A Cultural Perspective Of Organizational Justice

A Cultural Perspective of Organizational Justice

by

Constant D. Beugré
Delaware State University

INFORMATION AGE
PUBLISHING

Charlotte, North Carolina • www.infoagepub.com

Library of Congress Cataloging-in-Publication Data

Beugri, Constant D.
  A cultural perspective of organizational justice / by Constant D. Beugri.
     p. cm.
  Includes bibliographical references and index.
  ISBN-13: 978-1-59311-594-4 (pbk.)
  ISBN-13: 978-1-59311-595-1 (hardcover)
  1. Organizational justice. 2. Intercultural communication. 3. Industrial sociology.
  4. Industrial management--Cross-cultural studies. I. Title.
  HD6971.3B48 2007
  658.3'14--dc22

                                                                   2006038223

ISBN 13: 978-1-59311-594-4 (pbk.)
          978-1-59311-595-1 (hardcover)
ISBN 10: 1-59311-594-6 (pbk.)
          1-59311-595-4 (hardcover)

Printed in the United States of America

CONTENTS

Tables and Figures

ACKNOWLEDGMENTS

The idea for this book grew after my participation to the Academy of Management Meetings in New Orleans in August 2004. During this meeting, the OB division organized a workshop exploring future avenues of research in organizational justice. I was assigned to the subgroup focusing on organizational justice and culture. The discussions within this subgroup and the following discussion with the large group of participants demonstrated an increasing interest in the topic. I learned a lot during this workshop, which sharpened my thinking on the link between culture and organizational justice. I then began to explore how I could put the scant research on this topic together to write a book. Back in my hotel room, I started writing down a brief outline in my notebook. I am therefore grateful to the colleagues who participated to this Academy of Management's workshop. I am particularly grateful to Professor Joel Brockner of Columbia University who headed the subgroup focusing on the link between culture and organizational justice.

In writing this book, I also implicitly benefited from the global composition of the faculty of the School of Management at Delaware State University. Interacting with colleagues from different cultural, racial, and ethnic backgrounds convinced me of the importance of understanding the cultural implications of organizational justice. Thanks are due to all of them. I would also like to thank the Information Age Publishing team, particularly George Johnson and Benjamin Gonzalez for their enthusiastic support. Final thanks go to my wife Noelle and my son Jean-Christophe, for their emotional and social support. They just make my life meaningful. All errors, mistakes, and omissions are of my own making.

PREFACE

Globalization, offshoring, and multiculturalism have increased the potential for companies to operate in different geographic locations and employ people from various cultural backgrounds. Thus, a fundamental challenge facing today's organizations, is how to ensure an effective management of their main assets—human capital. One way of successfully managing this global workforce is to ensure that every employee is treated fairly. However, it is not clear whether everyone agrees on the meaning of fairness. What is fair for one person may be perceived as unfair by another person. Moreover, the standards of fairness may vary from culture to culture. Even in the same country, different social groups may have different views of what constitutes fairness. How then can organizations ensure that employees are treated fairly when there is no agreement on the very notion of fairness?

This book addresses this question. In so doing, the book analyzes the impact of culture on organizational justice. Organizational justice scholars know that what people value and consider fair is subject to cultural socialization and may vary from culture to culture. However, it is also widely believed that all human beings share a common desire to be respected despite their different cultural backgrounds, implying that concerns for fairness and justice are universal values. Therefore, I am not necessarily looking for differences when studying the impact of culture on organizational justice. Rather, I assume that there are both universals and culture-specific aspects to the study of cross-cultural organizational justice. In an era of globalization, offshoring, and multiculturalism, it is important for organizational justice scholars to develop conceptual models and theories that may spark empirical research and serve as guidelines for management practice. This book is an attempt in that direction.

Constant D. Beugré, PhD
Dover, Delaware May 31, 2006

INTRODUCTION

This book analyzes the impact of culture on employee justice judgments and reactions to perceptions of fairness and unfairness. I start this book with the following two questions. Why is a book on culture and organizational justice needed? What does such a book add to the extant literature on organizational justice, especially, after the publication of the landmark work of Colquitt and Greenberg (2005), *Handbook of Organizational Justice*? Although there are no easy answers to these questions, in the following lines, I explain the reasons why a book on culture and justice is not only needed but also timely.

There are at least three reasons for which a book on culture and organizational justice is needed. First, a book on culture and organizational justice is needed because "there are indications that culture exerts very important and wide-ranging effects on justice behavior including even generally shaping the likelihood that individuals will experience feelings of injustice" (James, 1993, p. 22). Second, globalization has led to the interrelatedness of world economies. Thus, most organizations not only operate in several countries, but they also employ people from different nationalities and cultural backgrounds. The resulting challenge is to find new ways of managing a culturally diverse workforce. Third, justice is inherent to any organized social group. As examples of social systems, organizations are arenas of justice concerns because their members compete for limited resources. The resources for which they compete include tangibles, such as money but also intangibles, such as status, power, and prestige (e.g., Tajfel & Turner, 1979; Turner, 1985). In the following lines,

I elaborate on the three reasons why a book on culture and organizational justice is needed and timely.

LINKS BETWEEN CULTURE AND ORGANIZATIONAL JUSTICE

Greenberg (1987a) introduced the construct of organizational justice to describe employee perceptions of fairness in organizations. Organizational justice encompasses the rules and norms in organizations that govern how outcomes should be allocated (distributive justice, Homans, 1961; Adams, 1963, 1965); the procedures that should be used to make decisions (Lind & Tyler, 1988; Thibaut & Walker, 1975); and how people should be treated interpersonally (Bies & Moag, 1986; Bies & Tripp, 1995). Although there are certainly objective features of fairness, organizational justice is generally construed as a perceptual phenomenon (e.g., Bazerman, 1993; Sheppard, Lewicki, & Minton, 1992). What individual X may perceive as just may not be so perceived by individual Y. Although all people may share a common interest in fairness, what they presume to be fair varies widely (Folger & Cropanzano, 2001). Thus, justice lies in the eye of the beholder (Sheppard, Lewicki, & Minton, 1992).

Justice is also context-specific. Rawls (1971) notes that what is just is what the parties involved in the relationship declared as such. It is therefore important to acknowledge that any definition of justice must incorporate the context in which the concept is embedded. This is particularly important in the study of organizational justice because economic organizations are embedded in the social systems in which they operate (Granovetter, 1985). Studying the impact of culture on organizational justice is important because cultural socialization plays an important part in the development of justice judgments. Moreover, actions, decisions, processes, and outcomes are all judged within a social context, including what others are getting, how they treat you, whether you are allowed to influence them, and whether they treat you appropriately (Davidson & Friedman, 1998). Although the desire to be treated fairly is a fundamental human preference, perceptions of fair treatment can be influenced by cultural beliefs and values (Pillai, Williams, & Tan, 2001; Tata, 2005).

In his book, *The Quest for Justice on the Job: Essays and Experiments*, Greenberg (1996) invited organizational justice scholars to conduct research on the cross-cultural aspects of employee perceptions of fairness. Specifically, he stated that "Whether organizational justice researchers are motivated by the desire to understand the universality of their phenomena or the operation of the global economy, now is the time to complicate our studies in the workplace by incorporating cross-cultural variables" (Greenberg, 1996, p. 406). Later, he reiterated this view by contending that "the study of people's perceptions of justice cannot be considered complete without understanding differences in national culture" (Greenberg, 2001a, p. 366). Since then, several scholars have undertaken empirical as well as conceptual studies to explicate the role of culture in organizational justice.

A particularly fruitful effort was conducted by Leung and his associates (e.g., Leung, 1987; Leung, 2005; Leung & Bond, 1984; Leung & Lind, 1986; Morris & Leung, 2000). Despite these efforts, more research is needed to explain the link between culture and organizational justice because we still know relatively less about how employees from other countries make fairness judgments and react to perceptions of fairness and unfairness (Skarlicki, 2001). A main reason for this relative paucity of knowledge may be because the impact of culture on justice judgments does not have a long history as a topic of investigation (Morris & Leung, 2000). It is therefore important for organizational justice scholars to develop conceptual models and theories that may serve as guidelines for further empirical research and management practice. This book is an attempt in that direction. Such an effort is timely in an era of globalization, offshoring, and multiculturalism.

GLOBALIZATION AND CROSS-CULTURAL RESEARCH IN ORGANIZATIONAL JUSTICE

Globalization refers to the interconnectedness of financial, technical, and human resources that engender the flow of goods, information, and services. The globalization of the workplace has led to an unprecedented interest in cross-cultural differences in work attitudes and behaviors (Brockner, Ackerman, & Fairchild, 2001). Proponents of globalization consider it as the way of the future, a mechanism to alleviate poverty and create wealth. Opponents, however, see in globalization the causes of all current evils, such as environmental degradation, increased gap between rich and poor nations, and unfairness in international trade. Whatever the position one may advocate, globalization does indeed, influence business practice. In particular, globalization impacts not only a company's customer base but also the management of its workforce. The impact of globalization on the movement of today's workforce is best summarized by the following quote.

> For more than a century, companies have moved manufacturing operations to take advantage of cheap labor. Now, human capital, once considered to be the most stationary factor in production, increasingly flows across national borders as easily as cars, computer chips, and corporate bonds. Just

as managers speak of world markets for products, technology, and capital they must now think in terms of a world market for labor. (Johnston, 1991, p. 115)

Because of globalization and multiculturalism, more and more employees are likely to work with people who are different from them in terms of demographic characteristics, such as race and sex (Chattopadhyay, Tluchowska, & George, 2004). These two trends have resulted in increased workplace diversity so much so that it is now common in many countries to find employees of various ethnicities or nationalities working together under the same roof (Leung, 1997).

International management scholars identified three types of employees in multinational corporations, home country nationals, host country nationals, and third country nationals. Migrant managers soon may become as migrant workers—moving from company to company as frequently as they move from country to country (Kanter, 1991). Managing such a diverse workforce or managing organizations in other cultures represents a challenge for global managers. Specifically, studying organizational justice requires an understanding of the cultural context in which judgments of justice and injustice are formed. What is fair may differ from society to society. Moreover, reacting to justice or injustice may also differ from society to society. Thus, justice issues in organizations are undoubtedly embedded in the social fabric of the environment in which organizations operate.

MANAGING A MULTICULTURAL WORKFORCE

Since the norms and values of fairness and justice constitute a fundamental feature of human life (van den Bos & Spruijt, 2002), it is important for organizational justice scholars to understand how people form justice judgments across cultures and how they react to perceptions of justice or injustice. Tyler, Boeckman, Smith, and Huo (1997) explained the importance of culture in the study of justice. They specifically contend that

> In a world in which mass migrations, international business ventures, and global politics are becoming commonplace, cross-cultural interactions are more likely to occur than ever before. Cultural differences in perceptions of morality and fairness can lead to open conflict and disrupt important relationships. Hence, it is important to understand whether there are any observable differences in people's views about justice across cultural contexts and how such differences would impact cross-cultural interactions. (p. 232)

We know that perceptions of justice or injustice are made based on some standards. When their expectations are not met, people experience a sense of injustice. These expectations are not always culture-free. In explaining the role of culture in judgments of distributive justice, Steiner (2001) pointed out that "Culture influences expectations by determining which distributive rule should be applied in a given context and according to which rules" (p. 122).

The literature on culture and management generally comprises two schools of thought, the "cultural relativism school" and the "cultural universalism school." The first school assumes that cultures are different and therefore management practices differ from culture to culture (e.g., Hofstede, 1980, 1991). One of the implications of this school is that theories developed in one part of the world could not and should not be applied elsewhere without major refinements. The second school, however, contends that they are principles, values, and behaviors that cut across cultures and are similar everywhere. This school also contends that cooperation among nations may result in similar patterns of work practices, leading to the *cultural convergence hypothesis.* Although there is a grain of truth in the arguments of each of these two schools, each also has its own limitations.

What people value and consider as fair is subject to cultural socialization and may vary from culture to culture. However, it is also true that concerns for justice are universal (James, 1993). It is widely believed that all human beings share a common desire to be respected despite their different cultural backgrounds. The concept of justice is probably universal across cultures, but it may be manifested in different ways (Pillai, Williams, & Tan, 2001). As Tyler, Boeckman, Smith, and Huo (1997) acknowledge, justice exists in the minds of all individuals. Kahneman, Knetsch, and Thaler (1986) specifically pointed out that people (1) care about being treated fairly, (2) resist unfair organizations even at a cost, and (3) have implicit rules that specify which actions of organizations are considered unfair.

Thus, in this book, I am not necessarily looking for differences when studying the impact of culture on organizational justice. Rather, I assume that there are both universals and culture-specific aspects in regard to organizational justice. This position is in line with previous arguments advocated by Campbell (1964) and Tannenbaum (1980) who emphasized that cultural similarities are as important as cultural differences, for cultural differences are more readily understood relative to cultural similarities. However, I acknowledge that although concerns about fairness are universal in nature, the operationalization of justice and its components may be culture-specific (Leung & Tong, 2004; McFarlin & Sweeney, 2001; Steiner & Gilliland, 1996; Tyler, Boeckman, Smith, & Huo, 1997). For instance, Leung and Tong (2004) note that although justice rules are universal, their relative salience and the way they are implemented are likely to be culture specific. They developed a conceptual framework of justice including three constructs: justice rules, justice criteria, and justice practices. Justice rules refer to abstract principles of justice and are universal. Justice criteria refer to the manner in which justice principles should apply. A justice practice is a concrete way in which justice criteria are operationalized and implemented, and may involve concrete standards, verbal or nonverbal behaviors, and social arrangements (Leung & Tong, 2004).

The present book is divided into six chapters. The first chapter discusses the foundations of organizational justice, its dimensions, and its importance as a topic of scientific inquiry. The second chapter discusses the theories of organizational justice. The third chapter reviews several models of culture and analyzes their importance for the study of organizational justice. The fourth chapter discusses the relationship between culture and employee reactions to justice, whereas the fifth chapter analyzes the relationship between culture and employee reactions to injustice. The sixth chapter discusses the cross-cultural management of organizational justice. Specifically, the chapter suggests strategies for transcultural competence in organizational justice.

CHAPTER 1

FOUNDATIONS OF ORGANIZATIONAL JUSTICE

The study of justice and fairness is becoming one of the most flourishing areas of empirical and conceptual research in organizational behavior. Thus, understanding the nature and foundations of organizational justice is of paramount importance. However, raising the following questions is important when one tries to understand organizational justice. Why do people care about justice? When are justice issues salient? And is organizational justice a one-dimensional or a multidimensional construct? I attempt to answer these questions in this chapter. In so doing, I highlight the recent literature on organizational justice and explain why and when people care about justice in organizations. I then discuss justice as expectations and the dimensions of organizational justice.

FORMING JUSTICE JUDGMENTS

Why Do People Care About Justice?

To answer this question, one must consider people as recipients (or targets) as well as actors of justice behaviors. As recipients of justice-related behaviors, people care about justice for three fundamental reasons. First, people care about justice because it helps them control desired outcomes. According to Colquitt and Greenberg (2001), people attend to fairness insofar as it allows them to gauge the degree to which their long-term economic interests are enhanced or protected (p. 221). Thus, the first reason for which people care about justice is purely instrumental. Second, people care about justice because it helps them assess their standing and acceptance in a group implying that the reason people care about justice is relational. People care about fairness insofar as it allows them to gauge the degree to which they are valued by the collective to which they belong (Colquitt & Greenberg, 2001, p. 221). Third, people value justice simply because it is the right thing to do (Colquitt & Greenberg, 2001; Folger, 2001). These three reasons are summarized by Cropanzano and Rupp (2002) who suggest that justice can provide at least three things: economic benefits (instrumental issues), validation of close interpersonal relationships (relational concerns), and the sense that moral principles are being upheld (moral issues). These three elements represent what Cropanzano, Rupp, Mohler, and Schminke (2001) call the three roads to organizational justice.

As people care about justice when they are recipients of behaviors, they also care about justice when they act toward others. Most research in organizational justice has considered people as recipients of justice judgments. However, when we consider people's behaviors directed toward others, an important question arises. Why do people want to behave in a just manner unto others? One may answer this question by stating that people want to act in a just manner for five fundamental reasons. (1) People want to act justly to enhance their own reputation of fairness. Because behaving fairly conveys the message that one is trustworthy and a "good" person, people when given the opportunity would seek to act fairly unto others to enhance their social status in the eyes of others and their community. (2) People want to act fairly to impress others. Here, fairness is used as an impression management tool (see Greenberg, 1990a). Greenberg (1990a) argues that workers are concerned about projecting an image of themselves as fair. The appearance of fairness may be as important as actual fairness (Brockner, 2006; Greenberg, 1990a). The impression management view of organizational justice conceives of fairness as a label for a set of attributions regarding adherence to appropriate standards of conduct that enhances one's self-image and/or one's projected social image (Greenberg, 1990a, p. 116). (3) People seek fairness out of reciprocity. By acting fairly toward others, people gain the assurance that others will reciprocate by acting fairly themselves. (4) People may act fairly toward others to gain acceptance. One way of getting acceptance from others is to be fair oneself. For instance, a supervisor who acts fairly toward his or her employees would gain their respect and admiration. However, a supervisor who is biased would generate resentment and outright hostility. (5) Finally, people may decide to act fairly toward others, because it is the right thing to do. Here, acting fairly is seen as a moral virtue (see Folger, 1998, 2001).

These five reasons described above can be reduced to the three roads to justice described earlier. People may prefer to act fairly toward others for selfish reasons, to enhance their standing in a group or for moral reasons. In the five conditions leading a person to desire to act fairly, some are purely for selfish reasons while others are for gaining acceptance. A person who acts fairly to impress others or enhance his or her reputation is certainly motivated by personal gains. Similarly, a person who acts fairly because he or she expects the recipient to reciprocate during a future encounter is obviously acting in his or her self-interest. However, personal interest may not always dictate people's desire to act fairly. People may decide to act fairly as a way of gaining acceptance from others. Although this may indicate a desire to serve oneself, the outcome here is more relational. Finally, people may decide to act fairly because it is the right thing to do.

A recent analysis (e.g., Cropanzano, Goldman, & Folger, 2005; Gillepsie & Greenberg, 2005; Miller, 1999) indicates that the goals of justice are self-interested. The authors used a psychological definition of self-interest that contends that a behavior is self-interested when an actor ultimately is motivated to serve himself or herself regardless of the effects of his or her actions (Sober & Wilson, 1998). Gillespie and Greenberg (2005) argued that the ultimate goal of justice is belonging—that is, the need to form and maintain at least a minimum quantity of lasting, positive, and significant interpersonal relationship (Baumeister & Leary, 1995, p. 497). They also conclude that the purpose of justice is to promote a fundamental intrapersonal motive—the occurrence of affectively pleasant interactions in the context of a temporally stable and enduring framework of affective concern for each other's welfare (Baumeister & Leary, 1995, p. 497).

Although Gillespie and Greenberg (2005) consider justice as self-interested, self-interest does not preclude concerns for others or following ethical standards. Rather, one may simultaneously engage in a self-directed behavior while at the same time respecting the concerns of others. Following this line of reasoning, Gillespie and Greenberg (2005) argued that the self-interested pursuit of fairness does not necessitate personal advantage. Indeed, they contend that although individuals are motivated to pursue fairness because it ultimately serves the self-interested goal of belonging, the consequence of achieving fairness in events and fair relationships with entities is mutually beneficial insofar as it simultaneously serves both one's own interests and the interests of others (Gillepsie & Greenberg, 2005, p. 205). Addressing the question of "why" people care about justice both as recipients and as actors of behavior calls for another question, specifically "when do people care about justice in organizations?" This question is addressed in the following section.

When Do People Care About Justice?

In addressing this question, Greenberg (2001b) contends that there are four conditions under which people care about justice in organizations. First, concerns about justice are triggered when people receive negative outcomes (Greenberg, 2001b, p. 246). This argument was first suggested by Leventhal (1976), who noted that people pay attention to procedural matters when they are dissatisfied with the distribution of outcomes. However, people do not usually question the fairness of procedures when they receive positive outcomes. When people are treated with dignity and respect, they are unlikely to have any concerns about how fairly they have been treated (Greenberg, 1994). When people work in organizations, they expect to receive tangible as well as intangible rewards in return for their efforts. Tangible rewards include monetary compensation, such as pay and bonus, whereas intangible rewards include status and prestige.

People also compare their input—output ratio to that of others (see equity theory, Adams, 1965). When their *social calculus* fails to add up, people experience a sense of distributive injustice and begin to question not only the fairness of the outcome received but also the process that led to that outcome. However, when the outcome is perceived as fair, generally, people do not question the fairness of the process underlying the outcome distribution. As human beings, we expect our fellow human beings to treat us with respect and dignity. We feel entitled to fair treatment from others. Thus, receiving fair treatment from others is the minimum to expect. However, violation of expectations raises concerns for justice.

Second, justice evaluations are made salient by change. When an organization goes through a process of change, every member is concerned about what he or she will receive and the resulting uncertainty adds to concerns for justice. Folger and Skarlicki (1999), Novelli, Kirman, and Shapiro (1995) and Cobb, Wooten, and Folger (1995) underscored the importance of fairness in the change process. Folger and Skarlicki (1999) note that organizational fairness is a psychological mechanism that can mediate employee resistance to change, whereas, Novelli, Kirman, and Shapiro (1995) argue that effective change is not simply a matter of clearly articulating an energizing vision and getting people to buy in to the desired outcome of the change; it is crucial to focus on the justice aspects of the change process. Indeed, when employees are fairly treated, they develop positive attitudes and behaviors required for successful change, even under adverse conditions (Cobb, Wooten, & Folger, 1995).

Third, concerns for justice are also aroused by the scarcity of resources. Concerns about the fairness of resource allocation are trivial when these resources are plentiful. However, when resources are scarce, people are concerned about what they will get and how they will get it. Resource scarcity even affects how justice is defined (Tyler, Boeckmann, Smith, & Huo, 1997). Skitka and Tetlock (1992) found that in situations of scarcity, third party allocators are more likely to deny claims for those responsible for their predicament. Most organizations do not have unlimited resources. Thus, there is fierce competition over these resources. Such competition raises questions related to the amount to give and the process underlying the allocation of the outcomes.

Fourth, justice concerns are more likely to arise between people with differential powers. Although people may be concerned about how fairly they have been treated during the course of an informal personal relationship, the removal of a power differential between people often makes moot the issue of the allocation of rewards between them (Greenberg, 2001b). However, the effects of power asymmetry on justice judgments have not been studied in the organizational justice literature. Perhaps, future research may explore the effects of power asymmetry on justice judgments. Although Greenberg's four reasons explaining the conditions under which people care about justice are enlightening, they do not still answer a fundamental question. Is there a standard against which people measure others' actions and consider them fair or unfair? When someone considers a given action as fair or unfair, what is the referent point? I address this question below by discussing the construct of justice threshold.

Justice Threshold

When people judge others' actions as fair or unfair, they do so by relying on a reference standard. People form personal threshold to assess the fairness (or unfairness) of others' actions. Actions that meet these standards are perceived as fair, whereas actions that fail to meet these standards are seen as unfair. These standards help create justice expectations. Perceptions of justice are most likely to result when expectations of justice are met (Furby, 1986). In discussing how people form procedural justice judgments, Ambrose and Kulik (2001) note that people can evaluate the fairness of a particular procedure by comparing the elements of that procedure to their template of fairness. It is that comparison that helps create the sense of fairness or unfairness. People react more strongly to another party's actions that violate their previous expectations of how the other party is likely to behave (Brockner, Tyler, & Cooper-Schneider, 1992).

Findings from prospect theory (e.g., Kahneman & Tversky, 1979) may help better explain the concept of justice threshold. In prospect theory, the reference point usually corresponds to the current asset position, in which case gains and losses coincide with the actual amounts that are received or paid (Kahneman & Tversky, 1979). Alternatives are evaluated by deviations from some reference point. Values that exceed the reference point are viewed as gains, whereas values that fall below the reference point are seen as losses. In comparison, a situation of fairness may be seen as a gain and a situation of unfairness as a loss. The use of the reference point may help explain people's reactions to voice—that is, the extent to which people are given the opportunity to express their opinions (Folger, 1977). For example, Price, Hall, Van den Bos, Hunton, Lovett, and Tippett (2001) suggest that voice that exceeds expectations may be perceived as a gain and voice that falls below expectations may be seen as a loss. When a person responds to a stimulus, the response is a function of the level of the stimulus and the individual's reference point (Price, Hall, van den Bos, Hunton, Lovett, & Tippett, 2001). According to these authors, stimulus outcomes that compare favorably to the reference point are perceived as favorable outcomes, whereas stimulus outcomes that compare unfavorably to the reference point are perceived as unfavorable outcomes.

When forming justice judgments, people have their own expectations of what is fair or unfair. A sense of justice arises when others' behaviors meet our expectations of fair treatment. However, when our judgment reveals that others' behaviors do not meet these expectations, we experience a sense of injustice. Thus, people experience a sense of fairness when their expectations of justice are met and a sense of injustice when these expectations are not met. A recent letter to the editor of *Fortune Magazine* illustrates the sense of unfairness people experience when their expectations for fairness are not met. Responding to a previous article on *Fortune* magazine titled "The Truth About Halliburton" (2005, April 18), Jim Renfroe, Senior Vice President of Halliburton wrote:

"The Truth About Halliburton" (2005, April 18) was pretty explicit in its conclusion that the company's problems in recent years were simply an issue of poor leadership, and you directed that charge against our current chairman, president, and CEO, Dave Lesar. But I think the article failed in assessing the quality of Dave's leadership. When our share price plummeted because of the asbestos litigation and we employees were shell-shocked, Dave, under tremendous pressure, stood with his management team and told us that if we would just focus on the core business, he would get us through the asbestos issue. He didn't give up. We did our part, and he did his. The stock price is back up. Your magazine didn't give its readers a balanced view of our leader. Next time, try to get all the facts, and be *fair.* ("Leadership at Halliburton," 2005, p. 22)

This letter illustrates two things. First, people care about fairness. Second, people tend to react when they experience a sense of injustice not only to themselves but also to others. For the author of this letter, a fair appreciation of the CEO's leadership abilities would have been to underline his shortcomings as well as his successes—to provide a balanced view of his performance. Failure to do so probably created the sense of injustice that motivated the author to write this letter. This letter also implies that judging Halliburton's chairman in terms of fairness or unfairness of his behaviors would have required following his actions over an extended period of time instead of judging only one action. Thus, when organizational justice scholars study people's perceptions of fairness are they concerned about the fairness of a single event or the fairness concerning events that occur over an extended period of time? In other words, are people's judgments of fairness or unfairness based on repeated encounters with the target person or are they based on a single incident? In the following section, I address this question under the label, justice as relationship.

Justice as Relationship

When employees consider the actions of their bosses as fair or unfair, are they referring to a single event or encounter or do such fairness judgments incorporate a string of events? Organizational justice scholars have not addressed such a question although understanding the reasons why justice matters in organizations is the focus of most studies in the organizational justice literature. Such understanding may help capture the meaning people ascribe to justice in work settings and design strategies for creating fair working environments. However, some organizational justice scholars have begun to acknowledge that what people mean by fairness is not a single fair transaction but rather a fair relationship (Lind, 2001). Thus, one may differentiate fairness judgments based on only one encounter with another party from fairness judgments related to repeated encounters. Recently, Bies (2005) and Cropanzano, Byrne, Bobocel, and Rupp (2001) acknowledged this possibility. Bies (2005) introduced the "encounter perspective" of justice, which he described as justice issues that are not related to specific decisions.

For instance, he notes that employees often raise concerns about bosses who do not fulfill their promises, coerce employees, and divulge secrets.

In these cases, no specific decision is made. Similarly, Cropanzano, Byrne, Bobocel, and Rupp (2001) differentiate justice as events from justice as entities. The first type refers to exchanges at one point in time, an event occurring between two parties, whereas the second concerns justice over an extended period of time.

When considering the distinction between justice as exchanges and justice as encounters, one may speculate that fairness judgments in organizations may generally fall under the second category. The concept of justice as relationship goes beyond the encounter perspective described by Bies (2001, 2005). Specifically, it argues that employees have lasting relations with others (bosses and colleagues) during their tenure in their respective organizations. In the course of these repeated interactions, a sense of justice or injustice derives from the meaning that an individual ascribes to an event (Folger & Cropanzano, 2001). These justice judgments may form overtime and incorporate several interactions with bosses as well as colleagues. Thus, when employees assess the fairness or unfairness of their bosses or organizational units, they base their judgments on a string of past experiences rather than on a single event. Despite the fact that this notion is conceptually appealing, it does not solve another issue related to the target of justice judgments in organizations. When employees make justice judgments in organizations, are these judgments directed toward managers and other employees or toward the organization as an entity? In other words, what are the targets of justice judgments in organizations? I address this question in the following section.

Targets of Justice Judgments

Research in organizational justice has mostly focused on "individual justice"—that is, justice directed toward individual human beings. However, we live in a culture where besides the person, there is another type of person—the juristic person represented by organizations of all kinds. As social entities, organizations have rights and responsibilities. Modern societies tend to view organizations as social actors that can act and/or react. Since these organizations can act and react, there is the potential for them to do so fairly or unfairly. Thus, in this section, I discussed the concepts of *person-centered justice* and *organization-centered justice*. The former refers to judgments and fairness reactions directed toward the individual, whereas the latter deals with judgments and fairness reactions directed toward the entire organization or its units. Targets of person-centered justice include peers, supervisors, and subordinates, whereas targets of organization-centered justice include the entire organization or subunits within the organization. Blader and Tyler (2003a) also identified two sources of procedural justice, organizational rules and specific organizational authorities.

This dual perspective of justice judgments is not new. Indeed, Cropanzano, Rupp, Mohler, and Schminke (2001) identified two paradigms, events and social entities. Events refer to elements in the environment, whereas social entities include individuals, such as supervisors, groups, or the organization as a whole. In the event paradigm, people evaluate some elements of the environment, such as a performance allocation situation or a resource allocation situation. In the social entity paradigm, however, measurement of justice emphasizes general evaluative questions about behavior or intentions (Cropanzano, Byrne, Bobocel, & Rupp, 2001). Employees may make inferences about supervisors, organizational units or the organization as a whole, based on the events they experience. For instance, when an employee considers his or her annual performance as fair (event paradigm) he or she may conclude that the supervisor is a fair person (social entity paradigm). Even in the social entity paradigm, employees may have the ability to distinguish the feelings they have for their organizations from those they have toward their supervisors (Cropanzano, Byrne, Bobocel, & Rupp, 2001; Cropanzano, Rupp, Mohler, & Schminke, 2001).

Colquitt, Conlon, Wesson, Porter, and Ng (2001) termed this dual perspective, the agent-system model. Like Cropanzano, Rupp, Mohler, and Schminke (2001), they argue that employees are able to differentiate the fairness of interactions provided by supervisors from the fairness of procedures dictated by the organization. Beugré and Baron (2001) conducted an empirical study using four justice dimensions, distributive justice, procedural justice, interactional justice, and systemic justice. They defined systemic justice as perceptions of fairness related to the organization as a social entity. These authors found that the three justice dimensions predicted employee perceptions of systemic justice thereby demonstrating the existence of an agent-system model of justice judgments. When people make justice judgments in organizations, they are able to differentiate these judgments as they relate to particular individuals or to the organization itself. For example, Masterson, Lewis, Goldman, and Taylor (2000) found that procedural justice perceptions were focused on the organization, whereas interactional justice perceptions were directed toward the supervisor.

One caveat with the dual perspective, however, is that although organizations do have rights and responsibilities, they act only through their representatives, mostly managers. As Schneider (1987) put it "It is the attributes of people, not the nature of the external environment, or organizational technology, or organizational structure, that are the fundamental determinants of organizational behavior" (p. 437). Thus, fairness judgments directed toward organizations are in fact, fairness judgments derived from the behaviors of individual actors—specifically, managers. As representatives of their organizations, managers are responsible for enacting fair policies and treating employees in a dignified manner. Their behaviors are used as heuristics to judge their organizations. In fact, when the individual is the supervisor, organization-oriented justice and supervisor-oriented justice will invariably be correlated because the supervisor is often viewed as a representative of the organization (Cropanzano, Rupp, Mohler, & Schminke, 2001). Despite its promising assumptions, the dual perspective of justice judgments needs further theorizing and empirical validation. Specifically, one may research how this perspective may help explain the extent to which people would tend to make biased justice judgments. For instance, would managers and employees differ in their judgments of the fairness of their organization? Why do people tend to consider their own actions as fairer than the actions of others? The concept of egocentric fairness may help address these questions.

The Egocentric Bias in Justice Judgments

Although justice permeates every social system, people's judgments of what is fair or unfair tend to be biased—leading to the construct of egocentric fairness bias (e.g., Greenberg, 1983; Messick & Sentis, 1979; Messick, Bloom, Boldizar, & Samuelson, 1985). Tanaka (1999) identified three consequences of this egocentric fairness bias: (a) one tends to remember one's own fair behaviors and others' unfair behaviors; (b) one attributes more fair behaviors to oneself and more unfair behaviors to other people; and (c) one perceives that one's own behaviors are never unfair, that the behaviors of others are never fair, and that unfair behaviors of oneself and fair behaviors of others do not occur. Generally, people tend to consider their actions as fairer compared to the actions of others. They also tend to perceive as fairest those outcomes that best serve their interests (Greenberg, 1983). Grover (1991) found that the perceived fairness of corporate parental leave policies was positively related to employees' own plans to have children. Employees who planned to have children themselves tended to view the system as fair, whereas those who did not have such plans tended to view the system as unfair. In their seminal work on procedural justice, Thibaut and Walker (1975) found that defendants believe that legal verdicts are fair when they are found innocent than when they are found guilty. Likewise, in a study conducted on a sample of college students, Tyler and Caine (1981) found that students consider teachers as fair when they receive higher grades than when they receive lower grades.

The reasons underlying egocentric fairness still remain unclear. However, research on the construct of self-serving bias may provide some clues. Zuckerman (1979) found that people tend to attribute their successes to ability and skill, but their failures to bad luck. Such bias helps preserve one's self-esteem. The same may hold true when it comes to fairness judgments. People may tend to see their own actions as fair because they want to give a positive image of themselves and convince themselves that they are trustworthy and fair. Similarly, they will tend to consider others' actions as unfair compared to their own actions. Both attitudes help preserve one's self-esteem. Generally, people interpret information in a self-serving manner (Babcok, Lowenstein, Issacharoff, & Camerer, 1995). For instance, in negotiation settings, the egocentric bias can be regarded as a form of self-serving conclusion about which settlement point is more fair (Paese & Yonker, 2001).

Two reasons may explain the nature of the egocentric bias in forming justice judgments. First, justice judgments are fundamentally perceptual. Second, people prefer to present a positive image of themselves. Doing so helps people convince others that they are trustworthy and decent people. Perceptions play such an important role in justice judgments that one may contend that what is important is not reality itself but the perception of reality.

> A critical point in all such judgments is perceptions—for all intents and purposes, reality is not consequential, so differences between perceptions and reality are not relevant. We act on our own perceptions, and must deal with the perceptions of the people with whom we interact. (Sheppard, Lewicki, & Minton, 1992, p. 12)

As such, a fair act for one person may be an unfair one for another. Thus, justice lies in the eye of the beholder (Sheppard, Lewicki, & Minton, 1992). Bazerman (1993) argues that neither distributive nor procedural fairness operates as an objective state. Rather, systematic and perverse characteristics of how we assess competitive environments, independent of the reality of procedures and the distribution of resources, create our perceptions of (un)fairness (p. 186). These perceptions of justice, however, are embedded in a social context.

The Social Construction of Justice Judgments

Recent studies have acknowledged the social construction of organizational justice. What is just or unjust is socially constructed. Thus, it is important for organizational justice scholars to acknowledge this assumption when explaining why people care about justice and how their form justice judgments. Individual behavior can best be understood by study-ing the informational and social environment within which that behavior occurs and to which it adapts (Pfeffer & Salancki, 1978). What people believe to be fair depends on their exposure to consensually validated opinions regarding appropriate ways to distribute outcomes and to treat others. Repeated exposure to these standards breeds expectations that serve as the basis for assessments of fairness (Greenberg, 2001a, p. 365). Individuals who have been through the same socialization process would tend to share similar conceptions of justice and injustice. Thus, socializa-tion plays an important role in the formation of justice judgments.

In discussing the impact of socialization on justice judgments, Lee, Pil-lutla, and Law (2000) note that an individual's prior socialization influ-ences the value he or she places on justice. Thus, the study of organizational justice should undoubtedly integrate the social context in which justice judgments occur. At the organizational level, this social con-text includes peers and managers. At the societal level, this social context is larger and includes beliefs, values, and traditions espoused by members of the society. Thus, justice judgments by individual employees may be affected by information coming from embedded peers or managers. For instance, concerning work settings, Pfeffer and Salancik (1978) argue that when important aspects of the work environment are ambiguous, workers are likely to use social information in developing their perceptions of the work environment.

The social construction of justice may occur at two levels: (1) the extent to which employees' justice judgments are influenced by others (peers or managers) and (2) the extent to which their justice judgments are influ-enced by others' experiences. As employees make sense of events in their organization, they may be influenced by colleagues. There are generally two sources of influence when employees form justice judgments. The first source of influence involves peers. Specifically, embedded peers may influence employees' justice judgments. An embedded peer is a co-worker with whom the focal employee has close relations. The second source of influence is the employee's social capital. Social capital refers to the net-work of relationships in which an actor is involved, and is conceptualized in the workplace as the relationship an employee has with managers (e.g., Lamertz, 2002).

Lamertz (2002) found that an employee's procedural and interactional justice perceptions were positively related to the interactional justice per-ceptions of an embedded peer and that interactional justice perceptions were positively associated with the number of relationships an employee had with managers. Goldman and Thatcher (2002) developed a social information processing view of organizational justice. They suggest that employees' justice judgments may be affected by peers. They gave two examples related to the perceptions of justice and injustice. Specifically, they note that if coworkers argue that a supervisor's treatment of a worker is unfair, this judgment may have a powerful effect on perceptions of fairness. Likewise, the advice and information of friends, family, and coworkers may also play a role in the individual's reactions to perceived injustice. The social processes involved in fairness judgments may be direct or indirect (Lamertz, 2002). Lamertz (2002) notes that individuals directly compare their understanding of fairness to that of a significant other, indirectly construe the fairness of their experiences by consulting with a significant other in reference to the opinions and information of mutual friends or other third parties with whom they both interact in important ways, and may impute fairness through a mixture of direct comparison and indirect identification with the social in-group symbolized by significant others.

The social influence of fairness perceptions may also occur by incorporating others' experiences of fair treatment. When forming justice judgments about a supervisor, an employee may integrate his or her own experiences in dealing with that supervisor and also the manner in which this supervisor treats other employees. In fact, people do incorporate the experience of others into their own judgments of fairness (Ambrose & Kulik, 2001). They also consider their own experience when forming justice judgments concerning others. Kray and Lind (2002) found that participants were more sympathetic to the plight of their coworker when they had themselves experience a similar injustice with the same supervisor. However, when they had not experienced an injustice with the same supervisor they were relatively insensitive to their coworker's plight.

People may also adapt their fairness judgments to the expected behavior of their interaction partner (Hertel, Aarts, & Zeelenberg, 2002). This indicates that group norms may affect people's judgments of fairness. If the normative standards of a group expect a person to see fairness (or unfairness) in a given behavior, this expectation may shape that focal person's perceptions of fairness. Hertel, Aarts, and Zeelenberg (2002) conducted two experimental studies using student samples from the Netherlands and the United States to test the influence of group norms on fairness judgments in dyadic exchange situations. They found in both experiments that fairness judgments were affected by group norms. When both interaction partners had outcome control, cooperative ingroup norms led to more balanced and prosocial fairness judgments than competitive ingroup norms. However, when the participant was the only person of a dyad who decided about the outcomes of both interaction partners, no such ingroup effect occurred.

In the first section of this chapter, I have discussed how people form justice judgments. However, in explaining how people make judgments of fairness or unfairness, one should keep in mind Sheppard, Lewicki, and Minton's (1992) three implications: First, judgments about fairness are always relative. These relative comparisons can be made by reference to one's past outcomes as well as by reference to others' current and past outcomes (Folger, 1987; Thibaut & Kelley, 1959). Second, judgments about fairness are influenced by one's social motivation or social philosophy. Third, one's own group tends to influence judgments of fairness. Thus, judgments of fairness are socially constructed. Moreover, people tend to favor in-group members when making fairness judgments. Tajfel (1978) notes that people tend to pay others who are like themselves more than they will pay others who differ from themselves. For such people, this tendency seems fair, although others may see it as completely unfair. It is also important to acknowledge the multidimensional nature of organizational justice. After 30 years of research on justice in organizations, we can state with confidence that people care about the fairness of their outcomes, the fairness of the procedures to which they are subjected, and the fairness of the interpersonal treatment they receive (Ambrose, 2002, p. 805). Thus, justice judgments are made at three levels: distributive, procedural, and interactional justice. I discuss these three dimensions in the next section of the chapter. Since these dimensions have been extensively studied in the organization justice literature (see Beugré, 1998a; Cropanzano & Greenberg, 1997; Folger & Cropanzano, 1998), I will only focus on their main assumptions here.

JUSTICE DIMENSIONS

Distributive Justice

In modern organizations, questions of justice are fundamental whenever resources are distributed (Greenberg & Lind, 2000). People care about distributive justice because organizational resources are limited. Thus, people want to know whether they can get their fair share of these limited resources. When this happens, they experience a sense of distributive justice. However, distributive injustice occurs when a person does not get the amount of reward he or she expects in comparison with the reward some other gets (Deutsch, 1985). Distributive justice refers to perceptions of outcome fairness (Adams, 1963, 1965; Deutsch, 1985; Homans, 1961). Homans (1961) first coined the concept of distributive justice. He used the concepts of investments and profits to qualify the exchange relationship between two parties. Investments refer to inputs, to what the person brings to the relationship, whereas profits refer to what the person gets from the relationship. According to Homans (1961), profits should be proportional to investments, such that the greater the investments, the higher the profits. He contends that

> a man in an exchange relation with another will expect the profits to be directly proportional to his investments and when each is being rewarded by some third party he will expect the third party to maintain this relation between the two of them. (p. 244)

Thus, judgments related to distributive justice are based on social comparisons. Two models of distributive justice, equity theory (Adams, 1963, 1965) and Deutsch's (1975, 1985) allocation principles are widely discussed in the literature. They are briefly summarized here.

Equity Theory

Building on Homans's concept of distributive justice, Adams (1965) formulated a more explicit theory known as equity theory (see Adams, 1963, 1965). Equity theory contends that people compare their input-output ratio to that of a comparison other. A sense of equity and fairness arises when the two ratios are equal. However, a sense of inequity arises when these two ratios are unequal. Over-reward inequity occurs when one gets more than the comparison other and under-reward inequity occurs when one gets less than the comparison other. Adams (1963, 1965) argues that people are motivated to reduce inequity. People reduce under-reward inequity by reducing input (working less for example), complaining, improving outcomes (asking for a readjustment of one's output), changing a comparison other, or leaving the field (quitting). Although Adams (1963, 1965) contends that people reduce over-reward inequity by increasing their inputs, in practice, they tend to rationalize over-reward inequity. Indeed, when a person gets an outcome greater than that of a comparison other, this person may tend to explain that this outcome was somehow deserved. Walster, Walster, and Berscheid (1976, 1978) formulated a revised version of equity theory. These authors used the expressions *exploiter* and *harmdoer* to describe the beneficiaries of an inequitable relationship, and *victim* and *exploited*, to describe those who do not profit from such a relationship. Walster, Walster, and Berscheid (1976, 1978) contend that people would be more distressed by inequity when they are victims than when they are harmdoers.

One problem with equity theory, however, is the difficulty to often identify what constitutes inputs and outputs. Equity theory also tends to consider the working experience as a social exchange (e.g., Blau, 1964; Foa & Foa, 1974) in which employees exchange inputs against outputs. One must acknowledge, however, that people do not always try to maximize their objective outcomes. As Weick (1966) put it,

Man does not always live by equity alone. People have other motives besides the just motive, and sometimes these other motives give rise to feelings and behaviors that are in contradiction to those that would arise purely from equity considerations. (p. 27)

In his critique of equity theory, Deutsch (1985) notes that

My objections to equity theory, however, center not so much on its incompleteness but rather on several other concerns: The non-strategic characterization of the relationship between the parties in an exchange relationship; its motivational and cognitive assumptions; and the conception of justice that is implicit in the equity formulation. (p. 25)

Another problem deals with the equity principle itself. People may not always allocate resources based on the equity principle.

Deutsch's Allocation Principles

Deutsch (1985) identified three distribution rules: equity, equality, and need. A justice rule is defined as an individual's belief that a distribution or allocative procedure is fair when it satisfies certain criteria or ideal standards (Leventhal, Karuza, & Fry, 1980, p. 194). The equity rule of outcome distribution implies that the outcome is proportional to one's inputs. The equality rule of outcome distribution favors equal shares for all recipients. Equality rules signify that each member of the group has equal value as an individual (Kabanoff, 1991). The need rule of outcome distribution implies that each receives according to his or her needs. The use of each distribution rule is context specific. In cooperative relations in which economic productivity is a primary goal, equity rather than equality or need will be the dominant principle of distributive justice (Deutsch, 1975; Kabanoff, 1991). In cooperative relations in which the fostering or maintenance of enjoyable social relations is the common goal, equality will be the dominant principle of distributive justice (Deustch, 1975, 1985). In cooperative relations in which the fostering of personal development and personal welfare is the common goal need will be the dominant principle of distributive justice (Deutsch, 1975, 1985).

The need rule calls for integrating recipients' needs in outcome distribution. In modern organizations, need-based outcomes are provided in the form of family leave policies, flexible work arrangements, and the like. Only those employees who need these policies are likely to use them. However, the use of these distribution rules is not systematic. Moreover, these distribution rules do not always exclude each other although they may sometimes conflict. Since organizations are both task and social systems that involve simultaneous pressures for economic performance and the maintenance of social cohesion, it may well happen that these rules may be displayed in the same organization depending on the outcomes distributed. Under such conditions, the allocation principle would depend on the nature of the relationships between the people involved. As Lerner (1982) put it

> The form of justice that will be followed in making allocation decisions will depend on the nature of the relation between the parties involved in conjunction with the focus of the parties on each other as individuals or as occupants of positions. (p. 13)

Martin and Harder (1987) found that people used contribution rules to distribute financial rewards and equality and need-based rules to allocate socioemotional rewards. They acknowledge that some degree of harmony is often a prerequisite for productivity. Thus, they conclude that to the extent that management is successful in promoting friendly relations among employees, personal relationships at work may become an important source of reward, perhaps mitigating whatever feelings of financial exploitation lower paid employees may have (Martin & Harder, 1987, p. 245).

As I have observed earlier, distributive justice perceives the relationship between two parties as an exchange relationship (Blau, 1964; Foa & Foa, 1974), in which the person's ultimate goal is to maximize personal gains. In such an exchange relationship, the driver of a person's behavior is the extent to which he or she can maximize personal outcomes. Distributive justice is not limited to the distribution of tangible or monetary outcomes, however. It is viewed as being concerned not only with the distribution of economic goods, but also with the distribution of conditions and goods that affect well-being, which includes psychological, physiological, economic, and social aspects (Kabanoff, 1991). Despite the importance people attached to outcomes, people also do care about the process underlying outcome distribution. To acknowledge this, Folger and Greenberg (1985) introduced the concept of procedural justice into the organizational justice literature, which is discussed next.

Procedural Justice

Procedural justice focuses on the fairness of decisions underlying outcome distribution (Leventhal, 1976; Lind & Tyler, 1988; Thibaut & Walker, 1975). When justice researchers use the terms process or procedure, they are referring to something that is a method, manner, technique, or means by which something else is accomplished (Cropanzano & Ambrose, 2001, p. 128). Thus, procedural justice refers to people's perceptions of the fairness of these methods or means. Leventhal (1976) and Leventhal, Karuza, and Fry (1980) identified six procedural justice rules: *consistency* (procedures must be consistent to ensure fairness), *bias suppression* (procedures must be developed and implemented without considering the self-interests of those who elaborated them), *rule of accuracy* (procedures must be based on accurate information), *rule of correctability* (procedures must allow room for correction), *rule of representativeness* (procedures must integrate the interests of all parties), and *rule of ethicality* (procedures must follow moral and ethical standards). Thus, for a procedure to be considered fair, it must include the characteristics described above. One of the elements of procedural justice extensively studied is voice—the extent to which people are allowed the opportunity to provide inputs (Folger, 1977). Two models, the process control model (e.g., Thibaut & Walker, 1975) and the group-value model (e.g., Lind & Tyler, 1988), later renamed the relational model (e.g., Tyler & Lind, 1992) help explain why people seek voice in the decision-making process. I briefly discuss these two models in the following sections.

Process Control Model

Thibaut and Walker (1975) developed the process control model, which is in fact a self-interest model. Process control refers to control over the development and selection of information that will constitute the basis for resolving a dispute (Thibaut & Walker, 1975). Procedures are perceived to be most fair when disputants have outcome control and the opportunity to participate in developing the options that will be considered for the dispute's outcome. When people affected by a decision are given an opportunity to voice their concerns, facts, needs and options about the decision, they are likely to view the process as fairer than when they are not given such an opportunity (Thibaut & Walker, 1975). People value the opportunity to voice their opinions because it provides them with the opportunity to influence others' decisions (Thibaut & Walker, 1975).

Tyler (1987) reported the results of two studies testing the effects of the value-expressive model. He conducted two studies that examined the value-expressive components of process control effects in the context of citizens' experiences with the police and the court. The first study considered the conditions under which value-expressive voice effects occur. Results showed that a key precondition for such effects was an individual's beliefs that the authorities involved had considered his or her views. The second study used a panel data to examine the influence of an individual's prior views about the authorities encountered on his or her interpretation of experience. Results showed that participants with prior positive views were more likely to integrate low-decision control situations in a way that was more sympathetic to the authorities. The conclusions from both studies demonstrate that citizens value being treated politely—an element of interactional justice. Thus, it is not necessarily control but the promotion within-group relationships that people value in expressing voice. Positive feelings resulting from this fair treatment help employees stay within the system. Procedures can enhance feelings of inclusion by guaranteeing voice or access to decision makers, and they can enhance feelings of inclusion by carrying messages of value, through obviously dignified process or expressions of respect (van den Bos, 2001a).

The self-interest explanation for procedural justice effect is similar to the explanation generally offered for distributive justice in that it views people as being motivated primarily by a desire to maximize their managerial gains (Rahim, Magner, & Shapiro, 2000, p. 13). Procedures are perceived to be most fair when disputants have outcome control and the opportunity to participate in developing the options that will be considered for the dispute's outcome. Here, justice is valued because it creates a level playing field that protects one's self-interest (Colquitt & Greenberg, 2001). The major goal of the person is to influence the outcome by influencing the process leading to outcome distribution. However, despite its benefits in possibly controlling the resulting outcome, providing inputs may have value in itself. People may seek voice because expressing one's opinions has value in itself and may provide positive signals related to one's standing in a group. This conceptualization of voice led to the development of the group-value model, later renamed the relational model of procedural justice (Tyler & Lind, 1992).

Group Value Model of Procedural Justice
The group-value model of organizational justice (e.g., Lind & Tyler, 1988; Tyler, 1989) emphasizes the importance of being a member of a group. It contends that people value long-term relationships with groups (small work groups or large organizations) and this leads them to value procedures that promote group solidarity. Positive feelings resulting from this fair treatment help employees stay within the system. People expect an organization to use neutral decision-making procedures enacted by trustworthy authorities so that, over time, all group members will benefit fairly from being members of the group. They also expect the group and its authorities to treat them in ways that affirm their self-esteem by indicating that they are valued members of the group who deserve treatment with respect, dignity, and politeness (Greenberg, 1990b). In a study of citizens' interactions with political authorities, Tyler and Folger (1980) found that citizens placed great value on being treated politely and having respect shown to their rights.

In their model of procedural justice, Lind and Tyler (1988) suggest that the neutrality of the decision-making procedure, trust in the third party, and the information the experience communicates about social standing influence both procedural preferences and judgments of procedural justice. People value relationships because it is through relationships that they develop their self-identity and self-worth. Relationships give people the opportunity to validate the correctness of their beliefs and behaviors and to feel accepted, respected, and valued (Tajfel & Turner, 1979). Because people in organizations focus on their long-term associations with authorities, they expect organizations to use neutral decision-making procedures enacted by trustworthy authorities and to treat them with respect, dignity, and politeness so that, overtime, all group members will benefit fairly from being members of the group (Tyler, 1989, p. 837). The group-value model views violations of procedural justice as violations of basic group values and norms that engender negative affective reactions such as anger and dislike for the authority figure (Lind & Tyler, 1988).

The group-value model was later reformulated as the relational model of procedural justice (Tyler & Lind, 1992). The basic assumption of the relational model is that people are predisposed to belong to social groups and that they are very attentive to signs and symbols that communicate information about their positions within groups (Tyler, 1994). People seek group membership because groups provide a source of self-validation, giving their members information about the appropriateness of their attitudes and values, emotional support, and a sense of belonging (Festinger, 1954). The relational model links loyalty to whether groups provide their members with a positive sense of identity and feelings of self-worth and self-respect (Tyler, 1994). It maintains that the decision to comply with the directives of an authority depends on the degree of legitimacy of that authority; and that procedural justice judgments are the primary determinants of perceived legitimacy of authorities (Tyler & Lind, 1992). Both the group-value model and the relational model contend that relations are important insofar as they provide a sense of belonging and a standing within a group. Thus, the goal of justice is to enhance the sense of belonging (e.g., Gillepsie & Greenberg, 2005). Because it emphasizes treatment with respect and dignity, the relational aspect of procedural justice has been referred to as interactional justice (e.g., Bies & Moag, 1986).

Interactional Justice

Interactional justice refers to the quality of interpersonal treatment people receive during the enactment of organizational procedures (Bies &

Moag, 1986). Early conceptualizations tended to view interactional justice as the social component of procedural justice (e.g., Cropanzano & Greenberg, 1997; Greenberg, 1993a). However, recent theorizing (see Ambrose & Arnaud, 2005; Bies, 2001, 2005; Bobocel & Holmvall, 2001) and research evidence (Cohen-Charash & Spector, 2001; Colquitt, Conlon, Wesson, Porter, & Ng, 2001) favor the treatment of interactional justice as a separate dimension. Bobocel and Holmvall (2001) note that interactional justice can be distinguished from procedural justice at the conceptual level, if the definition of procedural justice is confined to represent people's concerns about the structure of decision procedures and we reserve the term interactional justice to represent people's concerns about the social or interpersonal aspects of decision making.

It is exactly this distinction that Bies (2001, 2005) refers to when he called for the separation of the two constructs. People compare the way they expect to be treated to the way they are actually treated. A discrepancy between the two would create feelings of interactional injustice. For example, an employee who is severely reprimanded by his or her supervisor in the presence of other employees may consider the incident as unfair and contemplate revenge. However, if doing so would lead to possible retaliation, the employee may decide to use obstructionism as an appropriate form of aggression or may not react at all. Greenberg (1993a) proposed two components of interactional justice, informational justice and interpersonal justice. The informational aspect of interactional justice includes the extent to which employees receive explanations and information about decisions concerning their working lives. The provision of such information is different from treatment with respect and dignity although the two may be correlated. Colquitt (2001) and Colquitt, Conlon, Wesson, Porter, and Ng (2001) recently validated this conceptualization of international justice. I briefly discuss these two components in the following sections.

Informational Justice

Informational justice refers to the adequacy of the information used to explain how decisions are made and the thoroughness of the accounts provided (Greenberg, 1994). Greenberg (1993a) contends that informational justice may be sought by providing knowledge about procedures that demonstrate regard for people's concerns. Examples of informational justice include the provision of causal accounts (Bies, 1987) and explanations underlying decisions (Bies & Shapiro, 1987, 1988; Bies, Shapiro, & Cummings, 1988). The open sharing of information, which is present in informational justice, enhances people's perceptions of fair treatment. Research on the impact of information sharing on fairness perceptions finds strong support for the explanation effect—the extent to which the provision of information promotes perceptions of justice. In introducing the construct of interactional justice, Bies and Moag (1986) conducted a study on job applicants' perceptions of fairness during a selection process. They used a sample of MBA applicants and found that job candidates found recruiters fair when these recruiters presented honest and candid information and reasonable justifications underlying their decisions. Further studies (Bies & Shapiro, 1987, 1988; Bies, Shapiro, & Cummings, 1988; Greenberg, 1993b, 1994) supported the positive impact of information sharing on perceptions of justice. Even informational justice tended to mitigate the impact of negative outcomes (Bies, 1987; Greenberg, 1994). Using socially fair treatment—that is, thoroughly explaining the reasons why negative outcomes occur and doing so in a manner that shows considerable interpersonal sensitivity facilitates people's acceptance of negative outcomes (Greenberg, 1994).

This positive effect depends on the fact that informational justice acts primarily to alter reactions to procedures, in that explanations provide the information needed to evaluate structural aspects of the process (see Colquitt, Conlon, Wesson, Porter, & Ng, 2001). Greenberg (1994) conducted a field study demonstrating the positive impact of information on employee acceptance of decisions. He found that providing a great deal of information about a ban's necessity (e.g., informational justice) and announcing it in a sensitive manner enhanced the degree to which employees embraced such a potentially threatening policy. When decision makers are honest in communications, people are more likely to infer that the underlying procedure is fair than when the decision makers are dishonest in their communications (Folger & Bies, 1989). Informational justice is important for two reasons. First, providing information may help reduce uncertainty about potential outcomes or processes underlying outcome distribution. By providing information to the recipient, the decision-maker helps alleviate the anxiety caused by uncertainty. Thus, information justice acts as uncertainty—reduction mechanism. Second, providing information may indicate that one is valued and respected by authority figures. By providing explanations, the decision-maker sends a signal to the recipient that he or she is valued and respected.

Interpersonal Justice

Interpersonal justice refers to the degree of concern and social sensitivity demonstrated over the outcomes received (Greenberg, 1994). It deals with treating people with respect and dignity, and being sensitive to their concerns. A manager who shows individualized consideration for his or her employees would promote interpersonal justice. By treating employees with respect and dignity, managers can enhance the sense of fairness in organizations. By contrast to informational justice, which focuses on knowledge of the procedures leading to outcomes, interpersonal justice focuses on the consequences of those outcomes directly (Greenberg, 1993a). Specifically, interpersonal justice is important when outcomes are negative. In fact, when people get negative outcomes or outcomes that fall short of their expectations, they tend to experience feelings of injustice. When this occurs, they are likely to question the process underlying the outcome distribution. Showing concerns for their plight may help alleviate their negative emotions.

Examples of interpersonal justice include treatment with respect and dignity, politeness, courtesy, and apologies to name but a few. Those elements are similar to those described by the group-value model (Lind & Tyler, 1988) and the relational model (Tyler & Lind, 1992). Apologies are likely to mitigate the impact of negative outcomes (Bies, 1987). Not only do they have a mitigating effect but they also provide a sense of relief and perhaps consideration for the recipient. Interpersonal justice acts primarily to alter reactions to decision outcomes because sensitivity can make people feel better about an unfavorable outcome (Greenberg, 1993b, 1994). Interpersonal justice is important because people very often express their experience of justice or injustice in terms of interpersonal interactions (Mikula, 1986). Such interpersonal interactions include rude and aggressive conduct, treatment that violates a person's dignity and self-worth, and actions that indicate disloyalty.

Although the two components of informational and interpersonal justice are distinct, they form the basis of interactional justice, construed here as a dimension, separate from distributive justice and procedural justice. Colquitt (2001) considered informational justice and interpersonal justice as two separate dimensions in his four-factor model of organizational justice. Colquitt conducted two studies, one in a university setting using a student sample and the other in two plants of a leading automobile parts manufacturing company. In both studies, informational justice and interpersonal justice were positively correlated with a correlation of .43 for the student sample and a correlation of .52 for the employee sample.

Despite the appealing nature of Colquitt's four-factor model of organizational justice (distributive, procedural, informational, and interpersonal justice), I have used here the three-factor model generally adopted in the organizational justice literature. In so doing, I have described the three justice dimensions as distinct from each other. Distributive justice refers to the fairness of outcome distribution, whereas procedural justice deals with the fairness of formal procedures enacted by organizational authorities. Interactional justice refers to treatment of employees with respect and dignity. Despite these apparent conceptual differences, I entertain the linkages as well as the differences among these dimensions. I also discuss the possibility of a concept of *overall* organizational justice.

Differences Among the Justice Dimensions

In this chapter, I consider the three dimensions as distinct and separate dimensions of organizational justice. There are both conceptual reasons and empirical evidence for this separation. Indeed, there is a clear conceptual distinction between distributive justice and procedural justice (Ambrose & Arnaud, 2005). Empirical evidence suggests that distributive justice and procedural justice have differential effects on organizational outcomes. Distributive justice is more strongly related to specific attitudes such as pay satisfaction and job satisfaction, whereas procedural justice is more strongly related to global attitudes, such as organizational commitment (Alexander & Ruderman, 1987; Folger & Konovsky, 1989). Empirical studies (e.g., Folger & Konovsky, 1989; Sweeney & McFarlin, 1993) and two meta-analytical studies (e.g., Cohen-Charash & Spector, 2001, Colquitt, Conlon, Wesson, Porter, & Ng, 2001) support this differential effect.

Folger and Konovsky (1989) found that perceptions of the procedures used to determine pay raises uniquely contributed to such factors as organizational commitment and trust in supervision, whereas perceptions of distributive justice were uniquely associated with one's own pay satisfaction. Recently, Brockner, Chen, Mannix, Leung, and Skarlicki (2000) found that employees were more supportive of decisions, decision makers, and the organizations that decision makers represent when procedures are perceived to be relatively fair. Lind and Tyler (1988) contend that procedural justice has especially strong effects on attitudes about institutions or authorities as opposed to the attitudes about the specific outcome in question. We believe that attitudes toward the organization as a whole, including such things as organizational commitment, loyalty, and work group cohesiveness, are strongly affected by procedural justice (Lind & Tyler, 1988, p. 179).

The same differential effect occurs when comparing procedural justice to interactional justice. Whereas procedural justice affects organizational outcomes, interactional justice affects supervisory outcomes (Ambrose & Arnaud, 2005; Rupp & Cropanzano, 2002). In reviewing the literature on the differential effects of procedural justice and interactional justice, Bies (2005) found that interactional justice perceptions were associated with direct supervisor evaluations, whereas procedural justice perceptions were associated with organizational system evaluations. This effect was supported in empirical studies (Barling & Phillips, 1993; Blodgett, Hill, & Tax, 1997; Cropanzano, Prehar, & Chen, 2002; Moorman, 1991; Skarlicki & Folger, 1997). In a meta-analysis examining the effects of distributive justice, procedural justice, and interactional justice, Cohen-Charash and Spector (2001, p. 317) concluded that "distributive, procedural, and interactional justice are strongly related, yet distinct constructs.... Thus, our findings support the need in having separate operationalizations of the construct." In a separate meta-analysis, Colquitt, Conlon, Wesson, Porter, and Ng (2001) arrived at the same conclusion of maintaining the justice constructs as separate and distinct constructs. They contend that the construct discrimination results suggest that procedural, interpersonal, and informational justice, are distinct constructs that can be empirically distinguished from one another. Despite this distinction, several studies have found a strong relation among the justice dimensions (e.g., Folger, 1987; Sweeney & McFarlin, 1997).

Similarities Among the Justice Dimensions

Even though the three justice dimensions are different, organizational justice scholars must acknowledge two things. First, the three dimensions of organizational justice are correlated. Several studies have found positive correlations between distributive justice and procedural justice, between distributive justice and interactional justice, and between procedural justice and interactional justice (e.g., Folger, 1987; Sweeney & McFarlin, 1997). For instance, Brockner and Wiesenfeld (1996) found that despite the differences between procedural justice and distributive justice, they do not always operate independently. Indeed, outcomes can influence procedures and vice versa. In fact, procedural evaluations are based in large part on outcomes attained (Thibaut & Walker, 1975). As an example, Brockner and Wiesenfeld (1996) found that the combination of low procedural justice and low outcome favorability engendered particularly negative reactions.

Second, the three dimensions are part of a same concept, organizational justice. It would certainly be interesting for future laboratory experiments and field studies to determine the existence of a general factor of organizational justice. Several authors (e.g., Ambrose & Arnaud, 2005; Colquitt & Shaw, 2005; Cropanzano & Ambrose, 2001; Greenberg, 2001a; Lind, 2001; Lind & Tyler, 1988; Shapiro, 2001) have advocated a holistic view of organizational justice. Specifically, Greenberg (2001a) notes that people make holistic judgments in which they respond to whatever information is both available and salient when they form impressions of justice. They are not concerned about a particular form of justice. Rather, they form a global perception of justice. It is perhaps, this global perception of justice that shapes their attitudinal and behavioral reactions. This argument is similar to the one formulated by Shapiro (2001) who contends that victims of injustice do not care about the number of justice dimensions included in their experience of injustice. What these victims consider important and react to is their general experience of injustice.

Emphasizing the unidimensionality of organizational justice, Cropanzano and Ambrose (2001) proposed a monistic model of organizational justice advocating the similarity between distributive justice and procedural justice. They reasoned that both distributive justice and procedural justice are derived from expectations of outcomes. In the case of distributive justice, these outcomes are economic, whereas in the case of procedural justice, they are socioemotional. This categorization of outcomes into economic and socioemotional, echoes Cropanzano and Schminke's (2001) dichotomy. These authors claim that distributive justice can have both economic and socioemotional benefits. For instance, having voice may help influence outcomes as proposed by the process control model. It may also help signal to someone that he or she is a respected member of a group. Similarly, as a tangible outcome, money can have both economic and noneconomic benefits.

Although using a holistic perspective may help advance research in organizational justice, it may raise some methodological issues. Researchers would have to develop a measure of total justice that can be used in both laboratory experiments and field studies. Colquitt and Shaw (2005) note that overall justice can be conceptualized in two ways, as a latent construct and as a global perception. As a latent construct, overall organizational justice could be modeled as a higher order latent variable that drives responses to the more specific justice factors (Colquitt & Shaw, 2005). However, this possibility implies that studies using overall justice as a latent construct should include at least three justice dimensions. When studied as a global perception, organizational justice should deal with overall perceptions of fairness related to outcomes, decision-making process, or interpersonal treatment. The items used to measure this construct should reflect this global nature. In suggesting the use of overall organizational justice as a global perception, Colquitt and Shaw (2005) argue that items measuring organizational justice as a global perception might best be utilized in research where justice is endogenous in the causal system. The authors suggest that such items could be used in the laboratory to assess the effects of manipulations of multiple dimensions on overall fairness, or could be used in the field as mediators of the relationships between indirect assessments and attitudinal and behavioral reactions (Colquitt & Shaw, 2005). This discussion paves the way for future laboratory and field studies using overall justice as an independent variable. Understanding linkages as well as the differences among the three justice dimensions is important for a better appreciation of organizational justice theories that are discussed in the following chapter.

CHAPTER 2

THEORIES OF ORGANIZATIONAL JUSTICE

In the previous chapter, I discussed the nature and dimensions of organizational justice. Specifically, I explained why people care about justice and how justice judgments are formed. I also discussed the three dimensions of distributive, procedural, and interactional justice. In the present chapter, I describe five organizational justice theories that attempt to answer the questions posed in the previous chapter. These theories are fairness heuristic theory, fairness theory, deonance theory, the group engagement model, and uncertainty management theory. Fairness heuristic theory focuses on whether people can avoid exploitation from groups they belong to. Fairness theory tries to understand whether people perceive fairness or not, whereas deonance theory focuses on justice as moral virtue. The group engagement model explains the extent to which one can cooperate in groups, and uncertainty management theory focuses on reducing uncertainty in groups or in relations with authority figures. These theories contain elements of distributive, procedural, and interactional justice. I discuss each of these five theories and contrast them by highlighting the similarities and differences among them. I then assess the limitations of these theories; specifically, the extent to which they do not integrate a cross-cultural perspective in their analysis.

A Cultural Perspective of Organizational Justice, 27–52
Copyright © 2007 by Information Age Publishing
All rights of reproduction in any form reserved.

FAIRNESS HEURISTIC THEORY

Fairness heuristic theory is based on Lind and Tyler's (1988) group-value model discussed in chapter 1. In fairness heuristic theory, fairness serves as a decision heuristic, a decision-making device that replaces a full exploration of the implications and possible motives of each directive from an authority (Lind, Kulik, & Ambrose, 1993, p. 225). Explicitly formulated by van den Bos (2001a) and Lind (2001), fairness heuristic theory posits two basic premises. First, fairness judgments are assumed to serve as a proxy for interpersonal trust in guiding decisions about whether to behave in a cooperative fashion in social institutions. Second, people are assumed to use a variety of cognitive shortcuts to ensure that they have a fairness judgment available when they need to make decisions about engaging in a cooperative behavior (Lind, 2001; van den Bos, Wilke, & Lind, 2001). Thus, fairness information is used as a heuristic substitute to decide whether or not an authority can be trusted (van den Bos, 2001a, p. 52). It is a way of anticipating one's reactions and dealing with others not only powerful others. In the workplace, people may use fairness information to react to immediate supervisors and colleagues. In such interactions, information about fairness greatly influences the person's actions. As van den Bos (2001a) put it

> If other persons' behavior seems to be fair, then people react favorably and acquiesce to demands or requests of those persons with little consideration of material outcomes. However, if a person is judged to be unfair, then people react largely in terms of the immediate material costs and benefits associated with various courses of action. (p. 54)

One of the main assumptions of fairness heuristic theory is that in order to explain how people form fairness judgments, it must be known what information is available to them (van den Bos, 2001a; van den Bos, Lind, & Wilke, 2001). The basis of fairness heuristic theory is the recognition that social relationships, including most relationships in organizations, involve repeated encounters with a very basic dilemma—the fundamental social dilemma (Lind, 2001). Social dilemmas are situations in which the reward or payoff to each individual for a selfish choice is higher than that for a cooperative one, regardless of what other people do; yet all individuals in the group receive a lower payoff if all defect than if all cooperate (Smithson & Foddy, 1999, pp. 1-2). Social dilemmas occur because as human beings, we are social animals and we feel the need to be part of something larger than ourselves. Yet, we also strive to have our individuality recognized.

> We humans are once individual and social beings. We live and work in social
> units, but we maintain a strong sense of self and of our individuality.... It is
> this tension between social impulses and individual interests that forms the
> context of much of our social and organizational existence. (Lind, 2001,
> p. 61)

The fundamental social dilemma is concerned with the notions of
exploitation and rejection (Lind, 2001). Thus, fairness is seen as an index
of the likelihood of exclusion and exploitation, two of the greatest threats
posed by social relations (Lind, Kray, & Thompson, 2001). Exploitation
refers to the extent that the person may not get the outcome he or she
deserves compared to his or her inputs or expectations. People generally
recognize that ceding authority to another person provides an opportunity for exploitation, so they worry about obeying orders that might be
guided by some covert, Machiavellian motive on the part of the authority
(Lind, Kulik, & Ambrose, 1993, p. 225). Rejection occurs when the person
does not feel accepted in a group with which he or she identifies. Life in
organizations is replete with experiences of unequal outcomes distribution or situations of discrimination and rejection (Beugré, 2005a). How
then do people resolve the fundamental social dilemma? Lind (2001)
argues that people routinely resolve the fundamental social dilemma by
using impressions of fair treatment as a heuristic device.

> If people believe they have been treated fairly by others in a given social
> context, then this prompts a "short-cut" decision to subordinate personal
> desires to the needs of the group, team, or organization.... Fair treatment
> leads people to respond cooperatively to the demands and requests of oth-
> ers and the group as a whole. On the other hand, if they believe that they
> have been treated unfairly, this cooperative orientation is rejected in favor
> of a self-interested orientation that decides every request on the basis of its
> implications for short-term self-interest. (p. 65)

Fairness heuristic theory identifies three cognitive phases of the justice
judgment: (1) the preformation phase, (2) the formation phase, and (3)
the postformation phase (van den Bos, 2001a). In the first phase, people
start forming justice judgments. The main issue here deals with why and
when people care about fairness. In the second phase, justice judgments
are formed. The main question is how are these justice judgments
formed? In the third phase, the most important question is what do people do with fairness judgments? In other words, how do people use fairness judgments to react to subsequent events and subsequent
information? According to van den Bos (2001a), people need fairness
judgments when they are concerned about potential problems associated
with social interdependence and socially based identity processes. Fair-

ness judgments are used to decide whether to obey group authorities, whether to accept compromises in the resolution of disputes, whether to exceed strict qui pro quo requirements in exchanges, and whether to trust other members of the group (Lind, Kray, & Thompson, 2001, p. 190). Procedural justice is an important element of fairness heuristic theory. Procedural justice information is often used to make relational inferences and influences attitudes toward outcome favorability (Brockner, 2002). This importance of procedural justice in fairness heuristic theory is found in Lind and Tyler's (1988) formulation of the group-value model. These authors note that because impressions of the process and procedure used by authorities are typically available to the perceiver prior to impressions of the outcomes they generate, judgments of the fairness of process and procedure form the heart of the fairness heuristic construct (Lind & Tyler, 1988, pp. 228-229). Because of the importance of procedural justice, fairness heuristic theory emphasizes the fair process effect—that is the positive influence of procedural justice on subsequent evaluations and behavioral reactions (Folger, Rosenfield, Grove, & Corkran, 1979).

Fairness heuristic theory includes two effects: the *primacy effect* and the *substitutability effect* (Lind, 2001; van den Bos, Lind, Vermunt, & Wilke, 1997; van den Bos, Vermunt, & Wilke, 1997). The primacy effect refers to the extent to which people use information that is readily available when making justice judgments. Information that is available first would be used as a decision heuristic compared to information that comes later (Lind, 2001). The theory also predicts that whatever justice-relevant information is received first will have the greatest impact on the general fairness judgment that forms the basis of fairness heuristic (Lind, 2001). The primacy effect was supported in several studies (e.g., van den Bos, Lind, Vermunt, & Wilke, 1997; van den Bos, Vermunt, & Wilke, 1997; van den Bos, Wilke, Lind, & Vermunt, 1998). Van den Bos, Vermunt, and Wilke (1997) conducted two laboratory experiments designed to test the primacy effect as well as the fair process effect. The first experiment used a scenario-based methodology in which participants (undergraduate students in the Netherlands) were informed about a procedure as well as an outcome. Participants received information about the procedure before they received information about the outcome or received outcome information before receiving procedure information. In the second experiment, participants, (again undergraduate students in the Netherlands) were asked to perform an estimation test consisting of 10 items. Participants received information about the outcome of the estimation test before receiving procedure information or procedure information before receiving outcome information. In both experiments, the authors found that what people judged to be fair was more strongly affected by information that was received first than by subsequently received information.

They also found two effects: a fair process effect (the positive influence of procedural justice on subsequent evaluations and behavioral reactions) and a fair outcome effect (the positive influence of distributive justice on subsequent evaluations and behavioral reactions). In assessing the primacy effect, fairness theory predicts that early fairness judgments will be especially potent and that there will be a substantial level of inertia in changing these judgments (Lind, 2001).

The substitutability effect occurs when information relevant to one type of fairness affects the underlying general fairness judgment during the judgmental phase, and this general fairness judgment then affects judgments of another type of fairness during the use phase (Lind, 2001). For instance, if a particular type of fairness judgment is missing, people will use other types of fairness to fill in the blank as they make fairness judgments (Lind, 2001, p. 74). This assumption supports the fair process effect. Several studies have also validated the substitutability effect (see van den Bos, Lind, Vermunt, & Wilke, 1997; van den Bos, Wilke, Lind, & Vermunt, 1998). When people do not have information about the fairness of their outcomes, they use information about the fairness of procedures as a heuristic for forming outcome fairness judgments. Similarly, when people do not have information about the fairness of procedures, they use the fairness of their outcomes as a heuristic substitute to assess how to respond to the procedure. As a result, the procedural judgments of those people show strong outcome effects.

However, when people receive information about the fairness of procedures, they rely less on the fairness of outcomes to make procedural judgments—thereby demonstrating weak outcome effects (van den Bos, 1999; van den Bos, Wilke, & Lind, 1998). Van den Bos, Wilke, and Lind (1998) demonstrated the substitutability effect in two experimental studies. In the first experiment, participants read a scenario in which they were asked to imagine that they were involved in a situation and to judge how satisfying and fair the procedure and the outcome were in this hypothetical situation. In the second experiment, participants directly experience the satisfaction and fairness of a procedure and an outcome. Results in both experiments showed that people's reactions to an outcome they received from an authority were strongly affected by procedural fairness when they did not know whether the authority could be trusted. Interpreting these findings, the authors note that when information about whether an authority can be trusted is not available, people rely on procedural fairness as a heuristic device to deal with this authority. However, when people know that an authority can or cannot be trusted, they are less in need of procedural fairness information.

Two lessons can be drawn from fairness heuristic theory. First, the theory encompasses elements of reciprocal justice. The type of behavior a person displays depends on how he or she feels treated. When the person feels fairly treated, he or she will engage in a cooperative behavior. Such a cooperative behavior has a long-term orientation and its main goal is to contribute to the welfare of the group, organization, or community. However, when the individual feels unfairly treated, he or she is likely to adopt a less cooperative behavior and more likely to engage in a self-serving behavior. Second, the theory implies that fairness in organizations should be viewed as "relational fairness" to the extent that what people generally mean by fairness is not a single fair transaction but rather a fair relationship. To paraphrase the literature on psychological contract, one may argue that fair treatment creates a situation of *relational fairness*, whereas unfair treatment creates a situation of *transactional fairness*. Relational fairness occurs when the person engages in a cooperative behavior within the group, generally over an extended period of time. Transactional fairness occurs when the person seeks his or her self-interest because of past injustice that leads the person to adopt a noncooperative behavior.

Fairness heuristic theory may also be construed as an extension of the group-value (e.g., Lind & Tyler, 1988) and the relational (e.g., Tyler & Lind, 1992) models discussed in the previous chapter. By focusing on relationships and the person's status and standing in groups, fairness heuristic theory espouses key assumptions of these two models. Indeed, these models argue that people are concerned about their relationship with others and fair treatment acts as a key determinant of whether one is accepted as a valued group member. Fairness heuristic theory also argues that people are concerned about their standing and relationship in group settings. Fair treatment then provides information about such standing and whether to cooperate or withhold cooperation. Fairness heuristic theory is based on information processing. To determine how people form justice judgments, one should consider what situation they are reacting to. Thus, to understand what people judge to be fair we have to carefully assess what information they are reacting to (van den Bos, 2001a). In addition, when people do no have information available to make justice judgments, they use shortcuts as demonstrated in the studies reported above. One of the practical implications of fairness heuristic theory is for managers to create early impressions of fair treatment. Since people use such information for subsequent justice judgments, it may help instill trust and compliance early on. However, fairness heuristic theory suggests that managing for fairness is a very powerful tool for some particularly important organizational issues, but it is not a panacea for all the problems that might arise in organizational life (Lind, 2001).

One of the limitations of fairness heuristic theory is that it does not clearly explain whether the decision for a person to cooperate or engage in a self-serving behavior is a reaction to a previous act of justice or injustice or the expectations that justice or injustice would occur in the future? If the decision to cooperate or behave egoistically is based on a previous action by another party, then the person's reaction becomes an example of revenge or retaliation. *I will cooperate with them because they value me or I will look after myself because they do not care for me*—a way of evening the score. A person may also decide to engage in a cooperative behavior not because of previous experiences of justice but because of expectations of fair treatment. If I expect others to treat me well or if I expect the group to help me in the long run, I may well cooperate today. Expectations of justice or injustice may influence current behaviors.

There are also two methodological caveats related to studies designed to test fairness heuristic theory. First, most studies were conducted in laboratory settings thereby limiting their generalizability to work settings. Second, these experimental investigations mostly operationalized procedural justice as voice (see van den Bos, 1999; van den Bos, Wilke, & Lind, 1998; van den Bos, Wilke, Lind, & Vermunt, 1998; van den Bos, Lind, Vermunt, & Wilke, 1997). Using only voice narrows the scope of procedural justice. Another limitation of fairness heuristic theory is that it does not discuss the concept of accountability in justice judgments, a key element of fairness theory (e.g., Folger & Cropanzano, 1998, 2001) that is discussed next.

FAIRNESS THEORY

Fairness theory draws from referent cognitions theory (e.g., Folger, 1986; Cropanzano & Folger, 1989). In referent cognitions theory, the driver of a person's justice judgments is the cognitive representation comparing a hypothetical situation to an alternative (what happened compared to what might have happened). The theory posits that individuals evaluate their work experiences by reflecting on what might have been under different circumstances and conditions (Folger, 1986). A comparison of what happened and what might have happened had the decision-maker acted differently creates a sense of justice or injustice. Fairness theory is built on counterfactual thinking—cognitive representations of what might have been (Colquitt & Greenberg, 2003, p. 177). Counterfactuals are simulated events contrary to the facts (Colquitt & Greenberg, 2003). According to the proponents of fairness theory, there are three counterfactuals, "**Would,**" (compares a current state to an alternate state) "**Could,**" (assesses whether the other feasible behaviors were available to the authority) and "**Should**" (compares an authority figure's actions with prevailing moral standards). All three counterfactuals are necessary for inferring injustice although they do not move in a linear order. A key assumption of fairness theory is that what triggers fairness judgments is an injurious condition or state of affairs (Folger & Cropanzano, 2001).

According to Folger and Cropanzano (1998, 2001), fairness theory includes three elements: (1) existence of an unfavorable condition; (2) the event must be due to the volitional, discretionary actions of the target person whose accountability is assessed; and (3) harmful actions must violate some ethical principle of interpersonal conduct. For a person to be held accountable for an injustice, that person must harm another person by behaving in a way that violates some ethical principle of social conduct (Folger & Cropanzano, 2001). Injury, conduct, and standards are the constituent elements from which blame is built (Folger & Cropanzano, 2001). Without harm, accountability cannot exist and without accountability, injustice cannot occur. The cognitive simulation experienced by people follows two points: (a) people respond to discrepancies between a counterfactual and an actual event, and (b) the magnitude of the discrepancy is related to the emotional and motivational strength of responses to it. The easier it is for people to imagine a positive alternative, the more likely it is that a negative event will cause distressful emotion (Folger & Cropanzano, 2001).

In fairness theory, the central topic of social justice is the assignment of blame (Folger & Cropanzano, 2001). Indeed, issues of fairness in social relations imply making judgments about another person's conduct and therefore imply a social target upon which people focus attention (Folger & Cropanzano, 2001). Perceptions of justice are based fundamentally on attributions of cause and responsibility (Cohen, 1982). As Folger and Cropanzano (2001) put it,

> When people identify an instance of unfair treatment, they are holding someone accountable for an action (or inaction) that threatens another person's material or psychological well-being. If no one is to blame, there is no social injustice. For this reason, the process of accountability, or how another social entity comes to be considered blameworthy, is fundamental to justice. When people ascertain the fairness of someone's actions, they are trying to decide whether to hold that person accountable for those actions. (p. 1)

If a person cannot attribute blame, no injustice has occurred. If either component fails to reach a bonding threshold, the bond is broken, and the initially accused party cannot be held accountable after all (Folger & Cropanzano, 1998, p. 189). Thus, justice judgments have special moral gravity (Folger & Cropanzano, 2001).

Gilliland, Groth, Baker, Dew, Polly, and Langdon (2001) conducted three studies using fairness theory as a conceptual framework. Based on the three counterfactuals, the authors identified three types of explanations. "Would Reducing" explanation suggests to the recipient that a more positive outcome would be unlikely, even with different circumstances. A "Should Reducing" explanation suggests that the decision process was appropriate and that alternate procedures should not have been used in the decision-making process. "Could Reducing" explanation suggests that the rejection was beyond the company's control. Gilliland, Groth, Baker, Dew, Polly, and Langdon (2001) found that "Would Reducing" explanations, which provide referent information to suggest why the outcome was justified, demonstrated positive effects on fairness perceptions. "Would Reducing" explanations, which suggest that alternate actions were unfeasible, similarly demonstrated positive effects on perceptions of fairness. The results were mixed for "Should Reducing" explanations, which the authors explained based on the context of each of the three studies. In Study 1, no "Could Reducing" explanation was offered, and an offer was actually extended to an applicant. However, in Study 2, no offer was extended. Finally, in Study 3, a "Could Reducing" explanation was offered but the hiring process was terminated before an offer was made (Gilliland, Groth, Baker, Dew, Polly, & Langdon 2001, p. 699).

Folger and Cropanzano (1998, 2001) contend that an individual will be held accountable for a misdeed if the following three conditions are met: (a) a current state of affairs is not favorable as an imaginable alternative (*Would*); (b) the action that produces this state of affairs could have been avoided (*Could*); and (c) the action violated a moral standard (*Should*). When a person is held accountable for an act, then he or she may be required to face the appropriate consequences. However, fairness theory does not make specific predictions regarding the effects of counterfactuals on different types of fairness perceptions. Rather, the existence of counterfactuals is hypothesized to reduce the perceived fairness of the negative event (Gilliland, Groth, Baker, Dew, Polly, & Langdon, 2001).

Fairness theory can easily integrate other theories of organizational justice. The three counterfactuals could easily manifest themselves in assessing distributive, procedural, and interactional fairness. Although the three counterfactuals play out with events that have positive consequences, proponents of fairness theory have focused more on events with negative consequences—equating fairness theory with a theory of reactions to unfairness. Both fairness heuristic theory and fairness theory consider justice as a means to an end rather than an end in itself. In fairness theory, justice judgments occur in response to unfair treatment, whereas in fairness heuristic theory, justice judgments are used as means to determine how one should behave in the future. None of these models has considered justice as an end in itself. Indeed, if "justice is the first virtue of social institutions" (Rawls, 1971, p. 3), concerns for justice among people should be guided by morality. This is exactly what Folger (2001) had in mind when he proposed his theory of justice as deonance that is discussed next.

DEONANCE THEORY OF JUSTICE

Folger (2001) proposes a theory of deonance to explain situations where justice is perceived as an end in itself. The fundamental premise of deonance theory is that people are concerned about justice because it is the right thing to do (Folger, 2001). Deonance theory assumes that people try to govern their own interpersonal conduct, and that of others, on grounds of moral accountability (Folger, 2001). Folger (2001) contends that deonance theory includes two elements: *selfvishness* and *bounded autonomy*. The construct of selvishness includes both the self and others. It is therefore different from both selfishness and altruism. A selfish motive refers to an end state concerning only oneself; whereas an altruistic motive refers to an end state desired for some person or persons other than the individual (Folger, 2001). Deontic justice refers to *perceptions of fairness as a moral obligation*. Essential to this definition is the concept of moral obligation. "People value justice simply because it is moral" (Colquitt & Greenberg, 2001, p. 221). These perceptions of fairness as moral obligation impact people's behaviors in dealing with others and their reactions when justice is violated.

Deonance theory claims that fairness concerns are like altruism in that they refer not only to desired conditions for oneself but also to conditions desired for another person or persons (Folger, 2001, p. 10). This implies that deonance is close to altruism but is the opposite of egoism. In deonance, the individual does care about him or herself as well as his or her fellow human beings. Thus, his or her subsequent behavior would be influenced not only by what happens to him or her but also what happens to others. In contrasting deonance and egoism, Folger (2001) contends that egoistic explanations account for behavior by considering the pursuit of egoistic ends as the only motivated drive in human beings. However, a deontic motive involves a desire for a type of end state juxtaposed with an end state referring to another person (Folger, 2001). A behavior is fair as long as it conforms to norms of moral obligations not only for oneself but also for others. Folger (1998, 2001) identified two principles essential to deonance theory: *bounded autonomy* and the *human covenant*.

Bounded autonomy refers to socially constructed and sanctioned constraints as contours of human freedom (Folger, 1998, p. 26). It implies that the individual's behavior is constrained by moral obligations toward others. These moral obligations prevent people from behaving only in their own self-interests. Fairness-as-virtue calls for principled conduct that rises above ordinary self-interest in seeking to preserve human dignity (Folger, 1998). For example, I am a free person but my freedom ends where my fellow's freedom starts. At work, I am free to take a break, but I am not free to force others to take a break. In highlighting the importance of bounded autonomy, Folger notes that recognizing the appropriateness of having your autonomy limited is implied by accepting moral obligations as legitimate grounds for being held accountable regarding your conduct toward others (Folger, 2001, p. 11). Bounded autonomy acts as a regulator of human behavior. Accepting that one's freedom is limited is a ground for accepting that one should act in a fair manner toward others.

The principle of human covenant is related to bounded autonomy and links it with the fairness-as-virtue of tacit understanding about how to treat others (Folger, 1998). The human covenant has respect for human dignity as an inviolable core germane to unique fairness claims on an irreducible minimum of deserved social treatment (Folger, 1998). A person has a moral obligation to act fairly toward others. An implicit covenant exists among fellow human beings and one should not violate it. It acts as a link that should not be broken and lead people to react negatively to unfair treatment of others (Folger, 1998). The human covenant implies that deontic justice is the caring for oneself and others. As formulated by Folger, deonance theory has two implications. First, if acting in a fair manner is perceived as a moral obligation, then how would people react when others violate the 'human covenant?' Second, how far would people go to restore justice? Fairness theory (e.g., Folger & Cropanzano, 1998, 2001) may help answer the first question. Justice as deonance strongly implies accountability—a key concept in fairness theory. People who adhere to deontic justice would be likely to hold violators of organizational or societal norms accountable for these violations. When people holds another person accountable for wrongdoing, indications of blame and angry condemnation by the former essentially constitute reactions to misconduct as if it were an attack like activity for a counterattack (Folger, Cropanzano, & Goldman, 2005). Thus, accountability is a fundamental norm enforcement mechanism (Tetlock, 1992).

According to Schlenker, Britt, Pennington, Murphy, and Doherty (1994), attributions of responsibility are a direct function of the combined strengths of the following three linkages: (a) a clear, well-defined set of prescriptions is applicable (prescription—event link), (b) the actor is perceived to be bound by the prescriptions by virtue of his or her identity (prescription—identity link), and (c) the actor is connected to the event, especially by virtue of appearing to have personal control over it (identity—event link). For these authors, social control rests on a society's ability to hold people responsible for their conduct and to sanction violations of important prescriptions (Schlenker, Britt, Pennington, Murphy, and Doherty, 1994, p. 632). Self-regulation involves the anticipation of the consequences of one's actions (Bandura, 1982; Schlenker, Britt, Pennington, Murphy, & Doherty, 1994). A person who perpetrates an injustice is described as a *transgressor* in deonance theory. The transgressor is a person perceived as exerting willpower in pursuit of self-interest with indifference or even callous disregard both for others' concerns and for dictates known by that person as commonly held moral standards of conduct (Folger, Cropanzano, & Goldman, 2005, p. 217). Since fairness is a social norm that prescribes just treatment as a moral principle, third parties in the community will disapprove of a person who deals unfairly with others under his power, whereas the one whose dealings are just and fair earns general social approval (Blau, 1964, p. 157).

The occurrence of an injustice arouses a hostile response called the deontic anger, which is conceptualized as a reaction to the violated dictates of moral accountability rather than as the result of a substantive setback to personal self-interest (Folger, Cropanzano, & Goldman, 2005). According to deonance theory, people care about moral principles and become upset when those principles are violated (Folger, Cropanzano, & Goldman, 2005). Deontic anger precedes the deontic response. A deontic response is a strong emotional reaction following a perceived injustice. Folger and his colleagues consider five attributes of the deontic response: automaticity, short-term irrationality, retribution as its own reward, reconciliation mechanisms, and emotion as the driver of behaviors. The deontic response to an injustice is quick and immediate. Often, it is also irrational for that people may not always act in their best economic interests. In the deontic response, moral remedies are desired after the moral motive has been evoked and the intrinsic desire for justice can create a motivation to punish the transgressor (Folger, Cropanzano, & Goldman, 2005).

The second implication of deonance theory deals with the restoration of justice. This implication is directly linked to the previous one. It deals with the question of how far people can go to restore justice. Can they self-sacrifice to restore justice? One cannot administer punishment (or seek the administration of punishment) if the offender is not held accountable for the harm done. Thus, the first step in administering punishment after justice has been violated is to hold someone accountable for the injustice. However, when administering punishment, people should keep in mind that the punishment should fit the crime. Rozin, Lowery, Imada, and Haidt (1999) hypothesized that moral judgment and the condemnation of others, including fictional others and others who have not harmed the self, is a universal and essential feature of human social life.

Similarly, Fiske (1991) notes that people undertake to punish others when they have no concrete or immediate interest in doing so, when they have nothing directly to gain by punishing, and there may be some risk or cost in doing so (Fiske, 1991, p. 192). Two studies (e.g., Kahneman, Knetsch, & Thaler, 1986; Turillo, Folger, Lavelle, Umphress, & Gee, 2002) provide evidence for such self-sacrificial behaviors to restore justice. Kahneman, Knestch, and Thaler (1986) conducted an experimental study designed to assess the extent to which people self-sacrifice to punish an unfair allocator. Participants indicated a clear preference to divide $10 evenly with a fair allocator rather than divide $12 with an unfair allocator. These findings clearly imply that participants were willing to self-sacrifice (losing $1) to punish an unfair allocator.

Turillo, Folger, Lavelle, Umphress, and Gee (2002) replicated Kahneman, Knestch, and Thaler's (1986) study. Their results supported Kahneman, Knestch, and Thaler's (1986) findings that people were likely to self-sacrifice to punish an unfair allocator. In terms of deonance theory, these findings have two implications. First, fairness is important for people regardless of self-interest (e.g., Cropanzano, Goldman, & Folger, 2005). Second, because people value fairness for its own sake, they are likely to punish someone they believe violates fairness principles, despite incurring some losses. Although these two studies were not based on actual behaviors in a "real-life" situation, they do concur to the willingness of people to "reward good and punish evil." Moreover, they show that people sometimes seek to punish the moral transgression of others—even those with whom they have no relationship—not only without any instrumental self-benefit but also (at times) despite burdens imposed (Turillo, Folger, Lavelle, Umphress, & Gee, 2002, p. 839).

Two real-life examples may be indicative of the "reward good and punish evil effect." First, most whistle-blowers encounter adverse treatment within their own companies when they make their allegations public. Yet, most of them go ahead with these charges regardless of personal harm, such as losing one's job or being ostracized by colleagues. Despite pressures to remain silent and threat to their employment status within their organization (Alexander, 2004), most whistle-blowers go ahead with their claims of wrongdoing. In terms of deonance theory, whistle-blowers may perceive their organizations' wrongdoings as moral transgressions. Thus, the primary driver of whistle-blowers' decision to go public may be the desire to see justice restored rather than the benefit of personal fame. Second, although still limited, there is an emerging "socially conscious investment" movement in the United States. Socially conscious investors refuse to buy stocks of companies that they consider not being socially responsible despite the potential of positive return on investment. Thus, these types of investors may self-sacrifice by foregoing potential financial benefits to hold up their moral principles related to environmental justice or other social issues.

By arguing that justice should be perceived as an end in itself, deonance theory raises two issues. First, organizations should strive to create fair working environments because fairness standards will serve as regulators of employee behavior. Thus, the ultimate purpose of an organization must always be a moral purpose. If this is so, then managers should strive to inculcate the importance of fairness to employees. To consider fairness as moral virtue, organizations need virtuous people. But what is a virtuous person? According to Meara (2001), a just person is characterized by the virtues of veracity, prudence, humility, compassion, and respect. If organizations have to become institutions that value justice as moral virtue, then, they must protect their less powerful members, generally employees. As Meara (2001) notes

> We cannot forget, either in research or practice that the view of the least powerful may in the end be the most important view in building just organizations and in doing research about how to build them. They look to the organization to be virtuous and to honor their individual contributions and uniqueness, not just to compare them to others or evaluate their worth. (p. 233)

Deonance theory implicitly suggests that human beings can be moral actors (e.g., Cropanzano & Rupp, 2002) who are not always motivated by material self-interest.

Second, transgressors should be held accountable for violating standards of fairness and be punished consequently. Punishing transgressors goes beyond mere self-interest because fairness as virtue calls for principled conduct that rises above ordinary self-interest in seeking to preserve human dignity (Folger, 1998).

> Violations of human dignity call for rebuke not simply because of the consequences they cause, but also because of the stand against virtue that they take. They oppose the decency, goodness, and civility without which human life becomes solitary, poor, nasty, brutish, and short. Cheaters are to be punished because they cheat, period, not because it looks as if the cheating might help them win or cause someone else to lose. (p. 32)

It is only when everyone adheres to standards of fairness that groups and organizations can function smoothly. For instance, cooperation in organizations requires that organizational members be treated with respect and dignity. Such treatment will motivate them to engage in behaviors that benefit the group. This assumption is particularly important in the group engagement model, which is discussed next.

THE GROUP ENGAGEMENT MODEL

Tyler and Blader (2000, 2001, 2002, 2003a, 2003b) and Blader and Tyler (2003a, 2003b) proposed a theory of justice known as the group engagement model. Engagement in one's group refers to a willingness to cooperate as a member of the group. According to the group engagement model, people's willingness to cooperate with their group, especially cooperation that is discretionary in nature flows from the identity information they receive from the group. That identity information, in turn, is hypothesized to emanate from evaluations of the procedural fairness experienced in the group (Tyler & Blader, 2003b, p. 353). The group engagement model intends to answer a fundamental question. As members of groups, when do people commit to their groups or behave in a selfish manner? The model argues that people engage in cooperation within groups when they are treated fairly.

The group-engagement model identifies two types of motivation—instrumental motivations (actions motivated by outside factors) and internal motivations (actions from within the individual) that influence fairness behavior. Instrumental motivation is concerned with cases in which people cooperate with others because they expect rewards for cooperation or fear punishments (Tyler & Blader, 2000). Internal motivations are internal forces that reflect the person's desires and feelings of responsibility (Tyler & Blader, 2000). Internal motivations include attitudes and behaviors. Attitudes refer to the things that people want to do, whereas values represent the things that people feel that they ought to do (Tyler & Blader, 2000). For instance, if a person has a positive attitude toward a given object, this attitude may drive his or her subsequent behavior toward that object. Likewise, certain values may drive a person's actions leading him or her to engage in some behaviors or to refrain from engaging in other behaviors.

The model also identifies two forms of cooperative behavior: *discretionary* cooperative behavior and *mandatory* cooperative behavior. Discretionary behavior occurs when people engage in behavior that is not directly required by the rules or norms of group membership (Tyler & Blader, 2000). Discretionary cooperative behavior originates with the group member (Tyler & Blader, 2000, 2003b). Mandatory behavior, however, occurs when people engage in behavior that is dictated or required by group rules or norms (Tyler & Blader, 2000). These two types of behavior are differently motivated. Mandatory behavior is motivated to a greater extent by instrumental judgments and concerns, whereas discretionary behavior is motivated primarily by people's attitudes and values (Tyler & Blader, 2000, 2003b). The group engagement model argues that groups benefit when the people within them engage themselves in the group, and groups are particularly benefited when that engagement is based on internal motivations because cooperation does not then depend on the ability of the group to utilize incentives or sanctions (Tyler & Blader, 2003b, p. 353). Thus, one of the keys to induce cooperation is to intrinsically motivate people.

The two types of motivation lead to self-regulatory behavior (Tyler & Blader, 2000). However, the authors emphasize the preeminence of internal motivations over instrumental motivations. They contend that when people act out of intrinsic motivation, they take greater enjoyment and satisfaction in what they do (Tyler & Blader, 2000). This assumption echoes previous arguments from Deci's (1975) concepts of extrinsic and intrinsic motivation. Deci (1975) notes that intrinsic factors tend to have a stronger motivational impact than extrinsic factors. In a study to validate the group engagement model, Tyler and Blader (2000) found that internal motivations were better at explaining the degree to which people engage in discretionary cooperative behavior. For instance, for the discretionary cooperative behavior—*deference*, instrumental forces explained only 10% of the variance, whereas internal forces (values and attitudes) explained 27% of the variance. However, each motivational force (external or internal) had the same variance in explaining mandatory cooperative behavior. The authors also found that procedural justice was the key factor shaping people's attitudes, values, and cooperative behaviors. They identified two elements of procedural justice: quality of decision-making processes and quality of treatment. Quality of the decision refers to the manner in which decisions are made and quality of treatment deals with interpersonal treatment during the enactment of those decisions (Tyler & Blader, 2000).

As illustrated in Figure 2.1, the group engagement model identifies three elements that link groups to social identity: identification, pride, and respect. Identity reflects the degree to which people cognitively merge their sense of self and their evaluations of self-worth with their judgments of the characteristics and status of their group. Pride reflects the person's evaluation of the status of their group. Respect reflects their evaluation of the status within the group (Tyler & Blader, 2003b). Procedural justice leads to the two procedural elements of pride and respect that in turn determine identification with the group. Identification leads to cooperative behavior. The key argument of the group engagement model is that people's level of cooperation with groups is primarily shaped by the extent to which they identify with those groups (Tyler & Blader, 2003b). Distributive justice and outcome favorability influence resource judgments. These resource judgments also influence identity judgments. However, their effects on engagement and cooperation are mediated by identity judgments. Thus, identity judgments are the central

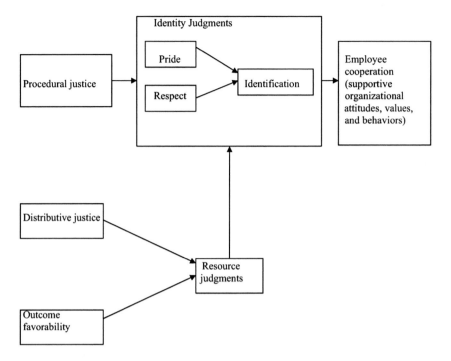

Source: Adapted with permission from Blader, S. L., & Tyler, T. R. (2005), How can theories of organizational justice explain the effects of fairness? In J. Greenberg & J. A. Colquitt (Eds.), *Handbook of organizational justice* (p. 337). Mahwah, NJ: Erlbaum.

Figure 2.1.   The group engagement model.

issue for predicting engagement and cooperation (Tyler & Blader, 2003b).

The conceptualization of people's willingness to cooperate with others explained by the group engagement model is similar to fairness heuristic theory (e.g., Lind, 2001) and contains some elements of the group-value model (e.g., Lind & Tyler, 1988) and the relational model of procedural justice (e.g., Tyler & Lind, 1992). According to Lind (2001), people decide whether to cooperate with others on the basis of whether they have been treated fairly or not.

> The judgment that procedures are fair constitutes acceptable evidence that the group is functioning properly and the individual can entrust fate to the group. This cognition acts independently of cultural collectivism, so even in the most individualistic societies, group oriented attitudes and behaviors can be evoked through fair procedures. (Lind & Tyler, 1992, p. 240)

As members of specific groups, people must balance two conflicting objectives: short-term personal gains and long-term relationship with the social group. How to maintain this balance depends largely on people's perceptions of fairness. If people think that they have been treated fairly, they are more likely to cooperate with others. However, if they feel unfairly treated, they tend to refrain from cooperating with others and pursue their own self-interest. Fairness heuristic theory underlines the importance of the fundamental social dilemma and contends that people would be likely to engage in cooperative behaviors when they are fairly treated.

The group engagement model also recognizes the importance of the fundamental social dilemma people face as members of particular groups. Using the concept of internal motivation, Tyler and Blader (2000) note that people help their group because they feel personally committed to group success, and they follow group rules because they feel a responsibility to do so. Such internal motivations are enacted by perceptions of fairness, and particularly, procedural fairness. Tyler and Blader (2000) also contend that people cooperate with groups because those groups perform an important role in sustaining a favorable social identity, a key concept discussed in the group-value and relational models of procedural justice. The group engagement model identifies three important identity-related variables (Blader & Tyler, 2005): (a) perceptions of the status or standing of the group (pride); (b) perceptions of one's status or standing within the group; and (c) the extent to which employees define themselves as members of the group. Pride and respect represent evaluative judgments, while identification embodies the extent to which cognitive representations of the self and group overlap (Blader & Tyler, 2005). Blader and Tyler (2005) note that when employees view their work organizations as operating and treating them in procedurally fair ways, they infer that the organization is one that they can be proud of and that they are respected members of the organization. However, when they are procedurally unfair, they evaluate their inter and intraorganizational standing in negative terms (p. 337).

The group engagement model emphasizes the role of procedural justice in fostering cooperation. Specifically, the model considers pride—the perceptions of status or standing in the group as an important variable. However, pride in an organization may also stem from an organization's social reputation. An organization's social reputation refers to the image outsiders have of the organization. An organization that has a positive image in a given community may instill pride in its members. For instance, the pride of a faculty member working in a prestigious research university may stem from the university's academic reputation than from procedural justice although such issues are not necessarily neglected. The group engagement model may be promising in an era where teamwork is valued in organizations. The model may also provide some insights in cross-cultural studies of organizational justice. For instance, in collectivist cultures, people emphasize the importance of the group. Is group engagement stronger in such cultures than in individualistic cultures? This question is an empirical one that can only be answered through cross-cultural studies. Another emerging theory is uncertainty management theory, which basically considers fairness as a means to manage uncertainty.

UNCERTAINTY MANAGEMENT THEORY

Lind and van den Bos (2002), van den Bos (2001b), and van den Bos and Lind (2002) recently proposed uncertainty management theory, which represents an extension of fairness heuristic theory. The uncertainty explanation developed out of research that was conducted following the fairness heuristic framework (van den Bos, 2005). Heuristic processes are a special case of how people deal with uncertainty (van den Bos, 2005). A key assumption of uncertainty management theory is that people use fairness to manage uncertainty. Uncertainty occurs either when a person confronts an inability to predict the future or when a person confronts an incompatibility between different cognitions, between cognitions and experiences, or between cognitions and behavior (van den Bos, 2002). The key element defining uncertainty is the salience of either the unpredictability of future events or the inconsistency between important cognitions, experiences or behaviors (van den Bos, 2002). What appears to be happening is that people use fairness to manage their reactions to uncertainty, finding comfort in related or even unrelated fair experiences (Lind & van den Bos, 2002, p. 21). Thus, fairness helps manage uncertainty because it gives people a feeling of general security with respect to their social milieu (van den Bos & Lind, 2002).

Uncertainty may be related to the trustworthiness of an authority figure, such as a manager or the fairness of an outcome. Receiving information about the trustworthiness of an authority figure may alleviate doubt about being unfairly treated in the future and reduce uncertainty about the outcome of a possible encounter with this authority figure. When we do not know that a person is trustworthy, we rely on fairness as a heuristic to deal with that person. Uncertainty management theory uses two principles, the substitutability principle and the primacy effect to explain why people care about justice and how they form justice judgments. The substitutability effect contends that because information about outcomes is not often available but information about procedures is often available, people rely on the latter to make judgments of fairness concerning their outcomes (van den Bos & Lind, 2002). The primacy effect contends that information which is first used to make judgments of fairness tends to influence subsequent fairness judgments. Information that comes first exerts a stronger influence on fairness judgments than information that comes second (van den Bos & Lind, 2002). This effect is a key element in fairness heuristic theory and has been validated in several studies (e.g., van den Bos, Vermunt, & Wilke, 1997; van den Bos, Wilke, & Lind, 1998).

The assumptions of uncertainty management theory find support in empirical studies (van den Bos, 2001b; van den Bos & Miedema, 2000). Several studies were conducted to test uncertainty management theory. Results of these studies showed that people were more likely to use fairness judgments as heuristic substitutes for trust when they were uncertain about authority's trustworthiness. Van den Bos (2001b) found that people react more strongly to perceived fairness when they are trying to deal with uncertain aspects of human life. The author concludes that uncertainty salience plays an important role in the psychology of social justice. Van den Bos and Miedema (2000) found that people react strongly to procedural justice when they are asked to think about their own death—a situation of uncertainty. Thus, fairness matters more when mortality has been made salient (van den Bos & Miedema, 2000).

When information about whether an authority figure can be trusted is not available, people rely on procedural fairness as a heuristic device to deal with this authority (van den Bos, Wilke, & Lind, 1998). People care more about fairness, and especially procedural fairness, when they are uncertain about whether they can trust authorities (van den Bos & Lind, 2002). They also showed that when facing uncertainty, people are likely to rely on fairness. Fairness tends to act as a buffer for uncertainty. The main goal of fairness judgments according to uncertainty management theory is to reduce uncertainty. Knowing that one is fairly treated may satisfy two purposes. First, it indicates that one is not excluded from the group and thus is respected and valued as a group member. Second, it indicates that perhaps, one would be fairly treated in the future. In this sense, fairness judgments alleviate fear of exploitation, exclusion, and future unfair treatment. Uncertainty management theory addresses a fundamental human desire—that of being in control of one's own destiny.

Uncertainty management theory is itself an application of uncertainty reduction theory (e.g., Berger, 1979; Berger & Bradac, 1982; Berger & Calabrese, 1975; Berger & Gundykunst, 1991; Mullin & Hogg, 1999) to fairness issues. Uncertainty reduction theory argues that people experience uncertainty in interpersonal settings. There are generally two types of uncertainty: *cognitive uncertainty*—the degree of uncertainty associated with attitudes and beliefs and *behavioral uncertainty*—the extent to which behavior is predictable. Uncertainty reduction theory develops seven axioms that are germane to interpersonal encounters. They include: verbal output, verbal warmth, information seeking, self-disclosure, reciprocity of disclosure, similarity, and liking (Berger & Bradac, 1982; Berger & Calabrese, 1975). Each of these seven axioms is related to uncertainty. For instance, verbal output contends that the more people exchange information, the lower the level of uncertainty would be. Similarly, the more freely people talk to each other (verbal warmth), the lower would be the level of uncertainty. Also, the better the information about the other party, the lower would be the level of uncertainty. When people interact with each other, they tend to reduce uncertainty by finding ways to predict others' behavior.

Uncertainty may be about what the other person is thinking or might do in the future. Applied to fairness, uncertainty relates to how fairly the focal person may be treated by authority figures. Since the most common way of reducing uncertainty is seeking information, when people feel uncertain, they may actively seek information that helps reduce the experienced uncertainty. This may be particularly true in situations of organizational change. In situations of organizational change, such as layoffs, downsizing, or offshoring to name just a few, employees are uncertain about their future within the organization. Fairness in implementing these changes may help reduce the level of uncertainty employees might experience. For instance, fairness concerns in time of organizational change include the provision of social accounts (e.g., Bies, 1987; Daly & Geyer, 1994; Kim & Mauborgne, 1997; Novelli, Kirkman, & Shapiro, 1995; Shapiro & Kirkman, 1999). Creating a climate of fairness may be an important precondition for effectively implementing organizational changes (Novelli, Kirkman, & Shapiro, 1995).

In general, people reduce uncertainty by engaging in information-seeking behaviors. When they do not have the information required to make judgments of fairness, people may rely of information provided by others. When social judgments are uncertain, people are likely to seek confirmation of their opinions (Festinger, 1954). Thus, when people lack information to make justice judgments, they may rely on information provided by others, however, incomplete this information might be. Uncertainty management theory raises an important issue that human beings have struggled with since the dawn of times. A fundamental human concern is to predict the future. Predicting the future helps to reduce uncertainty. Thus, uncertainty reduction is a fundamental human concern. From oracles in ancient Greece to modern day fortune-tellers and forecasters, the desire to predict the future in order to reduce uncertainty has preoccupied humans. Being able to predict how others will react toward us helps alleviate the anxiety that a lack of such knowledge brings. Uncertainty management theory was recently applied to reactions of unfair events (e.g., Tangirala & Alge, 2006). Tangirala and Alge (2006) found that information uncertainty makes fairness issues more salient to members of computer-mediated groups. They contend that this is due to the lack of familiarity among virtual team members.

A caveat of uncertainty management theory, however, remains the lack of a clear definition of uncertainty. Although van den Bos (2002) extensively explained the main assumptions of the theory and its applications, he did not explain what uncertainty really is leaving us with multiple interpretations of the construct. Uncertainty may concern the extent to which a person does not have information about a given situation, cannot predict the behavior of others, does not know how to react in a given situation or feels threatened. For instance, van den Bos and Miedema (2000) used terror management theory (e.g., Greenberg, Solomon, Rosenblatt, & Pyszczynski, 1990; Greenberg, Solomon, & Pyszczynski, 1997) to explain fairness as an uncertainty-reduction mechanism. In terror management theory, uncertainty may stem from a sense of vulnerability since people are especially afraid of their own death (Greenberg, Solomon, & Pyszczynski, 1997; van den Bos & Miedema, 2000).

Uncertainty management theory does not also explain how people should react when they face uncertainty. Suppose that a person does not have information about the fairness of group authorities. This lack of information generates uncertainty. How then should the person behave? Uncertainty management theory does not provide a clear answer. In this particular situation, one may suggest two types of behaviors, (a) building safeguards or (b) trusting the authority figure. The person may contemplate a worse case scenario, assuming that the authority will act in an unfair manner. As fairness heuristic theory indicates (see Lind, 2001) being member of a group runs the risk of exploitation and/or exclusion. By contemplating a worse case scenario, the person assumes that he or she will be the victim of exploitation or exclusion. This attitude will lead the person to build safeguards. Building safeguards may protect the person from deceitful behavior. The second behavior is to trust the authority. In trusting the authority, the person assumes that he or she will not be subject to exploitation and/or exclusion. This attitude has both advantages and disadvantages. By trusting the authority figure, the person may not incur the costs (social and/or emotional) that building safeguards entails. Under these conditions, trust may help reduce uncertainty. However, trust may leave the person in a vulnerable position should the authority fail to behave fairly. Thus, expanding the scope of uncertainty management theory may help better explain how people cope with uncertainty in social settings and why they care about fairness.

INTEGRATING ORGANIZATIONAL JUSTICE THEORIES

The organizational justice theories discussed so far are not mutually exclusive. Rather, each theory posits a psychological reaction to justice that may coexist with the reactions posited by the other theories (Blader & Tyler, 2005). For instance, fairness theory emphasizes the assignment of blame in the occurrence of injustice. When a person assigns blame to another party and experiences feelings of unfairness, he or she may use this unfair experience to decide whether to cooperate with the other party or pursue his or her self-interest. Thus, we see a clear link between fairness theory, fairness heuristic theory, and the group engagement model. Although fairness theory does not explicitly address the topic of cooperation, one may speculate that the attribution of blame leads to a perceived injustice. For instance, accountability judgments (the focus of fairness theory) may help address fears of exploitation and rejection (the focus of fairness heuristic theory), which in turn help group members feel a sense of security in their relationship with the organization (the focus of uncertainty management theory) that frees them up to cooperation (the focus of the group engagement model) (Blader & Tyler, 2005).

Fairness heuristic theory and uncertainty management theory contend that people use information about fairness to make judgments about their relationships with groups and others. Justice may provide information about one's standing within a group and influence the decision to seek one's own interest or to cooperate with the group. Fair or unfair treatment may also be used to assess further expectations of fairness or unfairness in a group—implying that fairness theory also contains elements of uncertainty management theory. When people enter groups, they do not know whether they will be treated fairly or not—thus, creating a situation of uncertainty. Treatment of fairness, especially procedural fairness helps reduce that uncertainty. Reducing uncertainty may pave the way for the person to engage in a cooperative behavior. Although fairness heuristic theory and uncertainty management theory do not address the link between justice and cooperation, their assumptions can be extended to make such a link.

The group engagement model and uncertainty management theory may relate to each other. For instance, if fairness motivates people to cooperate in groups as the group engagement model argues, one may evoke the principle of reciprocal justice. When people join groups, we do not know whether they will fully cooperate for the betterment of the group or pursue their own interest. Thus, fairness may help predict group members' behavior—thereby reducing uncertainty about their future behavior. When they are fairly treated, they will cooperate with the group. However, when they are unfairly treated, they will pursue their own interest and refrain from full cooperation. Such predictions help determine group members' future behavior.

A link may also be established between the group engagement model and deonance theory. When there is congruence between employees' personal values and organizational values, people may be motivated to engage in cooperation. In attempting to establish a link between the two theories, Blader and Tyler (2005) note that the level of congruence in moral values between the organization and the person may shape their level of identification with the organization, which in turn prompts cooperation and links the moral virtues and group engagement models (p. 346). Table 2.1 summarizes the key assumptions of the organizational justice theories discussed. It presents their main focus, the information required by people making justice judgments, the actions undertaken, and the theories' implications for management practice.

Although the different theories discussed so far help improve our understanding of how justice judgments are formed and how people react to situations of fairness and unfairness, they present two caveats worth mentioning. First, the unit of analysis is the individual person. Second, these theories do not integrate cultural issues in their assumptions. In all the theories discussed, the unit of analysis is the individual. However, recent attempts to expand the unit of analysis of organizational justice to teams and groups underscored the importance of new constructs, such as shared team justice and justice climate. Shared team justice refers to the shared perceptions of team members about how the team as a whole is treated (Roberson & Colquitt, 2005). Justice climate refers to shared perceptions of work unit treatment by organizational authorities (Colquitt, Noe, & Jackson, 2002; Mossholder, Bennett, & Martin, 1998; Nauman & Bennett, 2000).

Procedural justice climate is defined as distinct level cognition regarding how fairly the team as a whole is treated (Naumann & Bennett, 2000). Procedural justice climate has both a level and strength. Climate level refers to the proximity of the group mean to the positive endpoint of the response scale, whereas climate strength refers to the dispersion of respondents' climate ratings (Lindell & Brandt, 2000). Although such procedural climate issues are not addressed by current organizational justice theories, most of their assumptions may be applied to group level analysis. As group members share similar concerns about fairness, they may feel outraged when other groups are unfairly treated (deonance theory) or use available information to make inferences of fair treatment (fairness heuristic theory and uncertainty management theory). Teams may also decide to cooperate with other teams (group engagement model). Future research should explore the use of these theories' assumptions to study justice issues at the group level.

Table 2.1. Organizational Justice Theories and Justice Judgments

Theories	*Focus*	*Information Sought*	*Actions*	*Organizational Implications*
Fairness theory	Whether people perceive fairness or not	Accountability. Who is responsible of the injustice? Use of counterfactuals (Would, Should, Could)	Blame wrong-doer	Hold people accountable for injustice
Fairness heuristic theory	Whether one can avoid exploitation	Use of heuristics Use of available information	Make decisions about others' trustworthiness	Create situations of inclusion Avoid exploitation
Uncertainty management theory	Reduce uncertainty	Use of heuristics Use of available information	Use information that reduces uncertainty	Provide information to reduce uncertainty
Deonance theory	Justice as moral virtue Are actions morally fair?	Search for morality of actions and decisions	Punish transgressors	Set standards of fairness as moral virtue (moral code) Develop just managers Establish rules to punish transgressors
Group engagement model	Establish link between justice and cooperation	Information about how fair one is treated Fairness of procedural justice	Decision to cooperate or to hold off cooperation	Treat people fairly to win their cooperation

A second limitation of the organizational justice theories discussed is the lack of cultural variables in analyzing justice judgments. Although their assumptions may help explain justice judgments in other cultures, they do not acknowledge such issues. In discussing deonance theory, Meara (2001) remarks that our view of justice and virtue are very Western. Thus, the virtues and mores of other cultures need more attention (p. 233). It is certainly the lack of cultural issues in justice studies that motivates this present work. In an era of globalization, this represents an important weakness to remedy. Organizational justice scholars may wonder whether people from different social and cultural backgrounds use the same attributes when making justice judgments. Addressing this question is important for understanding the nature of justice across different social groups. To the extent that organizational justice scholars acknowledge that justice is a perceptual phenomenon (Sheppard, Lewicki, & Minton, 1992) it is worth integrating cultural variables in developing organizational justice theories and models.

Although the five theories studied did not underscore the importance of culture in the study of organizational justice, their main assumptions may help shed light on organizational justice across cultures. First, one must acknowledge that justice is a concern in every society (see Rawls, 1971). Whenever people interact with others, they are concerned about their status and positions in social entities, the rewards they get from these exchanges and the extent to which they are treated with respect and dignity. Thus, knowledge about theories of organizational justice may illuminate the cross-cultural study of organizational justice. Analyzing the different theories of organizational justice shows that pursuing justice can be based on instrumental, relational, and deontic purposes. When justice is instrumental, it is considered as a means to an end. Equity theory and the group/value relational model discussed in the previous chapter mostly express this view. Whereas the outcomes in equity theory are tangible, in the relational model, they are socioemotional. In both models, people seek justice because doing so helps them achieve important short-term and/or long-term goals. Fairness heuristic theory and the group engagement model both emphasize the importance people accord to group membership and the conditions under which they are likely to engage in cooperative behavior. It is possible that perceptions of fairness and particularly, procedural fairness may positively influence people's decisions to cooperate in groups regardless of their cultural background. The next chapter discusses different models of culture that may be relevant to the cross-cultural study of organizational justice.

CHAPTER 3

MODELS OF CULTURE

In chapter 2, I discussed the contemporary theories of organizational justice. The common thread of these theories is that they did not integrate culture as a meaningful dimension. In this chapter, I define the concept of culture and review five models of culture (e.g., Fiske, 1991; Hofstede, 1980, 1991; Schwartz, 1994; Triandis, 1995; Trompenaars, 1993; Trompenaars & Hampden-Turner, 1998). Understanding these models will help shed light on the importance of culture in the study of organizational justice. I first define the concept of culture. I then discuss each of the five models. Using the assumptions of these models, I identify four cultural syndromes that are relevant to the cross-cultural analysis of employee reactions to fairness and unfairness.

DEFINING CULTURE

Culture consists of patterned ways of thinking, feeling, and reacting, acquired and transmitted mainly by symbols, constituting the distributive achievements of human groups, including their embodiments in artifacts; the essential core of culture consists of traditional (i.e., historically derived and selected) ideas and especially their attached values (Kluckhohn, 1951, p. 86). Kluckhohn goes on to identify three components of culture: values, attitudes, and behavior. "A value is a conception, explicit or implicit, distinctive of an individual or characteristic of a group, of the desirable which influences the selection from available modes, means and ends of actions" (Kluckhohn, 1951, p. 395). Summarizing this conceptualization of culture, Hofstede (1991) defines culture as the collective programming of the mind that distinguishes the members of one group or category of people from another (p. 5). A culture is represented by its value system. Values are abstract ideals, positive or negative, not tied to any specific attitude object or situation, representing a person's beliefs about ideal modes of conduct and ideal terminal goals (Rokeach, 1973).

The cultural values that a person subscribes to are important components of his or her self-concept and, therefore, partially determine his or her normative beliefs (Lee, Pillutla, & Law, 2000). If culture is specific to a given society and includes people with the same mental programming, then people having the same cultural background should share similar values. This is not to say that people from the same culture always behave the same way. Despite the similarity of shared values and beliefs, culture also recognizes individual differences. Adler (1983) argues that the cultural orientation of a society reflects the complex interaction of the values, attitudes and behaviors displayed by its members. Research on culture has identified several models of culture. Reviewing all models of culture is beyond the scope of this chapter. However, in the following sections, I present five models of culture that may be relevant for the cross-cultural study of organizational justice. These models include Hofstede's model (e.g., Hofstede, 1980, 1991), Trompenaars's model (Trompenaars, 1993; Trompenaars & Hampden-Turner, 1998), Triandis's' four typologies of culture (e.g., Triandis, 1995), Fiske's (1991) four kinds of sociality, and Schwartz's (1992, 1994) theory of universal values.

HOFSTEDE'S TYPOLOGY OF CULTURE

Hofstede (1980) conducted an extensive study on a sample of 117, 000 employees of IBM working in 40 different countries. A factor analysis of his data led to the identification of four cultural dimensions: collectivism-individualism, power distance, uncertainty avoidance, and masculinity/femininity. Since these dimensions are well discussed in the scholarly literature (see Hofstede, 1980, 1991) as well as in major textbooks (e.g., Cullen & Parboteeah, 2005; Rodriguez, 2001; McFarlin & Sweeney, 2006), I will only review their basic assumptions here.

Collectivism-Individualism

This dimension is a binary one and opposes collectivism to individualism. Collectivism refers to the tendency for people to emphasize the importance of the group over the individual. In collectivist cultures, people emphasize relationships, whereas in individualist cultures, people focus on the economics of relationships—transforming interpersonal relations into social exchanges (e.g., Blau, 1964) in which personal interests dictate the outcome of these relations. An individualist acts as though he or she defines self as an entity consisting of a single person, bounded by his or her skin, but a collectivist acts as if he or she defines self as an entity extending beyond the individual to include a particular group of others, bounded by the social perimeter of that group. Thus, selfishness for an individualist implies attention to personal pursuits and inattention to group interests, but selfishness defined in the manner of a collectivist connotes attention to group interests and inattention to personal desires (Wagner, 1995, p. 154).

In collectivist cultures, people are more focused on displaying behaviors that enhance group harmony (Bond, Leung, & Schwartz, 1992; Bond, Leung, & Wan, 1982; Leung, 1997) than seeking their personal interests. Embeddedness in a network of relationships is a fundamental concern in collectivist cultures. Leung (1997) uses two constructs, *harmony maintenance* and *disintegration avoidance* to characterize the goals of interpersonal relations in collectivist cultures. Harmony enhancement refers to engaging in behaviors presumed to strengthen the relationships among interactants (Leung, 1997). Disintegration avoidance refers to avoiding actions that will strain a relationship and lead to its weakening and dissolving (Leung, 1997, p. 644). Examples of collectivist cultures include African, Arab, Asian, and Latin American cultures. In individualist cultures, the individual is a free agent, whereas in collectivist cultures, the individual is constrained by the social collectives (Menon, Morris, Chiu, & Hong, 1999).

An important characteristic of collectivist cultures is the sharp distinction between in-group and out-group members. An in-group member is a member of a group with whom the focal person is closely associated, such as the family, clan, or tribe. An out-group member, however, is a member of a group with whom the focal person has only loose relations or no relations at all. Members of collectivist societies make a clear distinction between in-group and out-group members compared to members of individualist societies (Triandis, 1989). Such distinction may strongly influence employees' social interactions in work settings. One must acknowledge that even if the ingroup/out-group distinction is prevalent in collectivist cultures, these cultures may not have the same view in regard to who belongs to the in-group (Ralston, Holt, Terpstra, & Kai-Cheng, 1996). Hall and Xu (1990) found that Chinese held the traditional view that family and trusted friends comprised the in-group, whereas Japanese viewed their company as the in-group.

Individualism, in contrast, focuses on the importance of the self over the group. What matters in individualist cultures is personal interest as opposed to group interest. In individualist cultures, the basic social unit is the individual, whereas in collectivist cultures, the basic social unit is the group. Examples of individualist cultures include the United States and other Western countries. However, one should acknowledge that not everyone in an individualist culture is individualistic. Similarly, not everyone in a collectivist culture is collectivistic. Hofstede's (1991) distinction between individualism and collectivism is illustrated in the following quote:

> Individualism pertains to societies in which the ties between individuals are loose; everyone is expected to look after himself or herself and his or her immediate family. Collectivism as its opposite pertains to societies in which people from birth onwards are integrated into strong, cohesive groups, which throughout people's lifetime continue to protect them in exchange for unquestioning loyalty. (p. 51)

These two dimensions of collectivism and individualism have been extensively studied in cross-cultural studies in industrial/organizational psychology, organizational behavior, and management (e.g., Triandis, 1995, 2002). Hofstede (1980) found that collectivism was positively correlated with another dimension, power distance, which refers to the acceptance of power inequalities.

Power Distance

Power distance refers to the extent to which less powerful members of institutions and organizations within a country expect and accept that power is distributed unequally (Hofstede, 1991, p. 28). It reflects an acceptance and expectation of social stratification (James, 1993). The United States is considered as moderate on power distance, whereas China is seen as high on power distance. Research on the effects of power distance shows that subordinates with low power distance orientation are likely to have strong connections to authorities and have a better understanding of the authorities they are dealing with. There is a difference, however, between power distance as a cultural dimension and power distance orientation. The former describes a culture, whereas the latter describes an individual's attitude toward the acceptance of power inequalities. In a society high on power distance, not every person is high on this dimension. Likewise, in a low-power distance society, not everyone emphasizes this cultural dimension. Employees with high power distance orientation tend to accept power inequality, whereas employees with low power distance orientation do not accept power inequality (Hofstede, 1980; Lam, Schaubroeck, & Aryee, 2002; Lee, Pillutla, & Law, 2000). A third dimension of culture identified by Hofstede (1980) is uncertainty avoidance.

Uncertainty Avoidance

Uncertainty avoidance refers to the fact that uncertainty about the future is a basic fact of human life with which we try to cope through the domains of technology, law, and religion (Hofstede, 1980). Uncertainty avoidance involves the extent to which people feel threatened by ambiguous (social) situations and have created beliefs and institutions that try to avoid these (Hofstede & Bond, 1984, p. 419). The three indicators that Hofstede used to identify uncertainty avoidance were rule orientation, employment stability, and stress. Rules and laws are some of the ways that societies use to prevent uncertainties. In high uncertainty avoidance cultures, there are many formal laws and/or informal rules controlling the rights and duties of employers and employees (Hofstede, 1991).

Countries were classified as high or low on uncertainty avoidance. Low uncertainty avoidance implies a greater willingness to take risks. High uncertainty avoidance, however, implies a lower willingness to take risks. Hofstede (1980) also notes that uncertainty avoidance may affect the types of relations occurring between young and old people. He contends that in a high uncertainty avoidance society, older people wait longer before leaving responsibility in the hands of younger people, and in such a society, its members will more often disapprove of the behavior of young people (p. 172). Thus, they would be more of a generational gap in high uncertainty avoidance societies, in which gerontocracy (old people's rules) would prevail. People in high uncertainty avoidance cultures are concerned about rituals and traditions, and often follow very complex rules and regulations (Miles & Greenberg, 1993).

Uncertainty avoidance also characterizes cultures where there is a preference for predictability, clear instructions, and expectations in the behavior of others (Steiner, 2001). Cultures are divided between low uncertainty avoidance and high uncertainty avoidance. Low uncertainty avoidance cultures include the United States, whereas high uncertainty avoidance cultures include Mexico and China. A high level of innovativeness and entrepreneurship characterizes low uncertainty avoidance cultures, whereas high uncertainty avoidance cultures are characterized by a preference for the status quo and a high level of resistance to change and novel ideas. Perhaps, this dimension may be related to the level of innovation and competitiveness of countries. However, no systematic study has analyzed the impact of uncertainty avoidance on the level of innovation and competitiveness across cultures. Perhaps, such a study may illuminate our understanding of the importance of this dimension.

Masculinity/Femininity

Masculinity refers to assertiveness or ambitiousness (Hofstede, 1980). The opposite of masculinity is femininity. These two dimensions describe traditional gender roles. Masculine goals are directed toward assertiveness, ambition, and the desire to accumulate material wealth. Feminine goals, however, are directed toward nurturing, caring, and compassion. The masculinity-femininity dimension distinguishes between cultures that are aggressive, greedy, and competitive and those that are more nurturing, compassionate, and caring (Miles & Greenberg, 1993). In masculine cultures, people are concerned about earnings, recognition, advancement, and challenge in the workplace (Hofstede, 1980). In a masculine culture, there is a strong emphasis on being rewarded based on one's individual efforts (Miles & Greenberg, 1993). In feminine cultures, however, people are concerned about having amicable relations at work, employment security, and cooperative relations with colleagues and managers. The dominant value in such cultures is caring for others. Organizations in masculine societies are more likely to reward people on the basis of equity, whereas organizations in feminine societies are more likely to reward people on the basis of equality (Hofstede, 1991).

In countries high on masculinity, the job takes a more central position in people's lives than in low masculine countries (Hofstede, 1980). In other words, in the former, people live to work, whereas in the latter, people work to live. The centrality of work may influence people's reactions to justice and injustice in the workplace. However, no systematic studies (to the best of my knowledge) have tested the impact of work centrality on employee perceptions of fairness (or unfairness). It is possible that when work is central to one's life, the person may be so dedicated to his or her work that situations of unfairness may lead to stronger feelings and possibly to an emotional breakdown. Such consequences may be less dramatic for those who do not perceive that their work is the center of their life space. However, without hard data, these assumptions are merely conjectures that await empirical validation. Expanding on the impact of masculinity on work values and behaviors, Hofstede (1980) contends that in a masculine culture, a humanized job should give opportunities for recognition, advancement, and challenge. In a feminine culture, the focus is more on cooperation and a pleasant work atmosphere than on interpersonal competition.

Hofstede's (1980) original work missed several countries, especially those from the developing world and the former Soviet Union. This was, however, remedied in 1991 when Hofstede conducted another study including some of these countries and regions. This study also included another dimension—time orientation. Hofstede's work, however does not account for differences within countries. It is obvious that national cultures are not homogenous. A particularly striking example is the United States where different subcultures coexist. Despite these limitations, Hofstede's model continues to have a tremendous impact on the field of international management and remains a valuable guide for interpreting the effects of culture on work behavior (McFarlin & Sweeney, 2006). One of the merits of Hofstede's study is that it has led to the development of cross-cultural research designed to test the impact of these dimensions on employee behavior and the applicability of management theories to non-Western cultures. Following in his footsteps, Trompenaars (1993) and Trompenaars and Hampden-Turner (1998) developed a cultural model that identifies seven dimensions.

TROMPENAARS'S MODEL OF CULTURE

Trompenaars (1993) and Trompenaars and Hampden-Turner (1998) developed a cultural model based on extensive interviews of a sample of more than 115,000 managers over a ten-year period. These managers represented 28 different countries. The authors identified five bipolar dimensions: *universalism-particularism*, *neutral-affective*, *specific-diffuse*, *achievement-ascription*, and *individualism-communitarianism*.

Universalism refers to the extent to which people believe that rules and practices should apply to everyone, whereas particularism refers to the extent to which rules and practices should be adjusted to each individual or situation (Trompenaars, 1993; Trompenaars & Hampden-Turner, 1998). The more universalist a country, the greater the need for an institution to protect the truth (Trompenaars & Hampden-Turner, 1998). Trompenaars and Hampden-Turner (1998) note that countries with strongly universalist cultures try to use the courts to mediate conflicts. The American culture is high on universalism, whereas the Mexican culture is high on particularism. Collectivist cultures tend to be particularistic and individualistic cultures tend to be universalistic.

The dimension neutral-affective refers to the extent to which people publicly express their emotions or suppress them. In neutral cultures, people tend to contain the public expression of their emotions. In affective cultures, however, people tend to express loudly their emotions. As Trompenaars and Hampden-Turner (1998) pointed out

> members of cultures which are affectively neutral do not telegraph their feelings but keep them carefully controlled and subdued. In contrast, in cultures high on affectivity people show their feelings plainly by laughing, smiling, grimacing, scowling and gesturing; they attempt to find immediate outlets for their feelings. (p. 70)

It is worth mentioning that neutral cultures are not necessarily cold or unfeeling, nor are they emotionally constipated or repressed (Trompenaars & Hampden-Turner, 1998, p. 70). Examples of neutral cultures include the Japanese culture and examples of emotional cultures include the Mexican culture.

The dimension specific-diffuse refers to the extent to which life is compartementalized or diffused. Specific cultures refer to cultures in which life is compartementalized and people play different roles in different situations. Diffuse cultures, however, are cultures in which roles are blurred. In such cultures, a position in one life space may carry over into other life spaces. As an example of a diffuse culture, Trompenaars and Hampden-Turner (1998) cited the French culture in which the boss played the role of a boss in several life spaces. Outside the organization, the boss is still the boss and his or her views must be considered as better than those of subordinates. In diffuse cultures, people may tend to solicit those who are in positions of power for matters for which they may not have the required expertise. Sully de Luqe and Sommer (2000) used the constructs of specific and holistic to describe these two types of culture. According to these authors, specific-oriented cultures compartementalize areas of life experiences (job, family, and education) commonly avoiding overlap between areas; whereas holistic-oriented cultures blend areas of life, seeing them as interdependent, rather than separate.

Cultures may also differ on how people gain social status and recognition. While some societies accord status to people on the basis of their achievements, others ascribe it to them by virtue of factors, such as age, class, gender, or education (Trompenaars & Hampden-Turner, 1998). Achievement cultures refer to cultures in which a person's status depends on his or her own performance. In such cultures, being the best at whatever it is that you do carries a great deal of weight (McFarlin & Sweeney, 2006). Ascription cultures, however, describe cultures where status depends on factors, such as age, connections, class, or gender. The dimension, individualism-communitarianism is similar to Hofstede's

(1980) individualism-collectivism dimension. Individualism emphasizes the preeminence of the self, whereas communitarianism emphasizes the importance of the group (e.g., Trompenaars, 1993; Trompenaars & Hampden-Turner, 1998).

Trompenaars (1993) and Trompenaars and Hampden-Turner (1998) also identified two other dimensions related to time orientation and attitude toward the external environment. According to the authors, time can be sequential—representing a series of passing events or synchronic—representing a series of past, present, and future events. In sequential cultures, people tend to set tight schedules, whereas in synchronic cultures, people tend to set loose schedules. How people manage time may influence how they organize work. This is particularly true within organizations. Trompenaars (1993) and Trompenaars and Hampden-Turner (1998) used two constructs to explain how people view and deal with their external environment. Outer-directed people are those who feel that life's outcomes aren't under their control, whereas inner-directed people tend to believe that they control their own destinies. These two dimensions are similar to the constructs of internal and external locus of control (Rotter, 1966). Most individualist cultures are characterized as inner-directed, whereas most collectivist cultures are characterized as outer-directed.

Trompenaars and Hampden-Turner (1998) considered that these cultural dimensions influence people's work values, attitudes, and behaviors. Their model, however, does not represent a radical departure from Hofstede's work. To the contrary, the dimensions described may be considered as an expansion and enrichment of this work. Another author that enriched Hofstede's work is Triandis (1989, 1995). Triandis (1995) formulated a cultural model by combining the power distance and individualism-collectivism dimensions to form four typologies of culture. This model is discussed in the following section.

TRIANDIS'S FOUR TYPOLOGIES OF CULTURE

Triandis (1995) developed a model of culture that includes four attributes: (1) definition of the self, (2) structure of goals, (3) emphasis on norms versus attitudes, and (4) emphasis on relatedness versus rationality. Triandis (1995) describes collectivist and individualist cultures along these four attributes. He contends that collectivists view the self as interdependent with others and resources are shared with others (Triandis, 1989). What one takes is in relation with what others get or may think about the sharing mechanism. Contrary to collectivists, individualists view the self as independent from others. Whereas collectivist cultures develop an interdependent self-construal, individualist cultures develop an independent self-construal (Markus & Kitayama, 1991). Decisions to share (or not to share) resources are made individually (Markus & Kitayama, 1991; Triandis & Bhawur, 1997). Collectivists set goals that are compatible with others, whereas individualists care less about the compatibility of their personal goals with group goals. Collectivists also focus on duties, obligations, and norms, whereas individualists focus on personal attitudes, needs, rights, and contracts. Collectivists emphasize unconditional relatedness, whereas individualists emphasize rationality (Triandis & Bhawur, 1997).

Relatedness refers to giving priority to relationships and taking into account the needs of others, whereas rationality refers to the careful computation of the costs and benefits of relationships. Triandis (2002) labeled collectivism and individualism cultural syndromes. A cultural syndrome is a shared pattern of beliefs, attitudes, self-definitions, norms, roles, and values organized around a theme (Triandis, 2002, p. 16). Triandis identified complexity as the organizing theme of cultural syndrome. He argues that in complex societies, there are several subgroups with different beliefs and attitudes. In other words, complex societies are characterized by a dominant culture and several subcultures. In simple societies, however, all individuals are in considerable agreement about their attitudes and beliefs.

Triandis (2002) also considers tightness of a culture as an element of cultural syndrome. Tightness refers to the existence of rules, norms, and ideas about right and wrong. In tight cultures, there are many rules and norms that people must follow. Any minor deviation from these norms is not tolerated. However, in loose cultures, where there are few rules, deviations from the norms are relatively tolerated. Triandis (1994) notes that cultural syndromes, such as collectivism and individualism emerge in societies based on their degree of complexity and tightness. He suggests that individualism emerges in societies that are both complex and loose, whereas collectivism emerges in societies that are simple and tight. Despite the soundness of Triandis's classification, it may have one caveat. Cultures do change and as they change, they may become more complex than they used to be. For instance, collectivist cultures, such as China, Japan, and South Korea are becoming complex as they become economically sophisticated. Perhaps, changes in a given culture may modify the dynamics related to complexity and tightness.

In Japan, a collectivist culture, there are several words for "I" and "you" (Triandis, 2002). However, the use of these two words depends on the relationship between the speaker and the target person. In short, there is no "I" by itself. The "I" depends on the relationship. This example illustrates the importance of relationships in collectivist cultures where the self is conceived as interdependent of in-groups (Triandis, 2002). Triandis (1995) considers that some cultural traditions may emphasize the same aspects of the self in relation to others. In homogeneous cultures, people do not want to stick out (Triandis & Bhawur, 1997). He labels cultures that emphasize the same aspect of the self, *horizontal*. In heterogeneous societies, the emphasis is on the self, and people tend to differentiate themselves from others. Such cultures are labeled *vertical*. Triandis (1995) combined the two aspects of the self (horizontal and vertical) with the aspects of interdependent and independent self to form a typology including four elements (see Table 3.1): *horizontal collectivism, horizontal individualism, vertical collectivism,* and *vertical individualism*. Horizontal collectivism represents a form of balance between individual and group goals but does not make the individual secondary to the group, as tends to be the case in vertical collectivism (Kabanoff, 1997). Gouveia, Clemente, and Espinosa (2003) examined the dimensionality and factorial structure of individualism and collectivism on a sample of 526 Spanish participants and found that a vertical versus horizontal attribute crossed with individualism and collectivism dimensions.

Vertical relations are more common in societies high in power distance, whereas horizontal relations are more common in societies low in power distance (Triandis & Bhawur, 1997). Despite these distinctions, it appears that affluence is shifting most cultures toward individualism (Triandis & Bhawak, 1997). In every culture, people create a structure of habits that guides their behavior. Take the example of a manager from the United States (an individualistic culture) who is sent to manage a subsidiary in China (a collectivistic culture). How should this manager behave once in China? We may anticipate that to be successful, the manager should adapt his or her structure of habits to the Chinese cultural context. As the old saying goes, "in Rome do as the Romans do."

Triandis's model shows that individualism and collectivism are not opposite dimensions. Indeed, individualism and collectivism can coexist (e.g., Schwartz, 1990; Triandis, 1995). Although individualists have multiple in-groups, the relationships with in-group members are superficial as opposed to collectivists who have fewer in-groups but strong emotional ties with in-group members. The interpersonal relationships and the individual's identification with the in-group are key factors in the definition of individualism and collectivism in Triandis's typology. There is a degree of

Table 3.1. Triandis's Four Types of Culture

	Collectivism	*Individualism*
Horizontal	HC—Horizontal Collectivism	HI—Horizontal Individualsim
Vertical	VC—Vertical collectivism	VI—Vertical Individualism

similarity between Triandis's typology and Fiske's (1991, 1992) four kinds of sociality, which is discussed next.

FISKE'S FOUR KINDS OF SOCIALITY

Fiske (1991) proposed four types of relational elements including *Communal Sharing* (CS), *Authority Ranking* (AR), *Equality Matching* (EM), and *Market Pricing* (MP) to explain the foundations of social relations. He contends that people use these four cognitive models to generate, understand, coordinate, and evaluate social relationships; and represent the source of both motives and norms. In the following lines, I explain each of these four elements.

Communal Sharing

Communal Sharing is a relation of unity, community, undifferentiated collective identity, and kindness (Fiske, 1991, 1992). In communal sharing, resource allocations are based on needs, to each according to his or her needs regardless of inputs. People simply take what they need and contribute what they can, without anyone attending to how much each person contributes or receives (Fiske, 1992). Communal sharing may lead to justice *of solidarity*. When people live together, their respective needs are intertwined so much so that satisfying one's own needs is the same as satisfying the needs of a fellow member. An illustration of this mode of sharing resources is common in traditional cultures of Native Americans and of sub-Saharan Africa. In these cultures, the land is a common property. Therefore, one takes what he or she needs. In modern societies, a city park is a common property (Triandis & Bhawur, 1997). According to this value of communal sharing, people have more the sense of "we" than the sense of "I." Consensus, unity, and conformity are the expressions of the structure in communal sharing decision-making and social influence (Fiske, 1992).

In communal sharing, people seek the sense of the group, contributing ideas not as individual positions but as part of the search for a joint judgment that transcends the separate attitudes of the participants (Fiske, 1992, p. 697). This value is similar to Hofstede's (1980) dimension of collectivism. As in collectivism, "in communal sharing, people have a sense of solidarity, unity, and belonging, and identify with the collectivity: they think of themselves as being all the same in some significant respect, not as individuals but as "we" (Fiske, 1991, pp. 14-15). However, defined broadly, collectivism encompasses both elements of communal sharing

Table 3.2. Adaptation of the Manifestations and Features of Four Elementary Relational Models

Domains and Features	Communal Sharing	Authority	Equality Matching	Market Pricing
Reciprocal exchange	People give what they can and freely take what they need from pooled resources. What you get does not depend on what you contribute, only on belonging to the group.	Superiors appropriate or preempt what they wish, or receive tribute from inferiors. Conversely, superiors have personal pastoral responsibility to provide for inferiors who are in need and to protect them.	Balanced, in-kind reciprocity. Give and get back the same thing in return, with appropriate delay.	Pay (or exchange) for commodities in proportion to what is received, as a function of market prices or utilities.
Distribution (Distributive justice)	Corporate use of resources regarded as a commons, without regard for how much any one person uses; everything belongs to all together. Individual shares and property are not marked.	The higher a person's rank, the more he or she gets, and the more choice he or she has. Subordinates receive less and get inferior items, often what is left over.	To each the same. Everyone gets identical shares (regardless of need, desire, or usefulness).	To each in due proportion. Each person is allotted a quota proportionate with some standard.
Contribution	Everyone gives what they have, without keeping track of what individuals contribute. What's mine is yours.	Noblesse oblige: superiors give beneficently, demonstrating their nobility and largess. Subordinate recipients of gifts are honored and beholden.	Contributions match each other's donations equally.	People assessed according to a fixed ratio or percentage.

Work	Everyone pitches in and does what he or she can, without anyone keeping track of inputs. Tasks are treated as collective responsibility of the group, without dividing the job or assigning specific individual duties.	Superiors direct and control the work of subordinates, while often doing less of the arduous or menial labor. Superiors control product of subordinates' labor.	Each person does the same thing in each phase of the work, either by working in synchrony, by aligning allotted tasks so they match, or by taking turns.	Work for a wage calculated as a rate per unit of time or output.
Decision making	Group seeks consensus, unity, the sense of the group (e.g., Quaker meeting, Japanese groups).	By authoritative fiat or decree. Will of the leader is transmitted through the chain of command. Subordinates obey orders.	One-person, one vote election. Everyone has equal say. Also rotating offices or lottery.	Market decides, governed by supply and demand or expected utilities. Also rational cost/benefit analysis.
Social influence	Conformity; desire to be similar to others, to agree, maintain unanimity, and not stand out as different. Mutual modeling and imitation.	Obedience to authority or deference to prestigious leaders. Subordinates display loyalty and strive to please superiors.	Compliance to return a favor ("log rolling"), taking turns deciding, or going along to compensate evenly or keep things balanced.	Costs and benefits incentives. Bargaining over terms of exchange. Market manipulation.
Social identity and the relational self	Membership in a natural kind. Self defined in terms of ancestry, race, ethnicity, common origins, and common fate. Identity derived from closest and most enduring personal relationships.	Self as revered leader or loyal follower; identity defined in terms of superior rank and prerogative, or inferiority and servitude.	Self as separate but coequal peer; on a par with fellows. Identity dependent on staying even, keeping up with reference group.	Self-defined in terms of occupation or economic role: how one earns a living. Identity as product of entrepreneurial success or failure.

Table continues on next page.

Table 3.2. Adaptation of the Manifestations and Features of Four Elementary Relational Models

Domains and Features	Communal Sharing	Authority	Equality Matching	Market Pricing
Moral judgment and ideology	Caring, kindness, altruism, selfless generosity, Protecting intimate personal relationships.	What supreme beings command is right. Obedience to will of superiors. Heteronomy, charismatic legitimation.	Fairness as strict equality, equal treatment, and balanced reciprocity.	Abstract, universal, rational principles based on the utilitarian criterion of the greatest number. Rational-legal legitimation.
Moral interpretation of misfortune	Stigmatization, pollution, contamination. Isolation as pariah. Victims seek and join support groups of fellow sufferers.	Have I angered God? Did I disobey the ancestors? (e.g., story of Job).	Feeling that misfortune should be equally distributed: "things even out in the long run." Idea that misfortune balances a corresponding transgression.	Was this a reasonably expectable risk or calculable cost to pay for benefits sought? Is this too high a price to pay?

and equality matching. Three words, *kind* (as in kindness), *kindness*, and *kin*, characterize communal sharing. People are expected to be kind and cordial with each other. Their relations are mostly with those who are close to them, such as relatives and friends.

People also believe that they have communal sharing relationships with nonhumans, immaterial beings, or ancestors, projecting the model onto a social vacuum in the absence of objective human partners (Fiske, 1992). As Fiske (1992) put it

> Communal sharing is a central element in most religions, emerging in the forms of communion rituals, sacrifices in which people share food with the gods, commensal meals, an ethos of universal love and caretaking, and the close bonds of religious communities. (p. 698)

Communal Sharing may exemplify the division between in-group and out-group members seen in collectivism. Fiske (1992) notes that when people are thinking in terms of equivalence relations, they tend to regard the equivalence class to which they themselves belong as better than others and to favor it. This implies the existence of a group bias, since people may see their own group as better than other groups. For instance, the egocentric fairness bias would exist not at the individual level but at the group level. People would tend to consider the values and actions of the equivalence class as fairer than those of other classes.

Authority Ranking

Authority ranking is a relationship of asymmetric differences commonly exhibited in a hierarchical ordering of statuses and precedence, often accompanied by the exercise of command and complementary displays of deference and respect (Fiske, 1991). In such a system, inferiors are deferential, loyal, and obedient, giving obeisance and paying homage to their betters (Fiske, 1991, p. 14). People are ranked according to the formal status they enjoy in society. Those higher in rank have prestige, prerogatives, and privileges that their inferiors lack, but subordinates are often entitled to protection and pastoral care (Fiske, 1992). When people think in terms of rank and order, they treat high rank as better (Fiske, 1992). Thus, in an authority ranking relationship, people would tend to view those of high status as better and rely on them for guidance and decision making.

Authority ranking is a linear ordering of people that obeys to the natural pecking order observed in nonhumans. In such a relationship, what determines outcomes allocation is the social status. When people transfer things from person to person in an authority ranking mode, higher ranking people get more and better things, and get them sooner than their subordinates (Fiske, 1992). Subordinates also accept as given this social order. In some ways, Authority ranking corresponds to Hofstede's (1980) dimension of power distance. In both high power distance cultures and authority ranking relationships, people accept the inequality of power and relations are dominated by social status. Those who have power are revered and rarely confronted about their use of power. However, in authority ranking, there is reciprocity between power holders and subordinates that is not observed in high power distance cultures. In authority ranking relationships, power holders are revered, whereas, inferiors are entitled to receive protection, aid, and support from their leaders (Fiske, 1991, 1992).

In authority ranking relationships, many material objects are used as status symbols. Quite apart from their transactional flows through exchange, material objects are static markers that serve to represent the rank and authority of the person displaying them (Fiske, 1992). In modern organizations, examples of such objects are represented by large offices for CEOs or reserved parking lots for executives and high ranking officials. Decision making is vested in power holders and subordinates are united in their obedience to authority figures. In authority ranking relationships, people channel information upward and hand decisions down through the chain of command (Fiske, 1992). Authority ranking also influences people's relationships with nonhumans. Most cultures in the world believe in the power of a supreme being who is the creator, whose word is truth and whose will is good (Fiske, 1992). Misfortune may therefore be interpreted as an act of retribution for having offended God or some nonhuman beings, such as ancestors or spirits.

Equality Matching

Equality matching relationships are based on a model of even balance and one-for-one correspondence, as in turn taking, egalitarian distributive justice, in-kind reciprocity, tit-for-tat retaliation, eye-for-an eye revenge, or compensation by equal replacement (Fiske, 1992, p. 691). According to this value, resources should be distributed equally. The emphasis is on reciprocity, justice, and fairness. In modern organizations, employees should work the same number of hours and receive the same time for their lunch break. In a university department, instructors should receive the same teaching load. When exchanging material goods in equality matching relationships, people consider that these goods have equal value. *I scratch your back once, you scratch mine once.* As a collective decision-making mechanism, equality matching often takes the form of a one-person, one-vote electoral process (Fiske, 1992). The most influential mechanism of equality matching is people's reactions and expectations when they receive favors from others. According to Fiske (1992), the operating principle is that when people related in an equality matching mode receive a favor, they feel obligated to reciprocate by returning a favor.

Equality matching is an egalitarian relationship among peers who are distinct but coequal individuals (Fiske, 1991). In such a relationship, exchanges are reciprocal and have equal value. Equality matching as distributive justice takes the form of an even distribution into equal parts, such that people are indifferent among the portions, and/or so that what each person receives is the same as what another person receives (Fiske, 1991, p. 15). Equality matching supposes that everyone should be treated the same. It corresponds in some ways to what is expected in collectivist cultures among in-group members and to the horizontal aspect of Triandis's typology. As such, it represents a component of the collectivism dimension (e.g., Hofstede, 1980). However, in equality matching, people's actions are differentiated unlike in communal sharing; people do also attend to the magnitude of imbalances, using addition and subtraction to calculate the net result of a series of interchanges (Fiske, 1992).

Equality matching may lead to justice of reciprocity. In equality matching relationships, the expectations are that people treat fairly those who treat them fairly. In this reciprocal justice, people often think about how much they have to give to reciprocate or compensate others or come out even with them (Fiske, 1992). Equality matching entails some kind of additive tally of who owes what and who is entitled to what (Fiske, 1992). It also involves a conception of distinct but equal individuals whose relationship is based on an assessment of socially significant differences between people; the reference point, the equilibrium point around which the relationship oscillates, is even balance (Fiske, 1992, p. 705). Although material goods are different in equality matching, the operating principle is that everyone gets the same thing unlike in Market Pricing, where some goods have more value than others.

Market Pricing

Market Pricing is the fourth mode of social relationships described by Fiske (1991, 1992). It refers to a relationship mediated by values determined by a market system (Fiske, 1991). Market pricing is used to organize the transfer of objects or benefits, and material goods have a value ascribed to them unlike in the previous three modes of social relations. "Market pricing transactions typically entail a transmodal standard of value (price or utility) by which all costs and benefits, all inputs and outputs, can be compared and any value-relevant feature of any commodity can be assessed" (Fiske, 1992, p. 706). In market pricing, people engage in exchanges when they think that doing so will yield a payoff. The main criterion in market pricing is proportionality and the exchange of objects depends on their market value. In market pricing, each individual receives resources in proportion to his or her contributions. Applied to organizations, those who contribute more should be compensated accordingly; thus justifying compensation systems, such as bonuses and merit-pay.

Market pricing is based on an intermodal metric of value by which people compare different modalities and calculate exchange and cost-benefit ratios (Fiske, 1991). The market pricing model is a socioeconomic model in which social behavior depends on the advantages (rewards) and disadvantages (costs) of the relationships (Triandis & Bhawur, 1997). This value is similar to equity theory (e.g., Adams, 1963, 1965; Homans, 1961) and corresponds to Hofstede's dimension of individualism. In distributing outcomes, the equity rule of distribution (e.g., Adams, 1965; Deutsch, 1975) prevails in market pricing. Rules governing market pricing should be explicit, universal, and formally stated (Fiske, 1992). Market pricing is also viewed as a directive force that guides coordinated action toward a goal and influences work organization, and how people react to misfortune. Because in market pricing, people believe in proportionality, they may question whether they are paying too much of a price when they experience misfortune. People may also believe that others get what they deserve; thus reinforcing the belief in a just world hypothesis (e.g., Lerner, 1981, 1982). By arguing that people everywhere have just these four fundamental models for relating to other people, Fiske's (1991, 1992) indirectly established a link between his model and Schwartz's (1992, 1994) theory of universal values.

SCHWARTZ'S THEORY OF UNIVERSAL VALUES

Schwartz (1992, 1994) and Schwartz and Bilsky (1987, 1990) developed a theory of universal values that explains the influence of culture on human behavior. Schwartz and Bilsky (1987, 1990) argue that the primary content aspect of a value is the type of goal or motivational concern that it expresses. They contend that values represent three universal requirements of human existence to which all individuals and societies must be responsive: (a) needs of individuals as biological organisms, (b) requisites of coordinated social interaction, and (c) survival and welfare needs of groups. These three goals are crucial to the survival of individuals and societies. Applied to social relationships, values help shape people's attitudes and the manner in which they organize social interactions among them. Schwartz gathered data from 1988 to 1992. The data set included 86 samples drawn from 41 cultural groups and 38 countries. Respondents included 38 samples of schoolteachers, 35 samples of university students, and 12 general samples of adults with widely varied occupations, and two adolescent samples. Data analysis revealed seven cultural types: *conservatism, hierarchy, mastery, affective autonomy, intellectual autonomy, egalitarian commitment*, and *harmony*. Conservatism is based on values that foster harmony in society. In societies high on this dimension, the interests of the individual person are not seen as different from those of the group or community. Cultures that value this dimension are primarily concerned with security, conformity, and tradition (Schwartz, 1994).

The dimension Hierarchy deals with the extent to which cultures rely on superiors to set goals. Schwartz recognizes that power is a universally recognized value at the individual level. The dimension Hierarchy is closed to the dimension, Conservatism. Perhaps, the hierarchical allocation of fixed roles is more compatible with cultures where people are viewed as enacting ascribed roles built into the social fabric than with cultures where people are viewed as autonomous individuals with the right to seek their own level (Schwartz, 1994). The dimension, Mastery emphasizes active mastery of the social environment through self-assertion (Schwartz, 1994). It involves making efforts to modify, to structure or restructure one's social or physical environment and is not significantly correlated with the dimension, Intellectual Autonomy although both include values that represent self-direction at the individual level (Schwartz, 1994). However, it is negatively correlated with Conservatism.

The dimension Affective Autonomy refers to the extent to which people put more emphasis on stimulation and hedonism. A dimension close to Affective Autonomy is Intellectual Autonomy, which puts more emphasis on self-direction. Both dimensions are strongly correlated and are the opposite of the dimension Conservatism. The dimension Egalitarian Commitment represents a social commitment that can occur among equals (Schwartz, 1994) and aims to advance the welfare of others. Egalitarian Commitment is negatively correlated with Hierarchy and Conservatism but positively correlated with both Affective and Intellectual Autonomy. Finally, the dimension Harmony emphasizes harmony with nature. This dimension relates closely to Egalitarian Commitment and is negatively correlated with the dimensions, Conservatism and Affective Autonomy but positively correlated with Intellectual Autonomy.

Schwartz (1994) compared his seven dimensions to Hofstede's (1980) four dimensions. Using his own data and Hofstede's data, he computed correlations between the two sets of cultural dimensions. Some of his findings were quite surprising. For instance, he found that his dimension, Conservatism was negatively correlated with Hofstede's dimensions of Individualism and Uncertainty Avoidance but positively correlated with Power Distance. No significant correlation was found between Conservatism and Masculinity. Hierarchy was negatively correlated with Individualism, whereas Mastery was positively correlated with Masculinity. Affective Autonomy was positively correlated with Individualism but negatively correlated with Power Distance. Intellectual Autonomy was positively correlated with Individualism and negatively correlated with Power Distance (but only in the student samples). Egalitarian Commitment was positively correlated with Individualism but negatively correlated with Power Distance (only in the student samples). Finally, Harmony was not significantly correlated with any of Hofstede's dimensions. When the two dimensions representing Autonomy (Intellectual and Affective) were combined, a positive correlation was found with the dimension Individualism and a negative correlation with the dimension Power Distance.

Based on these results, Schwartz (1994) argues that there are conceptual differences between his set of dimensions and Hofstede's four dimensions. He contends that the Hierarchy values emphasize the legitimacy of using power to attain individual or group goals in general. However, the Power Distance items refer quite narrowly to legitimacy of power inequality in employee-boss relations (Schwartz, 1994). Schwartz (1994) also calls for a distinction between two dimensions confounded in the Individualism-Collectivism literature: a dimension opposing conceptions of the person as autonomous versus embedded or related (Autonomy versus Conservatism) and one opposing pursuit of personal goals versus collective goals (Mastery and Hierarchy, versus Egalitarian Commitment and Harmony). Ralston, Holt, Terpstra, and Kai-Cheng (1997) applied Schwartz's Value Survey to the study of work values in four different countries, China, Japan, Russia, and the United States. They found that American managers reported higher scores on the Self-Enhancement dimension compared to managers from the other three countries. These findings indicate the willingness of American participants to stick out and enhance their individual worth. It also indicates the individualistic nature of the American culture, which is recurrent in all five models.

INTEGRATING THE MODELS OF CULTURE

There are at least three lessons to draw from the discussion of the different models of culture. First, the four models explain clearly the impact of culture on human behavior, although they use different dimensions to do so. Second, these cultural dimensions also overlap. The dimension, power distance (e.g., Hofstede, 1980, 1991) is similar to the dimensions of verticality (e.g., Triandis, 1995) and authority ranking (e.g., Fiske, 1991). These dimensions emphasize the extent to which people accord great attention to power differences. They also recognize that those who hold power are revered and subordinates often seek protection and guidance from leaders. The dimensions of collectivism (e.g., Hofstede, 1980, 1991), communal sharing (e.g., Fiske, 1991), communitarianism (e.g., Trompenaars, 1993; Trompenaars & Hampden-Turner, 1998), horizontal collectivism (e.g., Triandis, 1995), and conservatism (e.g., Schwartz, 1992, 1994) are also similar. They all emphasize the importance of harmony and interpersonal relationships.

Third, because these models explain the influence of culture on human behavior and social relations, they are important in helping to hypothesize the potential impact of culture on organizational justice. Using the different models of culture, I developed a typology of cultural syndromes (e.g., Triandis, 1996). Cultural syndromes consist of shared attitudes, beliefs, norms, roles, and self definitions, and values of members of each culture that are organized around a theme (Triandis, 1996, p. 407). This typology includes four cultural syndromes: (1) relation-centered, (2) self-centered, (3) status-centered, and (4) risk-prone. Like Sully de Luque and Sommer (2000) who also proposed four cultural syndromes (specific-holistic orientation, tolerance for ambiguity, individualism-collectivism, and status identity), I argue that this classification is not exhaustive nor is it intended to replace existing cultural classifications. Rather, this classification is used with the intention of making smooth the discussion of the impact of culture on organizational justice. Table 3.3 illustrates the four cultural syndromes, their characteristics, and their potential justice implications.

The present classification expands earlier work by Steiner (2001) who highlighted some of the dimensions relevant to the study of organizational justice. He used several cultural dimensions, such as collectivism, individualism, power distance, uncertainty avoidance, femininity, masculinity, ascription, achievement, locus of control, human nature as good or bad, pragmatic/idealistic, orientation toward time and Confucianism, to name but a few to explain the influence of culture on organizational justice. Since the impact of most of these dimensions on organizational justice was not previously studied, the author was not able to rely on empirical findings. Moreover, the relatively high number of cultural dimensions may confuse researchers assessing the impact of culture on organizational justice. To avoid this pitfall, the present book focuses on a limited number of cultural dimensions. This is particularly important because the cultural dimensions identified by several authors are not necessarily independent (e.g, Steiner, 2001). Thus, the present classification

Table 3.3. Cultural Syndromes Relevant to the Study of Organizational Justice

Cultural Syndromes	Cultural Characteristics	Distributive Justice Concerns	Procedural Justice Concerns	Interactional Justice Concerns
Relation-centered cultures Hofstede (1980, 1991) Leung et al. Trompenaars (1993); Trompenaars & Hampden-Turner (1998) Triandis (1995) Fiske (1992) Schwartz (1994)	Collectivism Confucianism Communitarianism Horizontal collectivism Communal sharing Egalitarian commitment	Preference for equality in reward allocations Preference for need in reward allocations In-group bias in reward allocations	Preference for procedures that benefit the group	Preference for interpersonal relations Importance of harmony in interpersonal relations
Self-centered cultures Hofstede (1980, 1991) Fiske (1992) Schwartz (1994) Triandis (1995) Trompenaars (1993); Trompenaars & Hampden-Turner (1998)	Individualism Market pricing Self-enhancement, self-transcendence Horizontal individualism Individualism	Preference for equity in reward allocations egocentric bias	Preferences for procedures that benefit the self	Treatment of respect and dignity as symbols of self-worth
Status-centered cultures Hofstede (1980, 1991) Fiske (1992) Schwartz (1994) Triandis (1995) Trompenaars (1993); Trompenaars & Hampden-Turner (1998)	Power distance Authority ranking Hierarchy Vertical individualism	Preference for status-based criteria in reward allocations	Preference for procedures that benefit those in power	Respect and deference to authority Tolerance of injustices emanating from authority
Risk-prone cultures Hofstede (1980, 1991) Sully de Luque & Sommer (2000) Trompenaars (1993); Trompenaars & Hampden-Turner (1998)	Tolerance to ambiguity Tolerance for ambiguity Achievement	Preference for equity in reward allocations	Preference for procedures that allow innovation and creativity	Interpersonal relations that foster change and creativity

differs from Steiner's in that it is based on a reorganization of different cultural models. In this classification, I have combined several dimensions together to form looser categories. For instance, the dimension, Relation-centered cultures includes collectivism (e.g., Hofstede, 1980), communal sharing (e.g., Fiske, 1991, 1992), horizontal collectivism (e.g., Triandis, 1995) and conservatism (Schwartz, 1992, 1994). In the following lines, I discuss each of the four cultural syndromes.

Relation-Centered Cultures

Relation-centered cultures emphasize interpersonal relationships and foster harmony and the importance of the group over the individual. This dimension is loosely defined and includes Hofstede's (1980) dimension of collectivism, Triandis's (1995) dimension of horizontal collectivism, Fiske's (1992) dimension of communal sharing, and Schwartz's (1994) dimension of conservatism. The social context would strongly affect justice judgments in cultures that emphasize relationships. Since the group is the primary unit of importance, individual judgments of fairness or unfairness would reflect more group or societal norms than individual standards. That is not to say that in such cultures people cannot set their own standards of justice. Another characteristic of relation-centered cultures is the fostering of harmony. Relation-centered cultures also emphasize the distinction between in-group and out-group members contrary to self-centered cultures. As indicated in Table 3.3, in such cultures, people may often prefer equality and need as outcome allocation criteria (e.g., Deutsch, 1985).

Self-Centered Cultures

Self-centered cultures refer to cultures that emphasize the pursuit of self-interest to the detriment of group interest. In such cultures, the primacy of the self over the group is the focus of individual behavior. In self-centered cultures, people highlight the individual as a focus of construal while deemphasizing the social context in which the individual is embedded (Kashima, Kashima, Kim, & Gelfand, 2006). This cultural syndrome includes the dimensions of individualism (e.g., Hofstede, 1980), Market Pricing (e.g., Fiske, 1991) and Autonomy (e.g., Schwartz, 1994). This cultural syndrome also includes such dimensions as Mastery (Schwartz, 1994), Masculinity (Hofstede, 1980), and Need for Achievement (McClelland, 1961). In self-centered cultures, the individual is the unit of concern and interprets events based on his or her personal standards. These standards may range from standards of fairness to the willingness to better oneself as an individual. For instance, self-enhancement is less direct in East Asia (a relation-centered culture) and involves an emphasis on the virtues of the group, and because the group has positive qualities one has positive qualities as a member of the group (Triandis, 2002). Triandis (2002) also notes that achievement motivation is socially oriented among collectivists and individually oriented among individualists.

Since the focus in such cultures is on the individual rather than the collective, justice judgments would be affected by personal standards of fairness rather than societal or group norms. Moreover, the quest for justice would be more instrumental than in relation-centered cultures. People would seek fairness because it serves their own interests. Likewise, the preferred rule of distribution would be equity. The preference for this rule is manifested in the Market Pricing dimension (e.g., Fiske, 1991). In self-centered cultures, the self is conceived as independent of in-groups, personal goals are given priority, attitudes determine much of social behavior, and interpersonal relationships are well accounted by exchange theory (Triandis, 2002).

Status-Centered Cultures

This dimension characterizes cultures that emphasize status differences among people. It includes the dimensions of power distance (e.g., Hofstede, 1980), authority ranking (e.g., Fiske, 1991), vertical collectivism (Triandis, 1995), and hierarchy (e.g., Schwartz, 1994). Although Schwartz (1994) did not find a significant correlation between hierarchy and power distance, I include these two dimensions in the broader dimension of status-centered cultures for two reasons. First, both dimensions describe the meaning that society ascribes to power and its use. Hofstede's (1980) dimension of power distance deals with the extent to which people accept the unequal distribution of power in society.

Criteria for creating hierarchy in society include age, gender, education, class, caste, race, and the like. Some of these criteria, such as gender and race are inherited, whereas others are acquired.

Schwartz's (1994) dimension of hierarchy, however, deals with the extent to which people accept that leaders should set goals for their groups. Although these two conceptualizations may seem different, they contain some similarities. Accepting that those who hold power should set goals is an implicit acknowledgement that power is unequally distributed among group members. Second, including these two dimensions implies that the concept of status-centered cultures is broadly defined here and has several subdimensions. A society may well recognize leaders' prerogatives to make decisions, even unilaterally, but may not tolerate abuse of power. Thus, power distance does not necessarily mean that power abuse is tolerated. This cultural syndrome embodies the notion that cultural members are stratified into categories or a hierarchy based on culturally salient criteria (Sully de Luque & Sommer, 2000). Such inequalities among people are internalized by members of the society. "Status inequality refers to modalities of expected behavior reinforced externally by formal or informal sanctions and expectations, and internally by the predisposing personality propensities set up by prior socialization" (DeVos, 1990). In high status-centered cultures, people are receptive to power differentials. Thus, unilateral actions from leaders are expected in such cultures. In low status-centered cultures, however, people are less receptive to power differentials.

Risk-Prone Cultures

The cultural syndrome of risk-prone refers to the extent to which cultures tolerate (or do not tolerate) ambiguity and encourage innovation and risk taking. Risk prone cultures tend to encourage individual initiatives, risk-taking and entrepreneurial endeavors. Risk-averse cultures, however, tend to favor conformity to rules, regulations, and traditions. This cultural syndrome encompasses Hofstede's (1980) dimension of uncertainty avoidance, and Sully de Luque and Sommer's (2000) cultural syndrome of tolerance for ambiguity. According to Sully de Luque and Sommer (2000), in low tolerance for ambiguity cultures, managers take fewer decision-making risks and there is extensive reliance on rules and procedures. Thus, adherence to procedures may represent an important aspect of organizational life in such cultures. Failure to follow these formal procedures may seem unfair because individuals are expected to conform to standard practices (e.g., Triandis, 1989). The propensity for low tolerance for ambiguity cultures is to avert risk and uncertainty, whereas the propensity for high tolerance for ambiguity cultures is to accept and be less threatened by risk and uncertainty (Sully de Luque & Sommer, 2000).

Hofstede's dimension of uncertainty avoidance helps capture the concept of risk-prone cultures. Coping with uncertainty is a fundamental concern in human life. How societies cope with uncertainty will shape how they evolve over time. Hofstede (1980) notes that coping with uncertainty belongs to the cultural heritage of societies and is transferred and reinforced through basic institutions like the family, the school, and the state. The dimension of risk-prone cultures may help illuminate some assumptions of uncertainty management theory (e.g., van den Bos, 2002). Some cultures tend to tolerate ambiguity, whereas others are more traditional and tend to maintain the status quo. For the former, success may lie in exploring new ideas and processes, whereas the latter may consider that respect for traditions and maintaining the status quo are important in ensuring a predictable future.

Although culture may help understanding justice behavior, we must acknowledge the importance of the underlying cognitive processes that make these cultural dimensions salient. For instance, how do individualists and collectivists construe a particular event as just or unjust? What cognitive mechanisms does a person with an individualistic orientation use to react to an abusive supervisor compared to a person with a collectivist orientation? Answering such questions requires the study of the cognitive processes that influence these cultural dimensions. People from collectivist cultures may construe an injustice to in-group members as a threat to oneself and therefore experience a stronger sense of unfairness. Similarly, people in individualistic cultures may construe the equity rule as involving the likelihood of showcasing one's performance and therefore should carry a meaningful message, helping to increase one's self-esteem and self-worth. Such cognitive interpretations make cultural dimensions more meaningful in explaining fairness or unfairness.

It is worth mentioning that the four cultural syndromes may interact with one another to influence attitudinal and behavioral reactions. A culture may be both self-centered and risk-prone or relation-centered and risk-averse or relation-centered and status-centered. As an example, one may consider the American culture as being both self-centered and risk-prone. Previous research (e.g., Hofstede, 1980, 1991; Triandis, 1995) have characterized the American culture as high on individualism and moderate on uncertainty avoidance. The four cultural syndromes may also apply to individual orientations within specific cultures. Some people may be "relation-centered," whereas others may be more oriented toward status identity. The extent to which these cultural syndromes interact echoes Sully de Luque and Sommer's (2000) contention that we must be aware that behavior is not only affected by specific differences on a single dimension but is also complicated by interactions across dimensions. Although some dimensions, such as collectivism-individualism and power distance have been studied in the organizational justice literature, very few empirical investigations have concerned the other dimensions. As illustrated in Table 3.3, the four cultural syndromes have implications for organizational justice. These implications serve as the basis for the following two chapters.

CHAPTER 4

CULTURE AND EMPLOYEE REACTIONS TO JUSTICE

In chapter 3, I discussed the different models of culture. Specifically, I re-classified the different cultural dimensions into four cultural syndromes. Using them, I focus on the impact of culture on employee fairness judgments and reactions to situations of fairness in this chapter. In doing so, I acknowledge the difference between perceptions of fairness and perceptions of unfairness. The experience of fairness is different from the experience of unfairness; and both elicit different cognitions and feelings. Injustice is different from justice because the two concepts are not end points of the same continuum (e.g., Bies, 2005; Finkel, Crystal, & Watanabe, 2001). The present chapter is organized as follows. First, it proposes a model of employee reactions to justice. Second, the chapter uses this model to analyze the relationship between each of the four cultural syndromes identified in chapter 3 and the three dimensions of distributive, procedural, and interactional justice.

A CULTURAL MODEL OF EMPLOYEE REACTIONS TO JUSTICE

Developing a cultural model of organizational justice is important because culture shapes the core values and norms of its members, and these values and norms are shared and transmitted from one generation

A Cultural Perspective of Organizational Justice, 81–103
Copyright © 2007 by Information Age Publishing
All rights of reproduction in any form reserved.

to another through social learning processes of modeling and observation as well as through the effects each person experiences as a result of his or her actions (Bandura, 1986). The cultural model of organizational justice (see Figure 4.1) contends that cultural variables influence perceptions of distributive, procedural, and interactional justice. Central to this model is the assumption that fairness judgments and employee reactions to perceptions of fairness have their basis in cultural norms. As Blau (1964) put it

> since fairness is a social norm that prescribes just treatment as a moral principle, third parties in the community will disapprove of a person who deals unfairly with others under his power, whereas the one whose dealings are just and fair earns general social approval. (p. 157)

The cultural variables included in the model are relation-centered, self-centered, status-centered, and risk-prone.

As the model illustrates, the occurrence of an event triggers justice judgments. Because the model focuses only on perceptions of fairness, these justice judgments are generally positive insofar as they indicate that the event is fair. These justice judgments result in perceptions of distributive, procedural, and interactional fairness, which may lead to positive attitudinal and behavioral outcomes. Regardless of their cultural backgrounds, employees tend to reciprocate for fair treatment with positive work-related attitudes, such as organizational citizenship behavior, organizational commitment, job satisfaction, and trust. The model also contends that culture may influence justice in two ways. First, culture may have a direct effect on justice judgments and reactions to justice. Second, culture enters the model as a moderating variable. In the following paragraphs, I describe the model and the manner in which culture influences justice judgments and reactions to justice.

Culture as Antecedent

As an antecedent variable, culture directly influences justice judgments and reactions to perceptions of justice. What is considered just is therefore embedded in every aspect of culture. Suppose that two individuals, Leo, a Chinese and John an American both work in the same organization. Suppose that we want to assess their preferences for outcome allocation rules. Because of their different cultural backgrounds we may suspect that Leo would prefer the equality rule of outcome distribution, whereas John would prefer the equity rule. Here, culture acts as an antecedent. There is ample evidence for this prediction. Stone and Stone-Romero (2001) con-

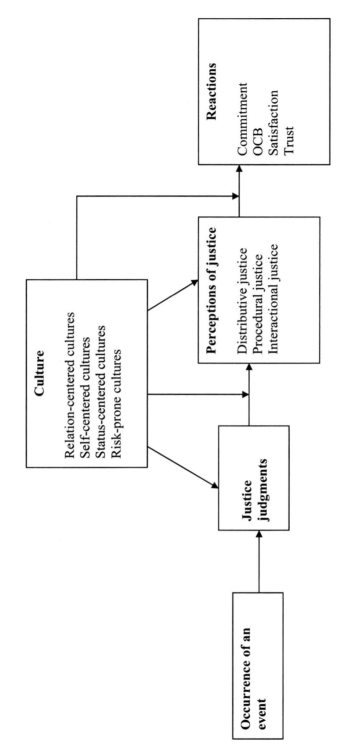

Figure 4.1.   A cross-cultural model of employee reactions to justice

tend that individuals from Western cultures may see allocations based on proportionality as fair, while those from Eastern cultures may view allocations based on equality or need as fair. According to the authors, the apparent differences may stem from religious beliefs.

Culture as Moderator

As a moderator, culture enhances or reduces the effects of justice judgments or reactions. For example, collectivists are known to favor the equality rule of distributive justice, whereas individualists are likely to favor the equity rule of distribution (Deutsch, 1985). Thus, when an organization applies a given rule of outcome distribution, employees may differently react to such rule depending on their cultural backgrounds. To illustrate the moderating effect of culture on justice, let us return to the previous example of Leo and John. Suppose that both Leo and John witness the same event. Despite their different cultural backgrounds, they make the same judgment. Both view the event as fair. However, their different cultural socializations may predispose them to react differently to this perception of fairness. Here, culture acts as a moderator. Using the model described above, I analyze the impact of culture on employee reactions to perceptions of fairness in organizations. This analysis uses the four cultural syndromes identified and the three dimensions of organizational justice.

RELATION-CENTERED CULTURES AND ORGANIZATIONAL JUSTICE

As indicated in the previous chapter, relation-centered cultures refer to cultures that emphasize the importance of the group over the individual. The impact of this cultural syndrome on the three dimensions of distributive, procedural and interactional justice is analyzed in this section.

Relation-Centered Cultures and Distributive Justice

There are four ways in which culture influences distributive justice (Greenberg, 2001a). First, people may differ in regard to how outcomes should be allocated. Some cultures may prefer the equity rule of distribution, whereas others may prefer the equality rule or the need rule of distribution. Second, people define justice differently across cultures (Greenberg, 2001a). For instance, there is not a word for "fair" in the Japanese language (Kidder & Miller, 1991; Tyler, Boeckmann, Smith, & Huo,

1997). The lack of word to mean fair in the Japanese language, however, does not imply that the Japanese do not care about fairness. Kidder and Miller (1991) acknowledge that concerns for distributive justice were very much important in Japan. Third, prevailing norms in various cultures may influence what is perceived to be fair in these cultures. Fourth, the dominance of some groups over others may influence distributive justice (e.g., Bierbrauer, 1990; Cook, 1990; Opotow, 1990).

A review of the literature on cross-cultural organizational justice indicates that individualism-collectivism is the dominant theoretical framework used for interpreting the results related to outcomes distribution across cultures (Leung, 1997). Specifically, cross-cultural studies using this dimension have identified several distribution rules that are culture specific. Productivity goals are linked with the equity rule, interpersonal harmony is tied to the equality rule, and personal welfare objectives are linked with need-based distributions (e.g., Deutsch, 1985). Cultural collectivism is related to the preference for the equality rule because equality is compatible with the emphasis on solidarity, harmony, and cohesion in collectivist cultures. In contrast, individualism is related to the preference for the equity norm because equity is compatible with the emphasis on productivity, competition, and self-gain (Leung & Bond, 1982).

Several studies (e.g., Bond, Leung, & Wan, 1982; Tornblum, Jonsson, & Foa, 1985) analyzed the impact of relation-centered cultures on allocation rules. Tornblum, Jonsson, and Foa (1985) found that in Sweden (a collectivist culture) people put the rule of equality first followed by the rule of need, then the rule of equity, whereas Americans viewed the equity rule as more important and resented the equality rule. Bond, Leung, and Wan (1982) conducted an empirical study that examined the impact of collectivism on outcome allocation. They identified two types of reward: (a) task reward (assignment of a grade to the recipient and willingness to work with the recipient again in the future) and (b) socioemotional reward (willingness to befriend the recipient). Their findings showed that the Chinese participants indicated a strong preference for an egalitarian allocation rule than their American counterparts for both types of reward. These findings were consistent with the prevailing view that collectivists tend to favor the equality rule of outcome distribution. Kim, Park, and Suzuki (1990) found that Korean participants followed the equality rule of distribution more closely than did Japanese and American participants. There was no difference, however, between the allocation patterns of American and Japanese participants.

Leung and Park (1986) conducted a comparative study on South Korean and American samples. They found that when productivity was emphasized, participants judged the equity rule to be fairer, used the equity rule to a large extent, and judge an allocator using the equity rule

as competent but less friendly. In contrast, when harmony was emphasized, participants judged the equality rule as fairer, used it more, and
judge an allocator using the equality rule as higher on social competence
and friendly than one using the equity rule. However, Korean participants
showed a stronger relation between the allocation rule a person uses and
his or her friendliness than did their American counterparts. They perceived an allocator using the equality rule as higher on social evaluation
and an allocator using the equity rule as lower on social evaluation than
did American participants.

Fields, Pang, and Chiu (2000) found that employees in both Hong
Kong and the United States consider both reward allocations and the
nature of an organization's dealings with employees in constructing judgments about job satisfaction, intent to stay, and evaluation of supervision.
Consistent with previous studies in the United States, they also found that
procedural justice has a larger influence on evaluation of supervision,
whereas distributive justice has a larger effect on intent to stay and job satisfaction in Hong Kong. However, contrary to previous findings in the
United States in which procedural justice did not moderate the relationship of distributive justice with evaluation of supervision, in Hong Kong,
procedural justice moderates the effects of distributive justice with job satisfaction and intent to stay.

These findings suggest both similarities and differences between the
two samples. Both samples recognize the importance of equity as a pro-
ductivity-enhancing behavior and equality as a harmony-enhancing
behavior. However, some differences emerge in regard to the link between
the allocation rule and the extent to which the allocator is perceived as
friendly or not. Korean participants may have seen an allocator using the
equality rule as friendlier than one using an equity rule. Their cultural
values may probably have affected their evaluation of the allocators. In
collectivist cultures, people are so concerned about the quality of interpersonal relations that an allocator's preference for a distribution rule
may be used as a proxy to judge the extent to which he or she emphasizes
social relations.

An allocator using an equality rule tends to be perceived as one valuing
social relations, whereas an allocator using an equity rule is seen as one
putting less emphasis on social relations. As Leung and Park (1986), put
it,

> Collectivists tend to perceive the consequences of the equity and equality
> rules to be markedly different and are more likely to make use of allocation
> rules to achieve an interactional goal that they perceive as appropriate to a
> given situation. (p. 118)

Perhaps, people from relation-centered cultures perceive that equality is the appropriate rule of distribution whenever a group is formed. Although the equity rule may be recognized as fostering better performance, it may be considered inappropriate when the objective is to maintain the quality of social relations. Each member of a system carries within him or her cognitive maps of allocation processes within that system (Leventhal, Karuza, & Fry, 1980). The development of these cognitive maps is subject to cultural influence. Other studies, however, did not support the 'culture-effect' of allocation preferences. Marin (1985) conducted a study on a sample of Indonesian and American participants. He found that both cultural groups preferred equity over equality regardless of the relationship between the allocator and the recipient. Leung and Iwawaka (1988) did not also confirm a culture effect. They found that cultural differences did not influence the allocation behavior of Japanese, Korean, and American participants.

Meindl, Cheng, and Jun (1990) conducted a field study comparing Chinese and American lower and middle-level managers. Results showed that the definitions of fairness and the preferences for highly differentiated, equity-based allocation schemes among Chinese managers were similar to those of their American counterparts. Both groups displayed allocations that reflected the rather highly differentiated patterns consistent with an equity logic when productivity was emphasized and interdependence among recipient was low (Meindl, Chen, & Jun, 1990). However, unlike American managers, Chinese managers were inflexible. When productivity values and high interdependence co-occurred, the Chinese managers deviated from what they considered fair (movement toward parity), maintaining instead the more differentiated patterns of an equitable logic. Interpreting these findings, the authors speculate that

> the somewhat inflexible adherence of Chinese managers to an equity logic may perhaps be symptomatic of an internal struggle with the necessity of becoming committed to forward-looking reforms and an attendant psychological reactance with the preferences and values that were associated with pre-reform ideologies of the past. (p. 233)

These findings were further confirmed by Chen (1995) who compared the allocation behavior of American and Chinese employees. He found that Chinese participants preferred the equity rule more strongly than their American counterparts. The author explained these surprising findings by invoking the extent to which China was moving toward a free market economy; therefore Chinese participants might have been more concerned about enhancing productivity—a key characteristic of market values than enhancing harmony.

Relation-centered cultures tend to divide people between in-groups and out-groups. An in-group is psychologically close, whereas an out-group is psychologically distant. Such a distinction may influence distribution rules in relation-centered cultures. Leung and Bond (1982, 1984) conducted several studies including Chinese and American participants. They found that in distributions involving in-group members, Chinese participants followed an equality rule when the allocator's personal input was high and an equity rule when it was low. With out-group members, however, Chinese participants followed the equity rule like their American counterparts. These findings support the view that in relation-centered cultures, exchanges between in-groups are perceived as relational, whereas exchanges with out-groups are perceived as transactional. They also raise an important issue related to the impact of the nature of the relationship between allocators and recipients on justice judgments. Leung and Bond (1984) argue that when allocators and recipients have an in-group relationship, collectivists are more likely to pursue the goal of harmony enhancement and employ a harmony enhancing allocation rule, such as the equality or the generosity rule. However, if allocators and recipients are not closely related, collectivists will pursue the productivity goal and employ the equity norm like individualists. Leung and Bond (1982) argued that collectivism is related to preference for equality because equality is compatible with the emphasis on solidarity, harmony, and cohesion found in collectivist cultures. However, individualism is related to equity because equity is compatible with the emphasis on productivity, competition, and self-gain in individualist cultures. This assumption was supported in other studies (e.g., Chen, Meindl, & Hui, 1998; Chen Meindl, & Hunt, 1997; Kashima, Siegal, Tanaka, & Isaka, 1988).

Kashima, Siegal, Tanaka, and Isaka (1988) conducted a study on two samples of Australian and Japanese participants. They found that Japanese participants perceived equity to be less fair and equality to be less unfair than their Australian counterparts. However, this cross-cultural difference was only in degree, but not in kind. Moreover, both samples tended to endorse a universalistic view of distributive justice; believing that equity rule was unalterable by legislation of the responsible organization or even by consensus of the people involved. Japanese participants considered the age of the employee as more important in determining justice judgments; whereas Australian participants considered the debt of the employees as a more important determinant of justice judgments.

Not all collectivist cultures are alike. Murphy-Berman and Berman (2002) demonstrated this aspect in a recent study using participants from Hong Kong and Indonesia, two collectivist cultures. They found that Hong Kong respondents perceived that the use of merit pay was fairer and more principled than the use of need. They also perceived the allocator who favored merit as less nice, more selfish, and likely to act without consideration of others' welfare. However, Indonesian respondents saw the use of need as being fairer than the use of merit, and they perceived that the allocator who favored the needy was nicer and acted more out of concern for others. The authors also found that cultural differences in respondents' perceptions were greater for the use of merit than for the use of need. Respondents from both cultures tended to rate the allocator more positively when resources were being given out than when resources were being taken away.

Recently, Conlon, Porter, and McLean-Parks (2004) conducted a study using eight allocation rules reflecting equity rule (past performance, future performance, and rank), equality rule (random draw and chance meeting) and need (business need and personal need) and political reasons. The study used a scenario-based methodology and was conducted on a sample of 514 students mimicking an organizational setting. Results showed that allocations based on past performance (equity) and random draw (equality) rules led to the highest fairness perceptions and the lowest expectations that the decisions made will lead to intragroup conflict. These findings support previous results indicating that the equity rule leads to perceptions of fairness, at least in the American context. Since past performance can easily be documented, using this rule makes the allocation process fair. Likewise, the random draw gives everyone the chance of winning thereby creating a sense of fairness. Other allocation rules include age and tenure. Morris and Leung (2000) hypothesize that in collectivist cultures where notions of devotion and sacrifice for the group are salient, long tenure should be valued as an indicator of loyalty and devotion to the group. In these cultures, factors, such as age and tenure may be perceived as legitimate inputs. Thus, elders or senior employees may receive more of an outcome than younger and employees with less tenure. In such cultures, people show respect and deference to older people probably because they have more knowledge and wisdom (Beugré, 1998b). Thus, these factors may represent inputs and be considered as legitimate outcome distribution criteria.

Relation-Centered Cultures and Procedural Justice

Although most research on culture and justice has focused on distributive justice, relatively little research has been conducted on the influence of culture on procedural justice (Steiner, 2001). Even within a national culture, people have different histories that lead them to develop different beliefs about the legitimacy of procedural elements (Brockner, Ackerman, & Fairchild, 2001). Greenberg (2001a) argues that concerns for procedural justice are more universal than concerns for distributive justice. Likewise, Leung and Morris (2001) note that the available cross-cultural evidence suggests that the content of procedural and interactional justice is largely similar across cultures. Lind, Tyler, and Huo (1997) supported the fair process effect across cultures.

In a study conducted in Japan, Sugawara and Huo (1994) found that relational issues were more important than instrumental issues in determining preferences for conflict resolution procedures. Leung, Smith, Wang, and Sun (1996) found that senior Chinese managers working in joint ventures reported lower levels of procedural justice and interactional justice. The authors explained this finding by arguing that the Chinese senior managers expected to be more involved in the decision-making process of their organization. Denial of such an opportunity created a sense of procedural and interactional injustice. Research on voice and expectations showed that when people expect voice and receive voice, this leads to perceptions of procedural justice (e.g., van den Bos, 1999). Perhaps, in relation-centered cultures, having voice may signify an acceptance of the individual as a group member.

An interesting aspect to consider when one analyzes the relationship between culture and procedural justice is the meaning of contracts. Contracts tend to have different meanings in relation-centered and self-centered cultures. For instance, in relation-centered cultures, contracts tend to be more informal and nonwritten, whereas in self-centered cultures, contracts are often formal and written. Contracts are assumed to be binding, concrete and precise in individualist cultures, whereas they are often taken as symbols of collaboration and general guidelines for future actions in collectivist cultures (Leung, 2005). Thus, the very meaning of procedural justice may differ from culture to culture. In some cultures, procedural justice may refer to the fairness of formal procedures, whereas in other cultures, it may just imply the fairness of the process used, be it formal or informal. Exploring such differences may help determine the nature of procedural justice across cultures.

The rule of consistency of procedural justice (e.g., Leventhal, 1976; Leventhal, Karuza, & Fry, 1980) may not always prevail in relation-centered cultures. Since in such cultures, people often make the distinction between in-groups and out-groups, different processes may be used depending on the type of relationship that exists between the decision maker and the recipient. Rules may be bent to accommodate an in-group, whereas they may be consistent when recipients are out-groups. The construct of "particularism" or "personalismo" may indicate such an orientation in relation-centered cultures. Empirical studies are needed to determine the extent to which procedures in relation-centered cultures vary according to the in-group/out-group distinction. In a field study, Sugawara and Huo (1994) found that Japanese participants were more concerned with the fairness of procedures than with the fairness of outcomes.

These findings indicate that Japanese were more concerned about the process than the outcomes. In this study, procedural justice included clarity of standards and procedures and openness of the procedures. These measures were more important for Japanese participants than the outcomes received. Perhaps, the Japanese culture with its emphasis on traditions, tends to value procedures and the extent to which these procedures are clearly explained. Another study conducted on German employees found that Germans accorded relatively more importance to procedural justice and showed less situation-based variation in the procedural justice importance ratings than did Americans (Barret-Howard & Lamm, 1986). These findings showed that Germans may be more sensitive to procedural justice matters than Americans.

Leung and Lind (1986) conducted a comparative study between Americans and Hong Kong Chinese using student samples. Their results showed that American participants preferred the adversarial procedure compared to the inquisitorial procedure, whereas their Chinese counterparts were indifferent about the two procedures. Interpreting these results, the authors noted that Chinese participants might have perceived the process control offered by the adversarial procedure to be desirable, but the confrontation and competitiveness inherent in this procedure might have mitigated their preference for it. Like the Americans, the Chinese saw the adversarial procedure as vesting more process control in the hands of the disputants. Schwartz's (1994) value of "Conservatism" may help explain people's reactions to justice. One may speculate that in cultures emphasizing Conservatism, employees may be less likely to expect and seek voice in dealing with superiors. In such cultures, employees may not often actively seek voice or explanations for management decisions. Therefore, they may be less likely to express feelings of unfairness and moral outrage when they do not receive voice. Similarly, in such cultures, justice judgments may be strongly influenced by the social context.

The social context would strongly affect justice judgments in cultures that emphasize relationships. Since the group is the primary unit of importance, individual judgments of fairness or unfairness would reflect more group or societal norms than individual standards. That is not to say that in such cultures people cannot set their own standards of justice. In a study including U.S. employees and employees from Hong Kong, Lam, Schaubroeck, and Aryee (2002) found that the outcomes of justice perceptions did not differ across societal cultures or levels of individualism, but the effects were of stronger magnitude among low power distance individuals than among high power distance individuals. When we describe cultures as collectivist or low-power distance, we are not assuming that every person in such cultures will score high on collectivism or low on power distance. As Triandis and Bhawur (1997) acknowledge, collectivists will not behave in a collectivistic way in all situations but only in most situations, and conversely, individualists will behave as collectivists do in a number of situations (p. 29). Instead, I assume that most of the time, individual judgments of justice in relation-centered cultures would be likely to integrate societal or group norms. Thus, what an individual considers as just or unjust in such cultures is what the group or society has labeled so. In such cultures, people are more likely to think of justice in terms of justice of groups such as their family or ethnic group rather than for themselves as individuals (Tyler, Boeckman, Smith, & Huo, 1997).

In relation-centered cultures, the goal of justice would be to maintain harmony and social standing in groups. The group-value model (Lind & Tyler, 1988), the relational model of authority (Tyler & Lind, 1992), and the group-engagement model (e.g., Tyler & Blader, 2003b) better illustrate this argument. As discussed in chapter 2, these three models emphasize the importance of group membership as a determinant of justice concerns. People are concerned about fairness because they want to be recognized as full members of groups.

Relation-Centered Cultures and Interactional Justice

Greenberg (2001b, p. 263) notes that the interpersonal determinants of justice—based on social norms and customs, are likely to be highly reflective of the cultural nuances that cause justice to be operationalized differently across cultures. Leung (2005) hypothesized that collectivists should display a higher level of respect toward in-group members and attempt to protect their face compared to individualists. Likewise, individual rights in the workplace, such as privacy, are more respected in individualist than collectivist societies. Interactional justice in relation-centered cultures may concern such issues as face saving, and in-group/out-group distinctions. For example, in most Asian countries, face saving plays an important role in interpersonal relations. Thus, in interacting with others, protecting their face is of paramount importance. Failure to do so may lead to perceptions of unfairness. Working on a sample of Turkish employees, Erdogan and Liden (2006) found that employees ranking high on collectivism were more likely to use soft influence tactics, such as ingratiation when they perceived interactional injustice. However, those who ranked low on collectivism did not use such tactics.

Research on relation-centered cultures has also emphasized the distinction between in-group and out-group members. Maintaining such a distinction may influence the scope of justice, thus limiting people's view of justice and injustice. Justice may be limited to in-group or applied differently based on the in-group/out-group distinction. Deutsch (1985) identifies two types of justice when discussing the effects of in-group and out-group membership on justice perceptions; inclusionary justice and exclusionary justice. Justice becomes exclusionary when individuals apply justice principles only to in-group members and inclusionary when justice principles are seen as universally applicable (Beugré, 1998a; Deutsch, 1985). Opotow (1990) suggests that moral exclusion occurs when individuals or groups are perceived as outside the boundary in which moral values, rules, and considerations of fairness apply (p. 1).

Deutsch (1985) also coined the construct of scope of justice to explain people's tolerance to injustice. When justice is exclusionary, the scope of justice is limited to in-group members. Social identity theory (e.g., Tajfel, 1978, 1982; Tajfel & Turner, 1979) may help understand justice judgments in collectivist cultures. Social identity theory contends that people evaluate their self-worth by considering aspects of self and the group to which they belong. The in-group out-group dichotomy may be more important in collectivist cultures than in individualistic cultures. In-group members would be part of the person's moral community, whereas out-group members would be excluded from this moral community (e.g., Boeckman & Tyler, 1997). It is then possible that injustice toward in-group members may elicit stronger negative feelings and reactions than injustice toward out-group members. Although this hypothesis is intuitively appealing, it requires empirical evidence. For now, it just remains a hypothesis, albeit a plausible one.

Justice is socially constructed (Umphress, Labianca, Scholten, Kass, & Brass, 2000). In cultures where people value group membership and rely on others' opinions before making a decision, justice judgments may be more influenced by peers than in cultures where people do not rely too much on others' opinions. Thus, in collectivist cultures, justice judgments may be influenced by concerns for aligning one's opinions on the group opinion. However, in individualistic cultures, people's justice judgments may be more influenced by personal opinions than by group opinions. Social influence on justice judgments may be more salient in collectivist cultures than in individualist cultures. Although fairness theory did not consider cultural variables in forming justice judgments, Folger and Cropanzano (2001) acknowledge that judgments concerning procedural events are relative to some referent standards. These referent standards may vary across individuals and cultures. All people might share a common interest in fairness, but what they presume to be fair varies widely (Folger & Cropanzano, 2001). Moreover, the same individual may have different standards depending on circumstances.

SELF-CENTERED CULTURES AND ORGANIZATIONAL JUSTICE

Self-Centered Cultures and Distributive Justice

Since the focus in such cultures is on the individual rather than the collective, justice judgments would be affected by personal standards of fairness rather than societal or group norms. Moreover, the quest for justice would be more instrumental than in relation-centered cultures. People would seek fairness because it serves their own interests. Likewise, the preferred rule of distribution would be equity. The preference for this rule is manifested in the Market Pricing dimension (e.g., Fiske, 1991). In a market pricing system, outcome would be proportional to individual inputs. Recipients who contribute more would receive more, whereas those who contribute less would receive less. Triandis (2002) notes that in individualist cultures, the self is conceived as independent of in-groups, personal goals are given priority, attitudes determine much of social behavior, and interpersonal relationships are well accounted by exchange theory.

The same reasoning may apply to procedural and interactional justice concerns. Superiors may often develop formal procedures with little input from subordinates in authority ranking relationships, whereas in communal sharing and equality matching, people may equally affect the enactment of rules and procedures. The opportunity for voice and the provision of social accounts may well be limited in authority ranking systems. However, such opportunities may exist in equality matching systems. Because justice judgments are strongly influenced by personal standards, the scope of justice would be universal and not limited to the in-group/out-group distinction often found in relation-centered cultures. Similarly, in self-centered cultures, the egocentric bias would be limited to the individual rather than the group and particularly the in-group. Therefore, people may tend to consider their personal inputs more favorably than that of others (Messé, Hymes, & MacCoun, 1986).

Self-centered cultures are described here as cultures in which people are more motivated by selfish motives. Central to these cultures is the extent to which people tend to look after themselves. Although they do not disregard the importance of the group, they are more motivated by satisfying their personal interests. This tendency would translate in a preference for outcome distribution rules that emphasize personal benefits. Previous scholars (e.g., Deutsch, 1975, 1985) note that in individualistic cultures, people tend to prefer the equity rule of distribution. In fact, the equity rule of distribution highlights personal contributions. Cultures with an emphasis on achievement are likely to prefer the equity rule in order to reward merit, whereas cultures emphasizing ascription will focus more on the rules and needs of equality that permit recognizing privileges from birth rather than individual accomplishments (Steiner, 2001).

Thus, people who pursue their self-interests would be more motivated by such allocation rules. In competitive societies like the United States, meritocracy is often recognized as the appropriate distribution rule. To justify the predominance of this rule, the common perception is that high intellectual ability accompanied by effort has a potential to contribute significantly to the common good, and therefore deserves a high reward (Lewin-Epstein, Kaplan, & Levanon, 2003). Although the need rule may be preferred in relation-centered cultures, one may argue that some examples in self-centered cultures allude to an application of this principle. In most developed countries, described as high on individualism, there are unemployment benefits. By helping the unemployed (the needy) these governments indirectly apply the need principle of outcome distribution. However, this action may have two major implications: (a) a moral one and (b) an instrumental one. Society may feel a moral obligation to help the needy (deontic justice) get back on their feet. Helping the unemployed may also contribute to the reduction of social upheavals.

Self-Centered Cultures and Procedural Justice

Organizational justice scholars have not extensively studied the impact of self-centered cultures on procedural justice. However, one may speculate that in such cultures, people may be concerned about the impact of formal procedures on the individual himself or herself. The extent to which procedures benefit the individual may be a major concern. Because interpersonal relations are "superficial" in self-centered cultures, formal contracts governing exchanges in organizations may be preferred. Moreover, employees may expect more voice in the decision-making process compared to employees in relation-centered cultures. The provision of voice may convey two important elements in self-centered cultures. First, voice may serve the self-interest motive insofar that it helps the individual express his or her opinions. By doing so, the individual may expect to influence the decision outcome (e.g., Thibaut & Walker, 1975). Second, voice may represent a status symbol. A person who is given voice may consider that he or she is a respected member of the group.

Procedural justice in self-centered cultures may also concern the provision of information and social accounts. To the extent that people in such cultures favor the self over the group, they would like to receive information related to their work tasks and environment. Receiving information helps the individual know and understand the circumstances surrounding a particular situation. It also indicates that the self is valued and respected. Thus, the existence of formal procedures is viewed as a way of enhancing the self, particularly when the individual contributes to their enactment.

Self-Centered Cultures and Interactional Justice

Self-centered cultures emphasize interpersonal competition among group members. Although this does not necessarily translate into hostile competition, one may speculate that interpersonal competition among group members may be more frequent and more intense in self-centered cultures than in collectivist cultures. In self-centered cultures, people may also tend to focus more on the content rather than the context of interpersonal communication. Thus, compared to employees in relation-centered cultures, employees in self-centered cultures may not be strongly concerned about "face saving." Rather, they would be concerned about interpersonal relations that help advance their personal agendas. Thus, interpersonal relationships in self-centered cultures would be more superficial and motivated by personal interests. Individual recognition and praise may be important determinants in ensuring interactional justice in self-centered cultures.

The tendency to make internal attributions for behavior is a product of an individualistic culture, in which people develop more independent forms of self-construal, whereas in collectivistic cultures, the tendency to make internal attributions is less pronounced (Brockner, 2003). Such differences in attribution may differentially affect judgments of fairness and unfairness. In relation-centered cultures, people would tend to make external attributions, whereas in self-centered cultures, people would tend to make internal attributions. These differences may result in conflict over responsibility and accountability for actions and outcomes. Thus, the fundamental attribution error may manifest itself differently across cultures. The fundamental attribution error refers to the tendency for people to attribute the behavior of others to internal factors rather than external factors (Ross, 1977). According to Brockner (2003), the fundamental attribution error is important in organizations because if managers have misperceived the root causes of certain problem behaviors, then their interventions are likely to be similarly misguided. This is particularly true in a cross-cultural setting. To the extent that culture influences attributions, it would indirectly influence justice by influencing the type of attribution people make when they experience justice or injustice.

STATUS-CENTERED CULTURES AND ORGANIZATIONAL JUSTICE

Status-Centered Cultures and Distributive Justice

Power distance may shape social comparisons (Morris & Leung, 2000). This cultural syndrome includes the cultural dimensions of Authority Ranking (e.g., Fiske, 1991), power distance (e.g., Hofstede, 1980) and vertical collectivism or vertical individualism (e.g., Triandis, 1995). These dimensions acknowledge power differentials between intertactants. The verticality rule of outcome distribution refers to outcomes allocation based on rank, status, or formally recognized position. Although the organizational justice literature has not recognized this principle of outcome distribution, I include it in this analysis. Two reasons explain the importance of this principle in assessing distributive justice. First, observations of organizations and societies reveal that this principle is in fact applied more often than acknowledged. In authority ranking, however, the distribution rule depends on the social rank of each recipient. High status recipients would receive more of the outcome than those of low status. The basis for ranking people may include attributes, such as formal status, age, tenure, and so forth. Where the social system accords respect and deference to elders, such attributes may be used in allocating resources.

In societies as well as organizations, people hold social positions that may influence how outcomes are shared. For instance, the president of the United States receives more protection than the average American citizen. Indeed, hierarchy is an outcome distribution criterion and is part of the distributive culture of the organization (Kabanoff, 1997). As such, those in high power positions may receive better shares of the resources than those who hold lower positions. In high power distance societies, superiors are given more power and privileges, and subordinates are expected to comply with instructions and not challenge superiors. In contrast, in low power distance societies, superiors and subordinates are assumed to have a more egalitarian relationship, and subordinates are given a freer hand in doing their work (Leung, 1997). The author also notes that in high power distance societies, people at the top of the organizational hierarchy are entitled to more privileges and deference than their counterparts in low power distance societies (Leung, 2005).

In allocating offices and parking lots, modern organizations may well follow an authority ranking principle. There are often reserved parking lots for top managers in business organizations or top administrators in universities and federal agencies. Everyone else has equal access to the remaining parking lots. In a company, some projects may be allocated based on an authority ranking system. Senior employees are often given the most important projects. As an example, in the U.S. Senate, senior senators are often given chairmanship of important committees. Rarely do junior senators head these committees. Similarly, in university departments, senior faculty members have more voice in academic matters than their junior counterparts. Modern organizations also follow an authority ranking principle when they allocate office spaces to senior executives.

People often tend to rely on interpersonal comparisons to other employees or groups of employees when judging the fairness of an outcome allocation (Runciman, 1966). Employees may compare themselves to other employees or groups of others may compare their groups to other groups within the organization leading to situations of relative deprivation (e.g., Crosby, 1976). In the United States, minority employees may see themselves as relatively deprived compared to majority employees. Group comparisons may often lead to distorting the reality of the situation because people are likely to consider their own group as more deserving (Tajfel, 1982). Groups that are powerful may ensure that their members get the larger portions of outcomes. Although few systematic studies have investigated the impact of power distance on outcome allocation, one may speculate that in status-centered cultures, people may use criteria, such as age, status, and tenure as distribution criteria. Because these criteria allow for differentiating people along power, they may be recognized as legitimate distribution criteria.

Status-Centered Cultures and Procedural Justice

Leung (2005) notes that in high power distance societies, procedures that involve a high-status third party as the decision maker are more accepted. This illustrates the "governance by status" principle. Decisions from high-status officials tend to be more accepted than those from low-status officials in high power distance cultures. Thus, one may expect conflicts with superiors to be less frequent in low power distance cultures and superiors would be more involved in conflict resolution among subordinates. In societies with high levels of power distance or inequality, employees pay strong respect to their superiors and avoid criticizing them (Erez, 2000). An element of procedural justice that has been extensively studied is voice (e.g., Folger, 1977). Recent studies on the cross-cultural aspects of voice indicate that power distance may influence not only expectations for voice but also employee reactions to voice. Brockner (2003) notes that people in high power distance countries are less likely to expect or want to have input into a decision making process relative to their counterparts in low power distance countries. Perhaps, in such cultures, the leader is perceived as powerful and knowledgeable who should make decisions for subordinates. Kabanoff (1997) echoes this assumption when discussing decision making in French companies. He argues that the decision-making process in France is elitist.

Brockner et al. (2001) conducted a study analyzing the voice effect involving participants from the United States, Germany (low power distance cultures) and China, Hong Kong, and Mexico (high power distance cultures). The authors found that regardless of whether voice is operationalized as an experimental manipulation or as a perceptual measure, the effect of voice on an assortment of dependent variables was more pronounced among those with low rather than high power distance beliefs. The authors concluded that the more cultural norms legitimize voice, the more likely are people to respond unfavorably to relatively low levels of voice. Thus, it is not the lack of voice per se to which people object. It is when the lack of voice violates cultural norms that people respond unfavorably (Brockner et al., 2001). These findings demonstrate two things. First, employees in high power distance countries may have been socialized to show obedience and deference to superiors. Thus, voicing one's opinions may be perceived as a challenge to superiors and contrary to societal norms. Perhaps, in high power distance cultures, subordinates may expect less voice than in low power distance cultures. They may also consider superiors as more knowledgeable, having the skills, knowledge and wisdom to make appropriate decisions. Requesting voice may be seen as challenging the superiors' ability to make good judgment. Second, the fair process effect may be strongly influenced by cultural norms. Cultural norms are one of the factors that have a moderating influence on people's reactions to voice (Brockner et al., 2001).

Procedures in status-centered cultures would be enacted with little input from subordinates. Because status-centered cultures believe in authority and the expertise that authority figures hold, they would be likely to entrust authorities. Questioning the decisions of authorities may be seen as questioning their legitimacy. Thus, employees in such cultures would rely on managers to make decisions and provide clear instructions. In such cultures, people may tend to rely on a person's formal position than his or her actual ability to solve a problem. Lee, Pillutla, and Law (2000) found that power distance orientation moderated the relationship between the two aspects of procedural justice (formal and interactional) and trust. Employees with low-power distance orientation perceived that procedural justice had stronger effects on their trust in supervisors. In contrast, perceived justice did not strongly influence high power-distance employees' trust in supervisors. Individuals low on power distance expect to have input into decisions that affect them and are less willing to accept arbitrary treatment from their superiors (Lam, Schaubroeck, & Aryee, 2002).

Status-Centered Cultures and Interactional Justice

Relationships between employees and managers may take a paternalistic flavor in status-centered cultures. Deference to authority may be considered as normal ways of dealing with superiors. In status-centered cultures, justice judgments may follow an ideology principle of justice, that is, justice norms would be dominated by powerful others. What is just or unjust is not what the group or the individual considers as such but what powerful others consider as such. However, in cultures where power is loosely distributed, leaders may be held accountable for their misdeeds, and justice judgments may be less likely to be influenced by power ideology. This assumption has not been empirically tested in the organizational justice literature. However, it represents a promising avenue for future research in cross-cultural organizational justice.

Research on the impact of power distance has demonstrated that people in such cultures tend to tolerate injustices, particularly, injustices emanating from authority figures. Specifically, when studying the impact of culture on organizational justice, one may well be advised by Morris and Leung's (2000) contention that "in high power distance cultures, people's acceptance of unequal social prerogatives promotes the tolerance of unfair treatment; whereas in low power distance societies, rejection of inequality makes people less tolerant of unfair treatment" (p. 117). Two reasons may explain these findings. The first reason lies in the belief of the leader's infallibility. For instance, the Catholic Church considers that the Pope is infallible. Thus, his decisions are never challenged. When subordinates believe in the infallibility of their leaders, they are unlikely to challenge their decisions or even consider such decisions as unfair. The second reason is more practical and deals with the aftermath of a complaint from a subordinate. In high power distance cultures, leaders are so powerful in distributing positive and negative outcomes (rewards and punishments) that it seems almost impossible for subordinates to challenge them. A challenge from a subordinate may run the risk of unwavering retaliation not only from the leader but also from colleagues who are socialized to obey leaders.

RISK-PRONE CULTURES AND ORGANIZATIONAL JUSTICE

Risk-Prone Cultures and Distributive Justice

Although few studies have been conducted on the impact of uncertainty avoidance on justice, the recent development of fairness heuristic theory and uncertainty management theory may help hypothesize the possible impact of uncertainty avoidance on distributive justice. Uncertainty avoidance deals explicitly with how cultures cope with situations of uncertainty. Some cultures tend to avoid uncertainty, whereas others embrace it. Thus, cultures that embrace uncertainty would be entrepreneurial, risk-taking, and innovative. In the face of uncertainty about outcomes, how would cultures low on uncertainty avoidance or high on uncertainty avoidance react? Because people in low uncertainty avoidance cultures tend to tolerate ambiguous stimuli, they would be less likely to express anxiety when they do not have information about distributive justice.

Van den Bos, Lind, Vermunt, and Wilke (1997) found that when people do not have information about distributive justice they use procedure information to make justice judgments. This tendency would be stronger in cultures high on uncertainty avoidance. There are pertinent reasons to formulate such a hypothesis. The lack of information about distributive justice creates anxiety and information seeking behavior. Since individuals in such cultures do not tolerate ambiguity, they will look for whatever information is available to reduce that uncertainty. Situations where information about the fairness of allocation rules is lacking may be perceived as more unfair in risk-averse cultures than in risk-prone cultures. Thus, providing detailed information about outcome fairness may enhance the sense of justice in risk-averse cultures. In such cultures, employees would prefer detailed information not only about outcome fairness but also about process fairness.

Risk-Prone Cultures and Procedural Justice

Here also, there are few studies assessing the effect of this cultural syndrome on procedural justice. Thus, the assumptions reported here are merely propositions based on conceptual analyses. One such conceptual analysis is provided by Steiner (2001) who contends that uncertainty avoidance is likely to impact the preferences for the application of a number of procedural rules. The author hypothesized that uncertainty avoidance would influence some of Leventhal's rules of procedural justice, such as consistency, correctability and accuracy. High uncertainty avoidance may lead employees to request more opportunities for voice. Thus, providing as much information as possible may help reduce uncertainty. Using the findings from fairness heuristic theory and uncertainty management theory, one may make the following propositions. First, when people lack procedural information, they may rely on outcomes fairness to make judgments of fairness related to procedures. Thus, they would be a strong outcome effect in high uncertainty avoidance cultures. Second, when people do not have information about procedures, they may use whatever information is available to make justice judgments. Thus, the primacy effect would be stronger in high uncertainty avoidance cultures than in low uncertainty avoidance cultures. Third, lack of procedure information may create more anxiety among people from high uncertainty avoidance cultures than among their counterparts from low uncertainty avoidance cultures.

In uncertainty avoidance cultures, people may believe that new procedures should be consistent with older procedures (Brockner et al., 2001). Thus, people from high uncertainty avoidance cultures may react especially unfavorably to a lack of procedural consistency. One may contend that the goal of procedural justice judgments in risk-averse cultures would be to reduce uncertainty about procedures. Although uncertainty reduction is a fundamental concern when people make judgments of fairness (e.g., van den Bos, 2002), the desire to reduce uncertainty may be stronger in risk-averse cultures than in risk-prone cultures. An interesting area of application of both uncertainty management theory (van den Bos, 2002) and fairness heuristic theory (e.g., Lind, 2001, van den Bos & Lind, 2002) is the area of culture and specifically the difference between risk-prone and risk-averse cultures.

Several questions may be asked when determining the impact of culture on procedural justice judgments. How might uncertainty management theory deal with cultures low or high on uncertainty avoidance? Perhaps, in cultures low on uncertainty avoidance, people may not always react to the lack of information as a strong impetus to seek information or use heuristic to reduce uncertainty compared to cultures high on uncertainty avoidance. Or it may be possible that when information about fairness is lacking, people may use rumors and other shortcuts to reduce this uncertainty. One may also wonder how people from risk-averse cultures react when they lack information in specific areas of justice. For instance, how do such people react when they lack information about the trustworthiness of authorities? Do they actively seek information about the authorities or do they assume blindly that these authorities can be trusted? Another important question is related to both the primacy and substitutability effects. How do these effects play out in risk-averse as compared to risk-prone cultures? These questions may generate research hypotheses that can be empirically investigated.

The lack of information may strongly increase uncertainty, whereas the provision of detailed information may help reduce uncertainty. Because people from risk-averse cultures are uncomfortable with ambiguous stimuli, they may perform poorly when detailed information is not provided. Thus, lack of detailed instructions and information related to one's job may be perceived as unfair. In discussing the possible link between uncertainty avoidance and procedural justice, Steiner (2001) hypothesized that this dimension would be associated with the importance of procedural rules that emphasize a clear definition of procedures. Employees from risk-averse cultures may also be reluctant to embrace organizational change. Not that they dislike the changes per se, but because changes increase the level of uncertainty these employees may experience. The norms of high uncertainty avoidance cultures may lead to the enactment of procedures that deviate little from one time or situation to the next.

Risk-Prone Cultures and Interactional Justice

Research on organizational justice has not focused on the impact of cultural dimensions, such as propensity to risk or uncertainty avoidance on interpersonal treatment. However, one may wonder whether such cultural dimensions influence people's perceptions of interactional justice? Interactional justice deals with treating people with respect and dignity but also with the provision of information. Thus, since employees in such cultures are likely to prefer opportunities for taking personal initiatives, a work environment that provides such opportunities would contribute to the enactment of interactional justice. When employees are not provided with opportunities to experiment new ideas and strategies, they may experience interactional injustice. No empirical studies exist to support these contentions.

However, research in cross-cultural management may provide some insights. Some cultures tend to be more creative and innovative than others. What then explains such differences? Research contends that power of traditions and the extent to which people are inclined to follow rules and regulations may prevent the exploration of new ideas and opportunities. Thus, where rules are cumbersome, employees may experience the sense of interactional injustice. Future studies in organizational justice may explore the extent to which the cultural syndrome of risk proneness enhances or inhibits interactional justice. Likewise, future research may explore the impact of this cultural syndrome on perceptions of injustice. The following chapter focuses on the relationship between the four cultural syndromes and employees perceptions of injustice.

CHAPTER 5

CULTURE AND EMPLOYEE REACTIONS TO INJUSTICE

In the previous chapter, I have discussed cross-cultural reactions to perceptions of justice. In the present chapter, I focus on cross-cultural reactions to perceived injustice. I made the distinction between reacting to justice and reacting to injustice because both experiences are not similar. The experience of injustice entails hot emotions. "People are inflamed and enraged or mad, angry, and bitter when they experience injustice" (Bies & Tripp, 1996, p. 254). As Finkel, Crystal, and Watanabe (2001) argued,

> the emotions that accompany unfairness are likely to have more heat and moral outrage than those accompanying fairness, and those hot emotions typically press for release and response in louder rhetoric and stronger action than one finds for fairness … emotions of unfairness have passion and insistence. (p. 348)

This is particularly true when we consider cross-cultural studies on employee reactions to perceived injustice. Past research on employee reactions to injustice found that unfairness was related to dysfunctional work behaviors, such as workplace aggression (e.g., Baron, Neuman, & Geddes, 1999; Beugré, 1998c, 2005a, 2005b), theft (e.g., Greenberg, 1987b; Greenberg & Alge, 1998), and revenge (e.g., Bies, 1987; Bies & Tripp, 2001a, 2001b; Folger, 1993; Skarlicki & Folger, 1997).

A Cultural Perspective of Organizational Justice, 105–125

Finkel (2000) contends that unfairness is ubiquitous in everyday life. "Unfairness claims are heard between friends, strangers, neighbors, roommates, and spouses, and between parents and children, employees and employers, students and teachers, and athletes and coaches" (Finkel, Crystal, & Watanabe, 2001, p. 345). Similarly, Beugré (2005a) notes that "the workplace is replete with examples of situations of unfairness and frustration. From daily irritations to severe cases of discrimination, employees encounter events that may arouse the sense of injustice" (p. 1131). The experience of injustice can be construed more as a process than as a state (Mikula, 1987).

The present chapter intends to explore the extent to which employee reactions to injustice are similar or vary across cultures. The chapter is organized as follows. First, I discuss the experience of injustice at work, including the construct of the triangle of injustice. Second, I develop a cross-cultural model of employee reactions to injustice. Third, using this model, I explore the impact of culture on employee reactions to unfairness.

THE TRIANGLE OF INJUSTICE

The experience of injustice includes three components: a victim, an offender, and an observer. The victim is the target of the injustice. The offender is the perpetrator of the injustice, and the observer is the person who witnesses the injustice. These three components of injustice are observable whenever an injustice occurs. Thus, they are relatively culture free. No matter the culture in which it occurs, injustice involves the three elements, a victim, an offender, and an observer (see Figure 5.1).

The victim may be related to the offender in different ways. The victim may be an employee and the offender a manager, or a colleague or even a

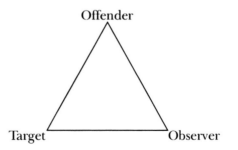

Figure 5.1.   The triangle of injustice.

subordinate. The offender and the observer may also be related. The observer may be an employee and the offender a manager or the victim's co-worker. Both the victim and the observer may also be related. They may be colleagues, friends, or in a hierarchical relationship. The types of relationships among the three parties may influence the experience of injustice. It is possible that witnessing an injustice done to a close friend may not generate the same intensity of indignation and moral outrage that witnessing an injustice to a stranger would trigger.

A CULTURAL MODEL OF
EMPLOYEE REACTIONS TO INJUSTICE

The cultural model of employee reactions to injustice (see Figure 5.2) contends that the occurrence of an event triggers fairness judgments. Because I consider unfairness here, this judgment is generally negative insofar that it indicates that the event is unfair. This judgment of unfairness may result in perceptions of distributive, procedural, or interactional injustice. Once these perceptions of injustice are formed, the target person will attribute blame (accountability). Accountability is at the core of injustice. Attribution of blame is necessary for a sense of injustice to exist (Folger, 2001; Shaver, 1985). Similarly, Cropanzano, Chrobot-Mason, Rupp, and Prehar (2004) contend that social injustices result in a quest for responsibility and accountability.

Perceptions of justice may also affect blame attribution. Barclay, Skarlicki, and Pugh (2005) found that the more employees deem the process or interpersonal treatment as fair, the less they attribute the blame for their unfavorable outcome to external sources and the more they can experience inward-focused negative emotions. However, when they found the process or interpersonal treatment unfair, the more they attribute the blame to external factors. The authors also argued that people may be more likely to evaluate and respond to fairness concerns when they are responding to a serious violation than when they are competing for a small price. In the following lines, I explain employee reactions to unfairness as well as the direct and indirect effects of culture on employee perceptions of unfairness.

Reacting to Injustice

Mikula (1987) identified four possible reactions to injustice: (1) restoration of justice, (2) punishment of the perpetrator, (3) leaving the field, and (4) resignation. Research on employee reactions to injustices has

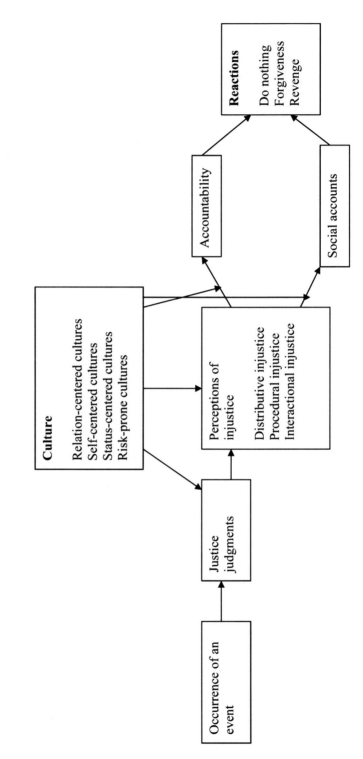

Figure 5.2. A cross-cultural model of employee reactions to injustice.

identified a range of behaviors, including aggression (e.g., Baron, Neuman, & Geddes, 1999; Jawahar, 2002), theft (Greenberg, 1990c, 2002; Greenberg & Alge, 1998); absenteeism (e.g., Boer, Bakker, Syroit, & Schaufeli, 2002); sabotage (e.g., Ambrose, Seabright, & Schminke, 2002), health complaints (e.g., Tepper, 2001); revenge (e.g., Bies, 1987; Bies & Tripp, 1996; Skarlicki & Folger, 1997; Tripp, Bies, & Aquino, 2002) and recently, sleep deprivation (e.g., Greenberg, 2006). A sense of injustice is both a major cause of conflict and a central barrier to its successful resolution (Leung & Tong, 2004). Likewise, mutual feelings of injustice and intense conflict may arise because of cultural differences in the notion of justice (Leung & Stephan, 1998).

Greenberg (2006) conducted a study on a sample of 467 nurses working at four hospitals where pay reduction was observed in two hospitals while pay levels were unchanged in the other two hospitals. Findings from self-reported measures of insomnia revealed that insomnia was significantly greater among the nurses whose pay was reduced than among those whose pay was unchanged. The degree of insomnia was significantly lower among nurses whose supervisors were trained in the use of interactional justice. These findings illustrate the extent to which injustice is harmful to individuals (e.g., Cropanzano & Byrne, 2001). The pay cut in the study may have led to feelings of distributive injustice. Rutte and Messick (1995) suggest that perceived unfairness will always affect the whole array of organizational attitudes, specifically job satisfaction, evaluation and trust in management, acceptance of decision, organizational commitment, loyalty, and work group decision (p. 254).

Equity theory (e.g., Adams, 1965) advocates that victims of perceived inequity would take several actions to reduce inequity. Such actions include reducing inputs, increasing outputs, psychologically distorting the situation, or leaving the exchange relationship. Although such reactions have been supported in laboratory and empirical studies, employees may not always be willing to jeopardize their positions by demanding corrective actions. Hegtvedt and Cook (2000) note that because employees may feel reluctant to threaten their job status by demanding higher salaries or lowering their inputs, they may opt for less obvious ways to cope with perceived inequity. Thus, people may react to injustices by a cognitive reevaluation of the situation.

Deutsch (1985) suggested that people have two broadly different sorts of reactions to unfair treatment. The first involves an experienced injustice that affects an individual not only personally but also as a member of a moral community whose moral norms are being violated. It evokes a sense of both frustration and injustice that involves a desire, even an obligation, to restore justice or to do something about it (Deutsch, 1985). When a person's sense of fair treatment is seriously violated, that person's major response is to reduce the sense of psychological belonging or commitment to the group rather than to try to decrease the direct inputs or increase the share of outcomes (Kabanoff, 1991). This assumption may find support in the group engagement model (Tyler & Blader, 2003b). Although the group engagement model does not directly address injustice, it contends that people are likely to engage or commit to a group when they feel fairly treated. In other words, perceptions of unfair treatment may reduce the sense of engagement to a group. Perceptions of injustice may also be explained by fairness heuristic theory. Unfair treatment may serve as a heuristic device helping people to decide whether to seek their own interest or engage in a cooperative behavior.

The experience of injustice may have meaning beyond the individual victim. This idea was explored by Bies (1987). Bies (1987) developed a predicament assumption which contends that an injustice is not merely a judgment; it is also a violation of a social norm that causes harm to someone. To be perceived as responsible for such a violation creates predicament for the harmdoer. A violation of justice norms represents an attack on the social group that endorses and supports those moral guidelines. Injustice tends to separate people from others, whereas justice brings them together (Cropanzano, Byrne, Bobocel, & Rupp, 2001). It also threatens people's sense of dignity and self-worth, tends to reduce self-esteem, and represents an attack on personal ego. "When personal norms of justice are violated by oneself, we have to expect guilt feelings, when others or institutions are violating the norms, resentment is expected—providing, excuses or justifications do not suspend these emotions" (Montada, 1998, p. 93). Injustice implies reproach and justifies claims for compensation or punishment. When injustice occurs, the party that violates the standards of justice is morally condemned (Montada, 1998).

To understand how people react to injustices, one must first understand the concepts of accountability (e.g., Gelfand & Realo, 1999; Tetlock, 1992) and blame attribution. Accountability refers to the perception of being answerable for actions or decisions, in accordance with interpersonal, social, and structural contingencies, all of which are embedded in particular sociocultural contexts (Gelfand, Lim, & Raver, 2004). To express resentment toward a person or retaliate against him or her, one should hold this person accountable for some action. Attributing blame for an injustice is at the core of fairness theory (e.g., Folger & Cropanzano, 1998, 2001). Once blame has been attributed, the victim may now decide what to do about the injustice. However, people do not always react to injustices. In fact, the possible individual response is for people not to react even though they recognize the situation to be unfair (Mikula,

1986; Tyler, Boeckman, Smith, & Huo, 1997). People may also decide to forgive the offender or suspend aggression (e.g., Beugré, 2005a).

Direct Effects of Culture on Employee Reactions to Injustice

To explain the impact of culture on reactions to injustice, one must understand how accountability is assigned across cultures. Individualist cultures may tend to assign blame to the actor, whereas collectivist cultures may tend to assign blame to the context. Blame assignment influences the manner in which the offender is treated. When blame attribution is internal, people may consider punishment as an appropriate way of dealing with an injustice. However, when blame attribution is external, people would consider rehabilitating the offender. The desire to punish rule breaking is prevalent across cultures (Hamilton & Saunders, 1992). However, cultures may differ in attributing blame for rule breaking. For instance, collectivist cultures may blame the system or society, whereas individualist cultures may blame the person. Similarly, cultures may also differ in regard to what type of punishment may seem appropriate for a rule breaker. Hamilton and Saunders (1988) for example, found that Japanese respondents favored sanctions that reintegrated the wrongdoer and restore relationships, whereas Americans favored sanctions that isolated the wrongdoer.

The model indicates that culture directly affects what people consider unfair. It also directly influences perceptions of distributive, procedural, or interactional unfairness and blame attribution. Indeed, social contexts influence people's judgments and responses to unfairness. Hegtvedt, Clay-Warner, and Johnson (2003) contend that social contexts, such as the group and legitimacy influence people's evaluations of an unjust act as unjust. When other group members argue that a given act is unjust, the victim may be reinforced in his or her own evaluation of the injustice. However, the lack of legitimacy provided by other group members and/or societal norms may lessen the perception of injustice.

Culture may directly influence third parties' accountability judgments and reactions. The model contends that third parties form accountability judgments and react to injustices. Although people place greater weight on their own experience of injustice than on that of others (Lind, Kray, & Thompson, 1998), they may be outraged by witnessing injustices done to others (e.g., Folger, 2001). Research shows that individualists tend to make dispositional attributions, whereas collectivists tend to make situational attributions (e.g., Morris & Peng, 1994). In some cultures, third parties may be more likely to hold offenders accountable for their perceived misdeeds, whereas other cultures may incriminate outside factors. Similarly, some cultures may prefer the punishment of offenders, whereas others may be more lenient. The need to punish harmdoers is present in any society. It is therefore important to know why people punish harmdoers (Darley & Pittman, 2003).

One of the many possible reasons may be that of moral outrage that often leads to a desire to inflict a just deserved punishment on the offender (Darley & Pittman, 2003). This is particularly so because the intentional infliction of wrong injures not just the victim but what might be called the fabric of society (e.g., Tyler & Boeckman, 1997). Moreover, what to do about a perpetrator of injustice is a fundamental human concern. Appropriately dealing with rule breakers is essential in ensuring the adequate functioning of any organized group. As Tyler, Boeckman, Smith, and Huo (1997) contend, the question of how to respond to rule breaking is central to the viability of organized groups. However, dealing with rule breakers may be socially construed. What is perceived as an appropriate measure to deal with rule breakers in one society may be considered as inappropriate in another. Take the example of the death penalty. Although the majority of Americans consider the death penalty as an appropriate punishment for certain crimes, Western Europeans have abolished it and even view it as barbaric and uncivilized.

Moderating Effects of Culture on Employee Reactions to Injustice

Culture also moderates the relationship between perceptions of unfairness and subsequent reactions. In some cultures, people may have a tendency to forgive offenders, whereas other cultures may have the tendency to punish offenders. The experience of injustice also includes the offender who may decide to provide social accounts in order to attenuate the negative impact of the perceived injustice. Bies (1987) identified four types of social accounts, (a) causal accounts, (b) ideological accounts, (c) referential accounts, and (d) penitential accounts. When a person provides a causal account he or she denies culpability but he or she does not deny the injustice. The offender may attribute his or her actions to external factors. When making an ideological account, one appeals to some higher value that legitimizes the wrongful action (Bies, 1987). Referential accounts represent attempts to change a wronged party's frame of reference (Bies, 1987; Folger & Cropanzano, 1998). There are two types of referential accounts, temporal and social. The former compares the person's current situation to a future one, whereas the latter compares the person's plight to the plight of another person.

Friedman and Robinson (1993) found that social accounts were less effective at diminishing perceptions of injustice for union officials and female managers when the hypothetical victim was an in-group to them. Although causal accounts do sometimes mitigate the negative effects of injustice, they do not always allay ill will. Culture moderates the relationship between the provision of causal accounts and victims' possible responses. Providing a social account can mitigate the negative effects of injustice because social accounts proffer new information regarding the nature of an injustice (Folger & Cropanzano, 1998).

In some cultures, responsibility to sanctioning offenders may be left to supernatural forces. For instance, in some collectivist cultures, such as Arab and African cultures, people tend to believe in what may be called "cosmic" justice. The idea behind cosmic justice is that supernatural beings, such as God, ancestors, and spirits, influence earthly events. Thus, they main intervene to restore justice when and where needed. In such cultures, harmful behaviors from others may even be seen as predestined, the offender being used as just a means to carry out the offense. Thus, the offender is not in fact, the real actor of the harmful behavior. A "negative" force is acting through the offender. Thus, retribution should not be done by the victim himself or herself. Rather, a powerful being may intervene to restore justice. This argument is in line with Leung and Morris's (2001) contention that certain belief systems reduce the centrality of retribution.

Cultural factors may also influence emotional expressions following perceived injustices. Lutz (1988) argued that emotions can be viewed as cultural and interpersonal products of naming, justifying, and persuading by people in relationship to each other. Emotional meaning is then a social rather than an individual achievement, an emergent product of social life (p. 5). Injustice would lead to ego-focused emotions, such as anger, frustration, and pride in individualist cultures and other-focused emotions, such as sympathy, feeling of interpersonal communion, and shame in collectivist cultures (Markus & Kitayama, 1991). Using their constructs of independent and interdependent selves, Markus and Kitayama (1991) contend that for those with independent selves, emotional expressions may literally express or reveal the inner feelings such as anger, sadness, and fear, whereas for those with interdependent selves, an emotional expression may be more often regarded as a public instrumental action that may or may not be related directly to the inner feelings. When experiencing injustices, these two types of individuals may react differently. Perhaps, people with independent selves may react to injustices by displaying anger and outrage, whereas those with interdependent selves may not overtly show their indignation for fear of alienating their relationship with others. As Markus and Kitayama (1991) contend, "anger may seriously threaten an interdependent self and thus may be highly dysfunctional" (p. 236). Using this cultural model, I analyze the impact of culture on employee reactions to unfairness.

RELATION-CENTERED CULTURES AND REACTIONS TO INJUSTICE

Relation-Centered Cultures and Distributive Injustice

In relation-centered cultures, distributive injustice may occur when outcomes are not allocated using equality or need rules. Hundley and Kim (1997) found that South Koreans' pay fairness judgments were more sensitive to differences in seniority, education, and family size, whereas Americans pay fairness judgments were relatively more sensitive to variations in individual performance and work effort. Despite these differences, the two samples considered individual performance as the most determinant factor of pay. Similar results were found by Giacobbe-Miller, Miller, and Zhang (1997). Working on two samples of American and Chinese managers, they found that Chinese managers emphasized equality while American managers emphasized equity. Need was also a significant criterion for Chinese managers but not for American managers. Both samples of managers considered equity as the primary criterion in allocating resources.

The implication of these two studies is that equity would not necessarily lead to perceived injustice in relation-centered cultures. However, the most common factors likely to foster feelings of distributive injustice may be the lack of equality or need considerations in allocating resources. However, in some relation-centered cultures, such as China, people prefer the equity rule of outcome distribution, especially with out-group members. Distributive injustice occurs when a person does not get the amount of reward he or she expects in comparison with the reward some other gets (Deutsch, 1985). How would people from relation-centered cultures react to distributive injustice? Although few empirical studies have addressed this issue, we may speculate about possible reactions to distributive injustice in relation-centered cultures. Gelfand, Lim, and Raver (2004) note that violations of conduct are evaluated in terms of contextual forces in collectivist cultures, whereas they are evaluated in terms of individual responsibility in individualist cultures.

Research conducted mostly in the United States shows that perceived unfairness of outcomes distribution leads to resentment and other forms of negative behaviors (Adams, 1965; Baron, Neuman, & Geddes, 1999; Greenberg, 1990b, 1993b). "The more of a man's disadvantage the rule of distributive justice fails of realization, the more likely he is to display the emotional behavior that we call anger" (Homans, 1961, p. 75). Greenberg (1990b, 1993b) found a significant correlation between distributive injustice and employee theft. Employees who felt unfairly rewarded tended to steal as compared to those who felt fairly rewarded. People may also experience unfairness even if they are not themselves victims of unfair treatment. Knowing that others are unfairly treated may arouse feelings of unfairness. This may be particularly true in cultures where group concerns are of paramount importance—leading to the sense of fraternal deprivation (e.g., Martin, 1981; Martin, Brickman, & Murray, 1984).

If injustice is culturally construed, then emotional reactions following a perceived injustice are also culturally construed. This assumption finds support in the anthropology literature. This literature suggests that emotions can be viewed as cultural and interpersonal products of naming, justifying, and persuading by people in relationship to each other. Emotional meaning is then a social rather than an individual achievement, an emergent product of social life (Lutz, 1988, p. 5). People in individualist cultures would tend to react on their emotions as compared to those from collectivist cultures. In so doing, the former may tend to confront the harmdoer, whereas the latter may remain silent or use other disguised forms of reactions. Emotions in collectivist cultures tend to embody the connectedness between individuals and their social environment, whereas emotions in individualist cultures appear to underline the disparity of self and others (Mesquita, 2001).

Emotional experiences differ fundamentally between collectivists and individualists (Mesquita, 2001). According to Mesquita (2001), collectivist emotions emerged as relational phenomena, embedded in relationships with others and perceived to reflect the state of those relationships. Individualist emotions, on the other hand, refer much less to the social environment (p. 72). To illustrate this assumption, let us assume that an employee from a collectivist culture and an employee from an individualist culture are both publicly reprimanded by their respective bosses. This case of obvious interactional injustice would be differently experienced by both employees. The employee from the collectivist culture would consider the event as causing him or her to lose face. He or she would also be concerned about what other employees would say. However, the employee from the individualist culture would view the event as a personal attack and express his or her outrage in terms of personal identity and self-esteem.

In relation-centered cultures, people may have the sense that injustice done to one is injustice done to all, particularly when the victim is an in-group member. To the extent that people strongly share the sense of belonging to the same in-group or clan, they may share in the plight of each member. When a member is unfairly treated, others may see in this unfair treatment an attack on the group. An anecdotal example from sub-Saharan Africa helps illustrate this tendency. In most sub-Saharan African countries, where a strong sense of the nation does not exist yet, people tend to identify more with their tribe than the nation. When a government official is sacked, his or her tribesmen tend to share in his or her plight by calling for mercy from the president or expressing "tribal" outrage. They often tend to rally behind their "son" or "daughter" who has been sacked.

Relation-Centered Cultures and Procedural Injustice

Perceptions of procedural injustice in relation-centered cultures would occur as a result of rigid and consistent procedures that do not integrate the specificity of individuals and situations. Relation-centered cultures may also influence employee reactions to perceived procedural injustice. Blader, Chang, and Tyler (2001) found that compared to American employees, employees from Taiwan were less likely to retaliate against their organization as a result of procedural injustice. Perceived injustice arouses less negative reactions if the salient norm is more tolerant of justice violations. Because primacy is attached to group membership in collectivist cultures, third parties would express more moral outrage when they witness injustice experienced by an in-group member than injustice experienced by an out-group member. People show more profound relational concerns when an injustice comes at the hand of a group with which they identify (Brockner, Tyler, & Cooper-Schneider, 1992).

People can also be moved by injustices experienced by strangers (Folger & Cropanzano, 2001). Likewise, in relation-centered cultures, the egocentric fairness bias may occur at the group level rather than at the individual level. People may tend to consider the inputs of their own groups more favorably (Messé, Hymes, & MacCoun, 1986). Collectivists may also use different allocation rules based on the in-group/out-group distinction. Leung and Bond (1984) found that the in-group/out-group distinction influenced allocation rules. Collectivists tend to use equality rule or the rule of generosity when rewarding in-group members and the equity rule when rewarding out-group members. Injustice toward in-group members may elicit stronger negative feelings and reactions than injustice toward out-group members. When people from collectivist cultures make external attributions when experiencing injustice, they would be less likely to blame the perpetrator of the injustice. In contrast, people from individualist cultures, would tend to directly blame the perpetrator of the perceived injustice and hold him or her accountable for the misdeed.

Relation-Centered Cultures and Interactional Injustice

To understand the effects of culture on interactional injustice one should acknowledge Inness, Barling, and Turner's (2005) contention that interactional injustice is arguably the most deeply personal type of injustice an employee may confront in the workplace. In relation-centered cultures, people care about interpersonal relations. They also care about face saving. Thus, social sensitivity and face saving are important factors to consider when interacting with members of relation-centered cultures. In such cultures, mistreatments that make someone loose face or threaten his or her standing in a group may be particularly considered unfair—raising the prospect of interactional injustice. Relation-centered cultures may also influence employee reactions to social accounts. Leung and Tong (2004) provide a particularly striking example. They describe the case of the USS Greeneville, a U.S. submarine that accidentally sank a Japanese fisheries training ship, the Ehime Maru in 2001.

> The captain of the ship, Scott Waddle, later issued a written statement in which he expressed his most sincere regret over the accident, which infuriated many Japanese. A relative of a victim told the press that Japanese refuse to accept the statement as an apology, and that a real apology required him to say it to each of the victims' relatives in person. Apology in person is in fact common in Japan to show the remorse felt and the willingness to shoulder the blame. Subsequently, Commander Waddle had an opportunity to apologize in person to the captain of Ehime Maru, Hisao Onishi, and expressed his wish to travel to Japan to apologize in person to the relatives of the victims. President Bush and key senior officers made high-profile, public apologies, and an admiral was sent to Japan to explain to the families of the victims the results of the enquiry of the accident. In this incident, the U.S. officials understood that in Japan, a major justice practice for the decision to absolve a wrongdoer requires his or her display of a deep sense of remorse and a willingness to shoulder the responsibilities, typically expressed in the form of elaborate apologies. Despite the initial uproar generated by the incident in Japan, the handling of the event in a culturally appropriate manner led to a satisfactory settlement without harming the U.S. Japan relationship. (pp. 329)

Collectivists tend to prefer mitigating tactics in social conflicts, such as apologies and excuses, whereas individualists tend to prefer assertive tactics, such as justifications and denial (Leung, 1987; Obhuci & Takahashi, 1994). Greenberg (1990c) found that the theft rate in a plant of underpaid workers was considerably lower when the basis for their underpayment was thoroughly and sensitively explained to them than when limited information was given in an insensitive manner. Bies and Shapiro (1988) also found that when a boss provided an explanation related to the refusal of an employee's request, the recipient felt less disapproval toward the boss and perceived greater fairness of the decision-making process than when no explanation was given. These findings show that providing employees with complete explanations regarding the procedures used in a way that showed sensitivity reduces their potential negative reactions.

Itoi, Obhuci, and Fukuno (1996) conducted a study on two samples involving Japanese and American respondents. They found that Japanese respondents preferred mitigating accounts, such as apologies and excuses, whereas their American counterparts preferred assertive accounts, such as justifications. Explaining these results, Beugré (1998a) content that "Japanese participants mitigating style reflects a stronger concern for relational and social harmony, whereas American participants' assertive style reveals a stronger concern for personal satisfaction" (p. 108). Collective feelings of injustice may be more present in collectivist cultures than in individualist cultures where personal feelings of injustice may predominate. Bies and Shapiro (1987) note that giving explanations related to the behavior performed helps subordinates to understand its causes and also ensures them that they are respected and valued. Accounts are important because they can smooth the troubled waters of relationships or can get one 'acquitted' for a misdeed (Hamilton & Hagiwara, 1992). However, keeping people in the dark might elicit negative feelings and reactions. Perhaps, such reactions may be more salient in self-centered cultures where employees tend to stick out.

SELF-CENTERED CULTURES AND INJUSTICE

Self-Centered Cultures and Distributive Injustice

Employees in self-centered cultures are concerned about their self-interests. Thus, outcome fairness would be of a paramount importance. In such cultures, people would experience distributive unfairness when they do not get the outcomes they think they deserve compared to others. Particularly, distributive injustice in such cultures would occur when equity rules of distribution are violated. Early studies on equity theory (e.g., Adams, 1963, 1965) found that inequity related to the lack of balance between one's input-output ratio compared to a comparison other led to perceptions of inequity. Subsequent studies have supported this effect. However, research at the cross-cultural level did not compare (at least not yet) self-centered and relation-centered cultures on reactions to distributive injustice. How do people from self-centered cultures react to distributive injustice compared to their counterparts from relation-centered cultures?

Emotions that people experience when they feel unfairly treated may influence their reactions to distributive injustice. The constructs of affective and neutral cultures (e.g., Trompenaars, 1993; Trompenaars & Hampden-Turner, 1998) may help explain such emotional reactions following perceived distributive injustice. In affective cultures, people may tend to overtly express their emotions when they experience injustice. However, in neutral cultures, people may limit the public expression of emotions following a perceived injustice. Such reactions may occur for the three types of injustice, distributive, procedural, and interactional.

Self-Centered Cultures and Procedural Injustice

In self-centered cultures, people care about procedures that benefit them personally, that are consistent and applied universally. They also tend to consider more the objective aspects rather than the subjective nature of those procedures. Thus, perceptions of procedural injustice would occur when procedures are inconsistent and violate the employee's individual standards. Employees from self-centered cultures would perceive subjective procedures as more unfair than objective procedures. How then would employees from self-centered cultures react to violations of procedural justice?

In self-centered cultures, procedural injustice may trigger an attempt to prompt actions that may help correct the procedures. However, in relation-centered cultures, people may not overtly react to unfair procedures, particularly when in-group members develop these procedures. In a study comparing American and Japanese reactions to social accounts, Takaku (2000) found that Japanese participants rated apologies as significantly more appropriate than did their American counterparts who rated justifications as more appropriate. Perhaps, for the American respondents, justifications may be seen as more assertive than apologies. Assertiveness is one of the characteristics of self-centered cultures. In addition, the status of the victim influenced Japanese participants' ratings of account appropriateness but not American participants' ratings. People raised in collectivistic cultures tend to make a conflict covert when possible, and tend to prefer mitigating than aggravating strategies, whereas people raised in individualistic cultures tend to make a conflict overt and employ assertive strategies (Leung, 1987; Obhuci & Takahashi, 1994; Takaku, 2000). Blader, Chang, and Tyler (2001) found that Americans were more likely to retaliate in response to procedural injustices. Such actions may characterize people from individualistic and low power distance cultures than those from collectivist and high power distance cultures.

Self-Centered Cultures and Interactional Injustice

As mentioned previously, in self-centered cultures, people are more concerned about the self than the group. Thus, in interpersonal relations, people will seek to enhance themselves. They may do so by advancing their own agenda or by avoiding to loose out in relationships. However, a situation that threatens one's self-interest would be perceived as unfair. How then will they react to interactional injustice? In individualist cultures, accountability rests with specific individuals, whereas in collectivist cultures, accountability rests with entire groups (Gelfand, Lim, & Raver, 2004). To the extent that people directly blame offenders, they would be likely to retaliate against them.

Previous studies, mostly conducted in the United States, found that perceptions of interactional injustice lead to dysfunctional behaviors (e.g., Bies, 1987; Baron, Neuman, & Geddes, 1999; Greenberg & Alge, 1998; Skarlicki & Folger, 1997). These reactions were observed in the United States, a self-centered culture. However, reactions to interactional injustice in the workplace in other cultures may not always follow the same pattern as in the United States. In self-centered cultures, fair interpersonal treatment may enhance an individual's standing and status within a group. People may tend to use such treatments as a sign of self-worth rather than a symbol of harmony with in-group members. When cultures emphasize the betterment of the self, people would prefer to be treated with respect and dignity as a sign of their individual standing and status. The betterment of the self may lead to positive self-esteem. Thus, unfair interpersonal treatment may represent an indirect attack on the person's self-esteem. Actions that are perceived as blatant acts of humiliation and personally degrading may be perceived as unfair. "Undignified and disrespectful treatment implies that the person is unworthy in the eyes of the group and this threat to one's personhood provokes extremely negative reactions to the procedure" (Lind & Early, 1992, p. 234). In self-centered cultures, people may tend to react overtly to such unfair treatments. However, in relation-centered cultures, people may tend to react covertly to situations of interactional injustice.

STATUS-CENTERED CULTURES AND INJUSTICE

Status-Centered Cultures and Distributive Injustice

Distributive injustice in status-centered cultures may stem from violating distribution rules such as age, tenure, status, and even gender. Because in such cultures, employees may consider age, status, tenure, and the like as inputs, they may expect that the distribution of outcomes integrate these factors. Failure to do so may result in perceptions of distributive injustice. However, in status-centered cultures, employees may be less likely to react to distributive injustice, especially when this injustice emanates from a powerful other. Because managers and bosses are very powerful in such cultures, employees would be less likely to directly confront them when their outcomes fall short of expectations. Indeed, with great power comes the potential for great injustice (Cropanzano, Chrobot-Mason, Rupp, & Prehar, 2004). This is particularly true in status-centered cultures where hierarchy is an important social arrangement.

When allocating rewards and punishments in self-centered cultures, allocators should not ignore recipients' status. Bosses in status-centered cultures may feel unfairly treated when allocation rules fail to consider their higher statuses. Doing otherwise may be perceived as unfair. People's social status may influence their reactions to justice or injustice. People with more resources and power prefer equity-based distributions, whereas those with fewer resources prefer principles of equality and need (Kabanoff, 1997).

Status-Centered Cultures and Procedural Injustice

Power distance also affects people's reactions to unfairness. The higher the power distance of a society, the less likely subordinates tend to react to situations of unfairness. This tendency may be explained by the fact that bosses in high power distance cultures tend to be so powerful that it is difficult for their subordinates to confront them directly. In such cultures, there are few occasions where bosses are reprimanded or punished for abusing their power. This sends a negative signal to subordinates that no matter the gravity of the incident, the boss is likely to prevail. As Beugré (1998a, p. 107) put it, "Cultures favoring unconditional deference and allegiance to authority may lead people to accept unfair practices and capricious decisions from authorities." James (1993) and Gundykunst and Ting-Toomey (1988) note that power distance influences tolerance to injustice.

Gundykunst and Ting-Toomey (1988) suggest that cultures that inculcate an acceptance of power differences lead individuals to expect, take for granted and, therefore, not get angry about injustices. Conversely, in relatively low-power distance cultures, there is less a tendency to defer to power, which inclines individuals to react negatively when situations or other individuals seem to be treating them unfairly. In high power distance cultures, people's acceptance of unequal social prerogatives promotes the tolerance of unfair treatment. By contrast, in low power distance societies, people's rejection of inequality makes them less tolerant of unfair treatment (Morris & Leung, 2000). Not challenging leaders for fear of retaliation is probably the reason why there are few opportunities for voice in high power distance cultures. In such cultures, employees may be less likely to have voice opportunities or even expect to receive voice. It is also possible that employees may be less angry when they do not receive voice compared to their counterparts from low power distance cultures. People may also tend to follow formal procedures in making request in status-centered cultures. Failure to follow these procedures may be perceived as unfair, especially by those in positions of power.

Status-Centered Cultures and Interactional Injustice

In status-centered cultures, employees may have fewer opportunities for voice. However, these employees may be less likely to react to such apparent injustices. Because, in such cultures, employees do not expect voice opportunities, they may not be offended by the lack of voice. For example, in a banquet, people in such cultures would expect seat arrangements to follow strict rules. Failure to do so may be perceived as unfair. Similarly, outdoor activities that require that employees mingle together with managers and executives without regard for their formal ranks in the organization may be resented in status-centered cultures. In fact, such activities may be perceived as unfair.

In status-centered cultures, bosses often set standards of conduct and accountability. For example, in high power distance cultures, standards of accountability are set by those in power and subordinates are expected to adhere to these standards without conditionality. In low power distance cultures, however, the standards of accountability are set by abstract principles and are mutually adhered to by both bosses and subordinates (Schwartz, 1994). Thus, in low power distance cultures, accountability is mutual, whereas in high power distance cultures, it is unidirectional. This probably explains why injustices from superiors tend to be tolerated in high power distance cultures.

In status-centered cultures, subordinates would experience interactional injustice when bosses do not personally take care of them. In high power distance cultures, bosses are expected to nurture their subordinates in return for allegiance and subordination. Failure to meet these expectations may result in perceptions of interactional injustice. However, subordinates may not overtly react to such perceived injustices. Blader, Chang, and Tyler (2001) note that individuals in high power distance cultures may be more tolerant of poor treatment of subordinates because such cultures may shape their expectations in ways that make treatment that would be regarded as disrespectful in low power distance cultures acceptable in high power distance cultures. In a society high on power distance, a verbal insult from a subordinate to a superior constitutes a threat to the social order and will therefore be more strongly condemned than in a society low on power distance. However, an insult from a superior to a subordinate would be tolerated (Bond, Wan, Leung, & Giacalone, 1985).

RISK-PRONE CULTURES AND INJUSTICE

Risk-Prone Cultures and Distributive Injustice

Research on organizational justice has rarely focused on the relationship between risk-prone cultures and perceptions of fairness or unfairness. However, in an era where change is the only constant, the organizational justice literature may gain by assessing the impact of this cultural syndrome on employee reactions to justice. In risk-prone cultures, the emphasis is on entrepreneurship, personal initiatives, and the sense of innovation. Thus, perceptions of procedural injustice may stem from a lack of reward for innovation, personal initiatives, and novelty. Employees would experience a sense of distributive injustice when they are not properly rewarded for their work contributions, such as creativity, innovation, and suggestions. How would they react to distributive injustice in such cultures?

Using previous findings on employee reactions to inequity, one may speculate about employees' potential reactions to distributive injustice in risk-prone cultures. According to equity theory, injustice creates an uncomfortable situation and the victimized party is motivated to restore equity (Adams, 1965). Individuals can restore equity in different ways. When individuals are underrewarded, they can reduce their inputs, increase their outputs (perhaps to influence their bosses), or terminate the exchange relationship. Individuals may also psychologically distort the situation—that is reinterpreting the situation in a more favorable way.

Such psychological and behavioral reactions may occur in risk-prone cultures as potential responses to distributive injustice.

In risk-averse cultures, however, distributive injustice may stem from a lack of reward for experience, respect for rules and policies, and the maintenance of the status quo. In such cultures, people would experience distributive unfairness when respect for existing rules is not considered as important. This may happen when management initiates change and insists on the adoption of new behaviors. Because people have a tendency for displaying behaviors for which they are rewarded, people would tend to reduce inputs by not following customary rules.

Risk-Prone Cultures and Procedural Injustice

In risk-prone cultures, perceptions of distributive injustice may stem from the existence of cumbersome rules, regulations, and policies. In organizations, such policies may include strict obedience to company rules, lack of voice, and lack of explanations of important decisions. How would then employees react to procedural injustice? Employees may react to such unfair procedures by "voicing" for the enactment of new procedures that allow the opportunity to innovate and take initiatives. For instance, in the United States, a culture described as risk-prone, empowerment is considered as important by most employees. Empowering employees provides them the opportunity to "own" their jobs. It also creates a sense of fairness since employees are given voice concerning critical aspects of their jobs.

In risk-averse cultures, however, procedural injustice may stem from many changes in existing procedures. Too much change may lead to uncertainty and uneasiness in such cultures. Although the same may occur in risk-prone cultures, the magnitude may be higher in risk-averse cultures. Employees in risk-prone cultures may tend to embrace change more often than employees in risk-averse cultures. Thus, frequent changes in an organization may be perceived as unfair and strongly resisted by employees in risk-averse cultures. Employees in risk-prone cultures may perceive the lack of voice opportunities during change initiatives as unfair. However, their counterparts from risk-averse cultures may tend to turn to management for guidance and direction. Thus, they may be less likely to perceive the lack of voice opportunities as unfair.

Risk-Prone Cultures and Interactional Injustice

Interactional unfairness in risk-prone cultures may stem from two aspects, informational justice and interpersonal justice. In risk-prone cultures, employees may easily work with partial information to accomplish their tasks. However, such partial information should not exclude the core information required for the job. In risk-averse cultures, employees may prefer to receive detailed information about their job. Lack of such information may create a sense of interactional injustice. Thus, the lack of information would be more likely to lead to a strong sense of informational injustice in risk-averse than in risk-prone cultures.

Interpersonal injustice in risk-prone cultures may stem from lack of recognition for people's ideas and suggestions. This does not necessary imply that people seek tangible rewards for their ideas. Rather, acknowledging people for their contributions may create a sense of justice in risk-prone cultures. Take the example of an employee who made a valuable suggestion to his or her manager. The manager reports the suggestion to his or her own boss without mentioning the employee. This may create a sense of interpersonal injustice since the employee was not properly acknowledged. Because people are eager to suggest ideas in risk-prone cultures, a lack of recognition for these ideas may be perceived as unfair. Fairness may then act as a motivator to encourage the generation of new ideas.

In the previous two chapters, I have discussed the impact of culture on employee reactions to justice and injustice. As the studies discussed in these chapters illustrate, there are both similarities and differences across cultures. Although not every individual in every single culture will behave the same, we can use the research tools, concepts, and theories presented in these chapters to make general predictions about a national culture's overall organizational justice preferences and tendencies (e.g., Conner, 2003). With this knowledge, managers may develop strategies to effectively motivate employees and ensure fairness wherever their organizations operate. This is particularly important because adaptability to different cultures and the ability to adjust management practices to specific cultures are essential to success in a globalized world. Indeed, the globalization of business is a reality that is redefining how people work together (Chao & Moon, 2005). Managing fairness in a global context is the focus of the next chapter.

CHAPTER 6

MANAGING JUSTICE ACROSS CULTURES

In the previous two chapters, I have discussed how people form justice judgments across cultures and how they react to situations of fairness and unfairness. Armed with this knowledge, I propose in this chapter strategies to manage justice in cross-cultural contexts. Managing justice implies the effective implementation of what Leung and Tong (2004) and Leung (2005) called justice practices. A justice practice represents the concrete standards, verbal and nonverbal behaviors, and social arrangements with which justice criteria are operationalized and implemented (Leung, 2005). The present chapter discusses strategies that may help organizations ensure justice not only across cultures but also across employees with different cultural backgrounds. Distinguishing the types of cultural influence on justice judgment clarifies a firm's options in the trade-off between standard versus locally sensitive policies (Morris, Leung, Ames, & Lickel, 1999). The chapter analyzes the management of justice issues along the four cultural syndromes identified in this book. It also discusses the management of justice in the network organization and the development of transcultural competence in organizational justice.

A Cultural Perspective of Organizational Justice, 127–149
Copyright © 2007 by Information Age Publishing
All rights of reproduction in any form reserved.

MANAGING JUSTICE IN RELATION-CENTERED CULTURES

As I have explained throughout this book, relation-centered cultures emphasize interpersonal relations and the preeminence of group welfare over individual welfare. Thus, multinational corporations operating in such cultures should integrate this value in implementing their justice practices. Bies and Greenberg (2002) asked an intriguing question that may be of concern to multinational corporations. "Given that global business corporations, such as Nike increasingly are faced with dealing with multiple constituencies across cultures, how can they present a consistent corporate image of justice?" (p. 333). This question is important for three reasons. First, it implicitly acknowledges the subjective nature of justice perceptions. If the multinational corporation encompasses several constituencies (as any organization does), it is more difficult to agree on what is fair or not. Second, since multinational corporations operate in an ever-changing environment, notions of justice may evolve over time, rendering difficult any agreement on what represents fair practices. Third, multinational corporations employ several types of employees who have different notions of justice. Thus, agreeing on fairness even within the multinational corporation is in itself problematic.

In light of these difficulties, multinational corporations must find ways of appearing fair if not being actually fair. These organizations should design and implement organizational policies and practices that promote fairness as a basic requirement for the effective functioning of organizations and the personal satisfaction of the individuals they employ (Lam, Schaubroeck, & Aryee, 2002). Such policies start at the level of individual employees who are the first recipients of situations of fairness or unfairness. In explaining how organizations can manage justice in relation-centered cultures, I considered the three dimensions of distributive, procedural, and interactional justice. These strategies are guidelines rather than absolute ways of managing justice in such cultures.

Managing Distributive Justice in Relation-Centered Cultures

There are two important issues one should consider when attempting to manage distributive fairness in relation-centered cultures. First, in such cultures, people tend to favor equality and need rules of outcome allocation. Second, most collectivist cultures, except Japan, belong to emerging or developing countries. One characteristic of emerging economies is that the economic sector is dominated by multinational corporations that employ a sizable number of expatriates. As a rule-of-thumb, expatriates often earn more than host country nationals working in the same ventures (Leung, Smith, Wang, & Sun, 1996). These two concerns make the management of distributive justice a complex endeavor in relation-centered cultures. Looking at distributive justice issues in international ventures in China provides a particularly illuminating example.

Joint ventures have become a major form of foreign investment in China since this country adopted an open-door economic policy (Shenkar, 1990). To run these ventures, expatriate managers are often sent from headquarters (Leung, Smith, Wang, & Sun, 1996). These expatriate managers enjoy much better pay and benefits compared to their local counterparts who hold similar positions. Such disparate treatment may result in perceptions of distributive injustice (Beugré, 2002; Leung, Smith, Wang, & Sun, 1996) and feelings of relative deprivation from local managers (Beugré, 2002). The basic proposition of relative deprivation theory is that the feeling of deprivation stems from a comparison between the rewards received by some other person or group, referred to as a comparative referent (Martin, 1981). The literature on relative deprivation identifies two types of relative deprivation: *egoistic deprivation* and *fraternal deprivation* (e.g., Martin, 1981). Egoistic deprivation occurs when a comparison to a similar referent causes a feeling of deprivation, whereas fraternal deprivation occurs when an upward comparison to a dissimilar referent causes a feeling of deprivation (Martin, 1981).

In collectivist cultures, both types of deprivation may occur. Egoistic deprivation may occur when a local employee compares himself or herself to another local employee working in the same venture or another venture. Fraternal deprivation, however, may occur when a local employee compares himself or herself to an expatriate. This employee may consider that on average, local employees receive lower salaries than expatriates. Therefore, as a group, local employees are relatively deprived. To reduce this sense of fraternal deprivation, managers should always explain the reasons underlying compensation disparities between host country employees and expatriates. Clear explanations may help reduce the animosity that such disparities may create. A study by Chen, Choi, and Chi (2002) supports this contention. Chen, Choi, and Chi (2002) found that ideological accounts had a main effect on host country employees' perceptions of distribute fairness when they compare their compensation to that of expatriates. Even though Chinese managers and employees received less pay than their expatriate counterparts, the provision of ideological accounts mitigated their perceptions of unfairness.

Although joint ventures may contribute to the growth of the economic output of a country when they raise issues of distributive justice, they may contribute to lowering host country employees' productivity. Thus, managers of multinational corporations may be well advised to design compensation measures that reduce the sense of inequity and relative deprivation. The existence of a sense of fraternal deprivation may deepen the social divide between host country employees and expatriates. Social identity theory (e.g., Tajfel, 1978, 1982; Tajfel & Turner, 1979; Turner, 1985) may help explain how this might occur. According to social identity theory, two types of identity, personal identity and social identity contribute to the self-concept. A social identity framework suggests that the most important distinction between fraternal and individual deprivation is not the comparison target but whether people think of themselves as group members or as isolated individuals (Tyler, Boeckman, Smith, & Huo, 1997). Because group membership is salient in collectivist cultures, fraternal deprivation may be more frequent than egoistic deprivation.

Concerns for fairness for host country employees should not lead managers to overlook concerns of fairness for expatriates. Although expatriates want to put their skills and knowledge gained abroad to use, they are often disappointed by the attitude of headquarters upon their return and by their new jobs (Black & Gregersen, 1999). When considering expatriates reactions to fairness, one should consider what they select as referents. Do they select host country or third country employees as referents or do they compare themselves to their home country employees? Konopaske and Werner (2002) contend that expatriates, especially American expatriates do not compare themselves to host or third country nationals. Rather, they compare themselves to home country expatriates and nonexpatriate peers. Because expatriates are vital to firms in today's global business environment, their attraction, retention, and motivation are vital to a firm's survival and success (Konopaske & Werner, 2002). To this end, justice issues should play an important role.

Managers should identify the factors that expatriates may consider as inputs. Expatriates may for example consider factors, such as the length of overseas assignments and the social economic distance between the home and host countries as legitimate inputs in addition to their work contributions. In addition to outcomes such as compensation and benefits, managers should also consider country attractiveness in making overseas assignment decisions. Although a host country may be economically poorer than a home country, an expatriate may consider it attractive if the host country presents characteristics that the expatriate values. For instance, India is economically less developed than the United States but some expatriates may consider India attractive because it offers a variety of tourist attractions or presents other characteristics that they value. Managers should therefore develop indexes of country attractiveness for expatriates. A country attractiveness index should highlight the positive characteristics that an expatriate may consider appealing when making an overseas assignment decision. Such an index may help identify which elements may attract expatriates and motivate them to take on overseas assignments.

Another example that is particularly striking in relation-centered cultures is performance-based compensation. By focusing too much on the individual's work performance, compensation-based pay may create animosity in such cultures. However, they may be situations where performance-based pay may be effective in relation-based cultures. For instance, when managers form work teams and link team members' compensation to the team's performance, performance-based pay may be successful because it does not single out an individual employee. Performance-based compensation is widely used in some organizations in individualistic cultures. Thus, it may be more effective in such cultures than in relation-centered cultures. In highly individualistic cultures, people focus on meeting their individual goals and expect to be rewarded for their individual effort (Miles & Greenberg, 1993). The same is not necessarily true in relation-centered cultures.

Because performance-based pay makes interpersonal competition more salient, it may be less appealing to employees in collectivist cultures. Multinationals willing to introduce such a compensation system in collectivist cultures may do it in a progressive manner or in an indirect way. They may set performance levels for each employee and encourage employees to help each other in reaching the assigned individual objectives. Also, where needed, teams may be established and assigned team tasks. Compensation will then be based on the performance of the team. Erez (2000) suggests that equal pay compensation should be offered in collectivist and low power distance cultures. As examples, the author cited Germany and the Netherlands. The author mentioned that only 4% of the workforce in Germany and only 19% of the workforce in the Netherlands receive payments by results.

Deciding what criteria to consider when making compensation decisions may be difficult in a cross-cultural context. In collectivist cultures, employees may consider nonjob related attributes as relevant in determining employee compensation. In individualist cultures, however, employees and managers alike may consider only job-related attributes in determining employee compensation. Thus, finding a proper balance for what is job-related can be a daunting task and a potential source of conflict in multinational corporations. For example, the *nenko* wage system in Japan is determined by age, education, seniority, and gender, instead of work-related contributions (Miles & Greenberg, 1993). Such a compensation system may appear unfair to most Americans. However, for Japanese employees, this compensation system is fair because it considers factors that are seen as inputs.

Managing Procedural Justice in Relation-Centered Cultures

Relation-centered cultures focus on harmony and the importance of the group. This orientation may have two managerial implications. First, procedures should help create or enhance harmony in an organization. Thus, using informal procedures to solve conflict would be more effective in relation-centered cultures. Second, emphasizing group and group allocation techniques may help increase group cohesiveness and effectiveness overtime. Procedures that encourage an equal treatment of employees should be emphasized. In relation-centered cultures, personal connections are often important and strongly influence work relations. Thus, the work experience may be construed as one entailing relations with special others, such as supervisors and colleagues (Hui, Lee, & Rousseau, 2004). The organization becomes an environment of "affect production," because relations and identification with supervisors and colleagues become more important than identification with the organization as an impersonal entity. Pearce, Branyiczki, and Bakacsi (1994) note that employees tend to rely on person-specific relationship in transitional economies. The cultures of these economies are often characterized as relation-centered.

Managers should also be concerned about third party reactions to their actions. Because in relation-centered cultures, people tend to favor group harmony and look after one another, they would be more affected by a manager's actions toward one of their own. For instance, a manager may build a reputation of fairness when he or she treats an employee's in-group member fairly. Similarly, a manager may build a reputation of unfairness when he or she is seen as treating an employee's in-group member unfairly. Thus, managers should cultivate group sensitivity when dealing with individual employees in relation-centered cultures. Perceptions of fairness in such cultures may be based on two types of experience, individual and vicarious. An employee may consider a manager as fair based on his or her own experiences with that manager. However, the employee may also develop fairness perceptions based on the experiences other employees, particularly in-group members have with the same manager.

Managing Interactional Justice in Relation-Centered Cultures

Although treating people with respect and dignity may be universal, the very practices that lead to fair interpersonal treatment may be culture specific. Leung and Tong (2004) identified two important concepts that are relevant to this discussion: (a) respect—meaning being polite toward others and (b) propriety—avoid inappropriate remarks and behaviors. They operationalized propriety as including social face and respect for individual rights. Social face involves putting the target in good light and avoiding acts that embarrass or belittle them, such as derogatory and abusive remarks, whereas respect for individual rights involves permitting people to exercise their rights, such as privacy rights or the right to be treated as innocent before being proven guilty (Leung & Tong, 2004). Social face is important in collectivist cultures, and it is expected that one should try to protect the face of others by not embarrassing them.

Leung and Tong (2004) speculate that in collectivist cultures, people should display a high level of respect and respectful social protocols toward in-group than out-group members and that respect would be unequally distributed in high power distance cultures. In such cultures, people of high status would be more respected than those occupying lower level status. Akasu and Asao (1993) note that it is rude for a boss to tell a secretary to copy something without saying "please" in the United States, but it is not considered rude in Japan to skip "please." Ordering relationships by status is a crucial element in Chinese society (Chi & Lo, 2003). The *wu-lun* principles specify people's roles and behaviors in relation to one another and serve as a referent norm of social interactions (Chi & Lo, 2003).

The implications for management practice are twofold: First, managers in multinational corporations should be aware of the extent to which in collectivist cultures, saving face is often more important than what is said. Thus, in reprimanding employees in collectivist cultures, managers should avoid remarks and actions that lead employees to lose face. Reprimanding an employee in front of other employees may be perceived as unfair, since the reprimanded employee may lose face in front of colleagues. Second, too much praise for a high performing employee may send a negative signal to his or her coworkers who may think that the manager does not acknowledge their personal contributions as well. Cushner and Brislin (1996) note that in Korea, employees would consider it rude to mention their mistakes in front of others because such behaviors make them lose face.

Managers should also be particularly cautious when dealing with employees from groups that have a history of past discrimination. Employees from such groups may tend to view current managerial actions in the lens of the historic relations between their own social group and their manager's social group. Since such employees may have internalized the "persistent injustice effect"—the tendency for people who have experienced injustice to continually see it (Davidson & Friedman, 1998; Shapiro & Kirkman, 2001) they may even consider a minor violation of fairness as reflecting the true nature and behavior of the organization and its managers. Davidson and Friedman (1998) studied the persistent injustice effect in managers in the United States. They found that because Black managers had more experience with unjust acts than White managers, they reported higher levels of past injustices, higher levels of expected injustices, and greater mistrust. Anticipating injustice may lead people to perceive injustice where there is actually none. Thus, the anticipation of injustice is likely to raise the probability of perceived injustice, which may lead to self-defeating organizational attitudes and behavior (Shapiro & Kirkman, 2001).

This effect may be extended to the analysis of relationships between managers from former colonial powers and employees from former colonies of Africa and/or Asia. Expatriates from former colonial powers, such as France and Britain often occupied managerial positions in these regions. Often, the relationships between expatriates from these countries and local employees and managers are strained because of what the locals describe as "condescending" behaviors from these expatriates. This 'condescending hypothesis' refers to the extent to which expatriates tend to demean local employees and managers by providing them with little opportunity for voice and empowerment. Rather, these expatriates tend to act in an autocratic manner and do not always trust local employees and managers. One way of improving these relations is to ensure fair interactional treatment. Indeed, creating fair working environments may help reduce such negative perceptions that may exacerbate the tension between host country employees and expatriates and reduce organizational productivity.

MANAGING JUSTICE IN SELF-CENTERED CULTURES

Managing Distributive Justice in Self-Centered Cultures

In self-centered cultures, the focus of the individual is on personal well-being as compared to group well being. Thus, in managing fairness issues in such cultures, managers should design policies that target individual self-interest. Self-interest is not viewed here as amoral. Rather, it is used as a motivational mechanism. Such a policy consists of relying on objective criteria for compensation and promotion decisions. In such cultures, the preferred rule of outcome allocation would be the equity rule as demonstrated by several studies (e.g., Deutsch, 1975, 1985). Outcomes in self-centered cultures include monetary rewards as well as promotion and individual recognition. Viewing the distribution of these outcomes as fair may enhance the recipient's self-esteem and his or her commitment to the organization.

Despite the importance of the equity rule in self-centered cultures, one should acknowledge that even in such cultures, need rules may apply under some conditions. For example, in the United States, the Family Leave Act and the Americans with Disabilities Act (ADA) are used only by those who need them. In discussing the fairness of accommodating employees, Colella (2001) argues that need rules may play an important role in determining distributive fairness judgments. Some employees may view the use of such "need" benefits as fair, whereas others may see them as unfair. The purpose of such policies, however, is to accommodate those who may need assistance in the workplace. Such policies may be effective in individualist as well as collectivist cultures. Managers should also provide challenging assignments and opportunities for training and development. These types of assignments may represent powerful motivational tools in individualistic and risk-prone cultures because they may be perceived as valuable job outcomes.

Managing Procedural Justice in Self-Centered Cultures

Managing procedural justice in self-centered cultures may include three elements: (a) the provision of voice, (b) the provision of explanations, and (c) the existence of procedures that foster and recognize individual contributions. By enacting policies that provide opportunities for voice, managers may help satisfy one fundamental need encountered in self-centered cultures. In such cultures, individuals prefer to voice their opinions because doing so helps them influence the decision-process. Thus, empowering employees may help gain their trust and commitment in self-centered cultures. Managers may also provide explanations to employees as a mechanism for fostering cooperation and a sense of personal worth. Finally, managers should constantly encourage individual contributions and design mechanisms to reward them. Managers may also enhance procedural justice in self-centered cultures by developing and assessing constantly the justice climate in their organizations. Because of differences in cultural backgrounds that may lead to misunderstanding, when people from different cultures work together, conflicts are likely to occur (e.g., Hofstede, 1980). One way to prevent the occurrence of such conflicts is to ensure that justice is served. This can be done by using a justice climate scale to assess the level of perceived justice in organizations. Doing so is important because justice climate and particularly procedural justice climate tends to be associated with helping behaviors (Nauman & Bennett, 2000).

Managing Interactional Justice in Self-Centered Cultures

Managing interactional justice in self-centered cultures may not be different from managing interactional justice in relation-centered cultures because the desire to be treated with respect and dignity tends to be a universal concern. However, in relation-centered cultures, relations tend to be warmer and enduring, whereas they tend to be superficial in self-centered cultures. Thus, in interacting with employees in self-centered cultures, managers should focus on developing "professional" relations. They should also avoid raising personal issues with employees and colleagues, especially if doing so conflicts with work outcomes. The workplace may be less likely to become an environment of "affect production" as compared to relation-centered cultures. However, treating employees with respect and dignity in self-centered cultures may help gain their trust and commitment. Interactional fairness may be seen as a mechanism through which managers can help enhance individual employees' sense of self-worth.

MANAGING JUSTICE IN STATUS-CENTERED CULTURES

Managing Distributive Justice in Status-Centered Cultures

In status-centered cultures, managers should be careful when designing compensation systems because employees may consider factors, such as age, gender, and tenure as legitimate inputs that should be considered in allocating rewards. Failure to recognize such elements may lead to perceptions of unfairness. For instance, the performance-based pay system commonly adopted in the United States, may not be effective in other cultures where efforts and individual productivity are not always perceived as legitimate inputs in determining employee compensation. Also, in status-centered cultures, superiors may resent the fact that a performance-based pay may help high achievers receive high level compensation that may be equal or even greater than their own. Pay differentials may be perceived as a way of maintaining the social order. In this "pecking order," those at the bottom are expected to receive less than those at the top. A mentality of "holding people down" may prevent the successful implementation of performance-based pay in status-centered cultures. Performance-based pay may be resented in such cultures not because it does not improve organizational productivity but because it disrupts the social order of status and reward.

When going overseas, companies have to contend with the differences not only in the principles or rationales that employees endorse but also in the concrete beliefs that guide how employees construe behavior of management and of their peers (Morris, Leung, Ames, & Lickel, 1999). In joint ventures, the scope of distributive justice has to be broadened because of the salience of social comparison processes (Leung, Smith, Wang, & Sun, 1996). Leung, Smith, Wang, and Sun (1996) indicate that local staff may have three types of comparison including expatriate employees who work in the same company, local employees who work in state-owned enterprises, and local employees who work in other joint ventures. To this list, one may add a fourth one; local employees who work in "local" ventures (companies owned by local entrepreneurs). Local ventures and state-owned enterprises in developing and emerging countries may have fewer resources compared to multinationals. Therefore, the level of compensation may be lower in the former than in the latter.

Leung, Smith, Wang, and Sun (1996) also indicate that expatriate managers, as a rule enjoy much better pay and benefits than their local counterparts who hold similar positions. Host country managers may see such disparate treatment as unfair. In their study, Leung and colleagues found that Chinese employees tended to compare themselves to other local employees as well as to expatriates. They also found that procedural justice and performance-based distributive justice were related to job satisfaction but interactional justice was not. When respondents compared themselves to other local employees, they reported a high level of satisfaction than when they compared themselves to expatriates. In addition, senior managers and supervisors reported a low level of procedural and interactional justice and regarded their pay as less fair when they compared themselves to local counterparts in state-owned enterprises. Perhaps, these reduced perceptions of justice may be related to the comparison other than to their actual outcomes and processes. Chinese managers working in international ventures, consider both locals and expatriates as comparison others. Because they received less pay compared to their expatriate counterparts, they may experience feelings of inequity. Moreover, they have the perception that their voices are not often heard. To the extent that critical decisions concerning the foreign ventures are often made by expatriates, local managers may experience reduced perceptions of procedural and interactional justice.

Managing Procedural Justice in Status-Centered Cultures

Culture affects the types of organizations that emerge in a country. Low power distance cultures may tend to have decentralized organizational structures, whereas high power distance cultures may tend to have centralized organizational structures. Although justice principles, perceptions, and actions may closely bound to the status, positional, and power systems of organizations, these factors have not often been included in research or theory in organizational justice (James, 1993). Kabanoff (1997) suggests that different types of organizations should be more or less prevalent in different national cultures. Using two of Hofstede's four cultural dimensions, Kabanoff (1997) developed four typologies: high power distance/high individualism, high power distance/low individualism, low power distance/high individualism, and low power distance/low individualism cultures. Examples of high power distance/high individualism cultures include Belgium, France, Italy, and Spain, whereas examples of high power distance/low individualism cultures include Brazil, Greece, Japan, Mexico, the Philippines, Singapore, and Thailand. Examples of low power distance/high individualism cultures include Australia, Canada, the Netherlands, the United Kingdom, and the United States.

These four types of culture lead to four types of organizations. High power distance/high individualism cultures lead to the emergence of elite organizations, whereas high power distance/low individualism cultures lead to the emergence of leadership organizations. Low power distance/high individualism cultures lead to the emergence of meritocratic organizations, whereas low power distance/low individualism cultures lead to the emergence of collegial organizations. Justice issues may vary in these different types of organizations. For example, employees in elite organizations may have less voice than their counterparts in collegial organizations. A particularly striking example relates to the characterization of French organizations. Hampden-Turner and Trompenaars (1993) and Toy (1995) described French organizations as elitist and French managers as minor deities. Specifically, Hampden-Turner and Trompenaars (1993) note that:

> For the French the very structure of the organization is a competitive weapon with a chain of command already in place. It remains for those to whom status has been attributed to act out its rationale in practice, for the engineer from the Haute Ecole Polytechnique to do the outstanding work for which he is qualified. The group's top leaders are propelled by the faith of their subordinates. *Le Chef, le Patron, le Seigneur, "Monsieur le Directeur,"* senior qualified engineers, often use *tu* instead of *vous* when talking down to a mere technician. This was, until recently, the habitual form of address for servants, a mixture of familiarity and subordination. "To be an engineer in France," explained a manager at Saint Gobain, "doesn't mean you can fix a machine. It implies something about outlook, about professional self-esteem and national pride." (pp. 360-361)

The implication for managers is how to structure their organizations when they move in different cultures and how to react to subordinates. Should organizations tailor their structures on the prevailing cultures or should they develop the same structure everywhere? Should managers provide employees the opportunity to voice their opinions even in cultures where employees do not expect voice? Although there are no easy answers to such questions, one may make some recommendations although with caution. To the extent that cultures may differ in their acceptance of voice and voice expectations, managers should adopt a contingency approach. Such an approach dictates that managers provide voice when the existing cultural values lead employees to expect voice. However, when employees do not expect voice, providing such an opportunity may be fruitless, even counterproductive. Such a contingency approach is particularly important because how organizations treat instances of injustice prompt employees to voice their opinions or remain silent (Pinder & Harlos, 2001).

Managing Interactional Justice in Status-Centered Cultures

Managing interactional justice in status-centered cultures may be different from managing intertactional justice in cultures that de-emphasize formal status. For example, asking employees for their input is welcome in low power distance cultures such as the United States. However, in high power distance cultures, employees may misinterpret such actions. They may lose respect for the manager and even consider that the manager is a slacker. Relations and harmony with fellow employees, including supervisors are important concerns in collectivist cultures. In collectivist cultures, relationships are assets. For instance, Chinese are very concerned about *guanxi*—that is interpersonal networks (Chen, Chen, & Xin, 2004). Thus, being part of an interpersonal context is an important aspect of managing employees in China. How then can managers help satisfy such a need?

In managing interactional justice across cultures, managers may well be advised to consider the prevailing values and traditions. In Asian cultures, face saving is particularly important. Thus, a decision should not lead an employee to lose face. In addition, the importance accorded to interactional justice in interactions with supervisors may vary across cultures. Leung, Smith, Wang, and Sun (1996) conducted a study that compared American and Chinese managers. They found that perceptions of interactional justice did not affect employee job satisfaction. The authors explained these findings by contending that because of the higher acceptance of hierarchy and authority figures in Chinese organizations, the level of interactional justice required by Chinese employees from their superiors might have been lower compared to their American counterparts. One may suspect that in low power distance cultures, employee expectations of interactional justice may be high, whereas in high power distance cultures, these expectations may be low. As members of a high status-centered culture, Chinese employees may have low expectations of interactional justice from their supervisors.

Employees may also have different interpretations of the fairness of human resource practices. In a field study, Leung and Kwong (2003) note that Chinese foreign partners often regard different human resource management practices as fair. The authors reviewed human resource functions in international ventures in China including recruitment, compensation, performance appraisal, training and development, and exit. They found that Chinese and the foreign partners often diverge on what constitutes legitimate justice rule and criteria. For Chinese, need and equity rules were often used together in making hiring decisions. However, the foreign partner was primarily concerned with the profitability of the international venture.

Scheer, Kumar, and Steenkamp (2003) applied equity theory to interorganizational relationships within American and Dutch companies. The study was conducted on a sample of 417 U.S. dealers and 289 Dutch dealers. In both countries, each dealer was asked to identify the automobile supplier whose product line accounted for the largest share of his or her firm's sales. This supplier was a manufacturer for U.S. dealers and an automobile importer for Dutch dealers. The authors found similarities as well as differences in American and Dutch dealers' reactions to inequity in their relationships with their automobile suppliers. Both positive inequity and negative inequity have detrimental effects on the reactions of Dutch firms. When undercompensated, Dutch dealers experienced hostility, and when overcompensated, they experienced guilt. However, U.S. dealers did not react negatively to positive inequity; only negative inequity had deleterious effects on them. The authors explained these findings by contending that the American culture is more competitive, whereas the Dutch culture is more egalitarian.

MANAGING JUSTICE IN RISK-PRONE CULTURES

Managing Distributive Justice in Risk-Centered Cultures

In risk-prone cultures, risk-taking, personal initiatives, creativity and innovation should be rewarded because they are considered as valuable inputs. In risk-prone and self-centered cultures, such as the United States, employees are often rewarded for their initiatives and novel ideas. In some cultures, being creative is perceived as a valuable input that determines the employee's importance in the organization. However, in risk-averse cultures, such elements may not be seen as valuable inputs. Rather, the tendency to maintain the status quo and follow rules and formal policies may be perceived as legitimate inputs and thereby be rewarded. Deviation from traditions and habits may be seen as a way of breaking the status quo and may not be rewarded.

Managers should therefore adjust their reward systems to such cultural syndromes. Such strategies may not be without costs. What should a company that relies on innovation do when operating in a risk-averse culture? Should it provide incentives for creativity and innovation or should it reward the status quo? How can the company change employees' cultures to align it to its own strategies? Although there are certainly no easy answers to these questions, organizations may be well advised to encourage innovation by rewarding employees accordingly. The generation of novel ideas may be an integral part of a company's compensation structure. However, managers should adopt a gradual process by first training employees to accept the system. They may do so by explaining the importance of novel ideas and idea generation to the prosperity of the organization to employees. Later, they may explain the rationale of the link between compensation and the generation of novel ideas and risk-taking. Such a strategy may ease employee resistance to risk-taking and consider personal initiatives and innovation as legitimate inputs that should be rewarded.

Managing Procedural Justice in Risk-Prone Cultures

The management of procedural justice in risk-prone cultures may include the formulation of policies and rules that foster creativity and innovation. Such a work environment may include the opportunity to provide voice, explanations for decisions, and employee empowerment. In such cultures, rules should be flexible and managers should empower employees. The company's compensation system should consider these elements are compensable factors. In risk-prone cultures, creating an environment that rewards creativity and innovation may help enhance procedural justice. However, in risk-averse cultures, managers should gradually include these processes in the organizational environment as suggested in the previous section. Such an approach is particularly important because creativity and innovation are core elements of a company's survival. Thus, managers cannot afford to maintain the status quo because a given societal culture is perceived as risk-averse. Shane (1992) examined the per capita number of invention patents granted to nationals of 33 countries in 1967, 1971, 1976, and 1980 and compared it with the values of power distance and individualism. He found that individualistic and nonhierarchical societies are more inventive than other societies. These findings show that procedural justice may serve as an innovation-enhancing mechanism. By creating a procedurally fair environment where employees are provided voice opportunities, managers may lay the basic foundations for inventiveness.

Managing Interactional Justice in Risk-Prone Cultures

Treating employees with respect and dignity may foster creativity and innovation. Using the relational model of organizational justice, one may assess why this is so. Lind and Early (1992) suggest that social behavior is affected by two sets of psychological processes; self-oriented processes and group-oriented processes. Justice judgments influence the process that will prevail. People are more inclined to suspend attempts to protect their own interest and more likely to give themselves over to group concerns when a state of justice exists. Conversely, when things seem to be working in an unfair fashion, people will abandon the group's interest and attend to their own individual interest (Lind & Early, 1992). This is particularly true when people have to contribute their ideas for the betterment of the organization. Thus, fair treatment may represent a motivational drive in risk-prone cultures.

Despite the importance of managing justice across cultures, justice issues in multinational corporations may seem complex insofar that they may go beyond individual employees and incorporate the network level. In the following section, I discuss justice issues at the network level. Organizations are internally structured groups that are located in complex networks of intergroup relations characterized by power, status, and prestige differentials (Hogg & Terry, 2000). Ghoshal and Bartlett (1990) conceptualized the multinational corporation as a network of exchange relationship among different organizational units, including the headquarters and the different national subsidiaries that are collectively embedded in a structural context.

MANAGING JUSTICE AT THE NETWORK LEVEL

Kim and Mauborgne (1993a) consider multinationals as differentiated networks in which principles of procedural justice govern strategic relationships between head offices and subsidiaries, and the enforcement of those principles varies according to the nature of a subsidiary's business. In an era of globalization and offshoring, organizational justice may also concern the fairness of the relationship between headquarters and subsidiaries (e.g., Kim & Mauborgne, 1991, 1993a, 1993b, 1993c, 1993d, 1995, 1996) as well as the different ventures in which an organization is involved. Norms of fairness about the way power should be distributed play a key mediating role between international joint venture (IJV) control structure and inter-parent conflict (Barden, Steensma, & Lyles, 2005). Contribution to the joint venture is perceived as an input by both local and foreign parents. The more a parent company contributes to an international joint venture, the more it is willing to exercise control. Failure to grant such control may be perceived as unfair. Fairness may facilitate the management of interdependence in multinational corporations. The "us" versus "them" mentality may prevail between subsidiaries and headquarter offices. This mentality may exacerbate the in-group/out-group distinction thereby making issues of fairness and unfairness salient. Fairness acts as both a motivator and a self-control mechanism for subsidiary managers.

An effective task for the successful execution of global strategies is to foster a sense of community in the organization's global network of subsidiaries (Kim & Mauborgne, 1991). Kim and Mauborgne (1991) conducted an empirical study designed to analyze the impact of procedural justice on higher-order attitudes (commitment, trust, and social harmony) and lower-order attitudes (outcome satisfaction among members of global units). They identified five elements of procedural justice: (a) the extent to which bilateral communication exists between managers and head offices and subsidiary units involved in global strategic decision making; (b) the extent to which head offices do not discriminate but apply consistent decision making procedures across subsidiary units; (c) the extent to which subsidiary units can challenge and refute the strategic views of head office managers; (d) the extent to which subsidiary units are provided a full account for the final strategic decisions of the head office; and (e) the degree to which head office managers involved in strategic decision making are well informed and familiar with the local situations of subsidiary units.

Working on a sample of 142 subsidiary top managers, Kim and Mauborgne (1991) found that procedural justice judgments had positive and significant effects on the higher-order attitudes of organizational commitment, trust in head office management, and social harmony between head office and subsidiary top managers. Procedural justice judgments also had positive effects on the lower-order attitude of outcome satisfaction. These findings are important in light of global strategy execution. As Kim and Mauborgne (1991) suggest, organizational commitment is essential to inspire subsidiary top management to identify with the global objectives of the enterprise and to pursue them to the best of their ability; trust in head office management heightens the propensity of subsidiary top management to sacrifice subsystem for system and short-term for long-term priorities and considerations; social harmony serves to strengthen the social fabric and inspire ongoing exchange relations of the effective and efficient kind of head office and subsidiary top managers. (p. 138)

Kim and Mauborgne replicated these findings in subsequent studies. Kim and Mauborgne (1993a, 1993b) found that procedural justice positively influenced subsidiary top management compliance with global strategies enacted by head offices. To the extent that these subsidiary top managers comply with the firm's strategies, they are likely to implement them. Thus, procedural justice serves here as a motivator for subsidiary top managers. The exercise of procedural justice inspires managers to go beyond the call of duty and engage in innovative actions, spontaneous cooperation, and creative behavior on behalf of the organization in their execution of decisions (Kim & Mauborgne, 1996).

Kim and Mauborgne (1995) also found a positive correlation between procedural justice and the quality of strategic decisions. Specifically, they found that procedural justice affects a multinational's ability to achieve its strategic objectives. For head office executives, procedural justice provides a way for top management to expand their sphere of influence beyond the controlling power that rests on formal authority and sanctions (Kim & Mauborgne, 1996).

Managing Distributive Justice at the Network Level

How can distributive justice be operationalized at the network level? Several factors may be considered as outcomes when one analyzes the relationship among the different units of the network. In a fully owned subsidiary what may be perceived as outcomes? Outcomes may be operationalized in terms of profit and the extent to which those subsidiaries that generate profits receive some types of windfall or not. Generating profits may also be considered as an input. By making profits, the subsidiary brings a valuable input to the organization. Outcomes may also include power and prestige enjoyed within the network. To the extent that a subsidiary generates profits, it may consider enjoying some type of prestige as a legitimate outcome. Managers should therefore assess what constitutes legitimate inputs from subsidiaries and how these subsidiaries would be rewarded.

This analysis may be extended to international joint ventures. When international joint ventures are formed, participating companies may seek to control the new venture. The reasons underlying such strategies may include participating companies' respective contributions. The more a participating company contributes to the establishment of a joint venture, the more control of the venture it may seek. Another factor that may increase a participating company's likelihood to control a new venture is related to the resources needed by the venture. Using resource dependency theory (e.g., Pfeffer & Salancik, 1978), one may speculate that a participating company would have more control over a joint venture when this joint venture depends on the participating company for critical resources. To the extent that the participating company controls the critical resources, it will control the joint venture. However, when a partner controls the critical resources needed by a joint venture but is denied the control of the joint venture, issues of unfair treatment may arise. Luo (2005) studied the impact of shared procedural justice on alliance performance on a sample of 124 cross-cultural alliances in China. He found that alliance profitability was higher when both parties perceived high rather than low procedural justice. Profitability was also higher when both parties' perceptions were higher than when one party perceived high procedural justice but the other perceived low procedural justice. These findings showed that procedural justice consensus was a facilitator of cross-cultural alliances.

Issues of fairness in the network may also expand beyond control and reputation. Whenever an organization is part of a network, it should be concerned about how each member of the network upholds standards of fairness and ethics. Suppose that a company uses a subcontractor to manufacture some of its components. Should this company be concerned by the actions of the subcontractor, especially when these actions raise issues of fairness and ethics? One consideration may be for the company to develop a code of conduct that may serve as guidelines. For instance, when a subcontractor uses child labor, should the company remain silent, express indignation, or break up the relationship? To avoid such ethical and fairness dilemma, organizations should develop acceptable ethical and fairness standards applicable to all network units, with the understanding that a violation of these standards would not be tolerated.

Managing Procedural Justice at the Network Level

Taggart (1997) analyzed the effect of subsidiary autonomy on procedural justice. Autonomy was defined as a decision process that evolves through bargaining between center and periphery in an organization. The author developed a combination based on two variables, autonomy and procedural justice. He hypothesized that the ideal combination is high procedural justice and high autonomy, characterized by excellent relations between headquarters and a highly proactive affiliate. Procedural justice is important in managing an intranetwork organization because it enhances network harmony (e.g., Kim & Mauborgne, 1988, 1991). Network harmony creates the right atmosphere of unity and cooperation between subsidiaries and headquarters (Kim & Mauborgne, 1988). Procedural justice enhances compliance of subsidiary managers with corporate strategic decisions, both directly and indirectly (Kim & Mauborgne, 1993a); and the exercise of procedural justice by corporate managers improves both the formulation and implementation of strategy (Kim & Mauborgne, 1993b).

Managing Interactional Justice at the Network Level

The management of interactional justice at the network level will focus more on how heads and executives of the affiliates are treated by headquarters. Are these managers treated with respect and dignity? Are they considered as part of the organization or as "remote others" whose decisions carry less weight? To this date, few empirical studies in organizational justice have addressed these questions. Even Kim and Mauborgne's studies did not specifically address the interpersonal treatment of subsidiary managers by head office executives. In the absence of empirical data, one may conjure that subsidiary managers are sensitive to both informational justice and interpersonal treatment from head office executives. Informational justice may occur when subsidiary managers are provided adequate information and explanations for decisions regarding not only their units by also the global corporation and the place of their units in it. It may also occur when subsidiary managers are provided voice opportunities. When these managers believe that headquarters listen to them and consider their views, such fair treatment may have two positive consequences. First, it may signal subsidiary managers that they are an integral part of the organizational network. Second, it may convey the message that these managers are not forgotten and their decisions carry some weight in the eyes of head office executives. Organizations should also effectively manage expatriates when they are on assignments and when they return home.

DEVELOPING TRANSCULTURAL JUSTICE COMPETENCE

The previous sections have suggested ways in which managers can develop transcultural competence in organizational justice. Managers should understand that as their organizations become global networks, issues of justice and fairness take paramount importance. Thus, managers should be successful not only in international contexts but also in managing a diverse workforce. Globalization enhances geographic mobility. Even though organizations may not move overseas, they may be confronted with multiculturalism insofar that they may have a workforce characterized by different cultural backgrounds and social diversity. It is now common in the United States that organizations employ people from various cultural, racial, ethnic, and national backgrounds. Thus, transcultural competence may help managers ensure fairness at two levels, domestic and global. However, the fact that some research findings point to similarities across cultures calls for exercising caution and avoiding an overemphasis on cultural differences. Thus, managers should design and implement organizational justice policies and practices that promote fairness as a basic requirement for the effective functioning of organizations and the personal satisfaction of the individuals they employ. In this section, I propose a model that may help managers develop transcultural organizational competence (see Figure 6.1).

The successful implementation of justice requires the existence of a fit between managers' justice practices and the values of the existing local culture. The construct of justice fit describes the existence of a match between justice practices and cultural values. There is a fit when justice practices of the organization match the existing culture. A fit will result in positive outcomes, whereas a lack of fit will lead to perceptions of unfairness. When a fit exists, managers would have demonstrated transcultural justice competence. However, when managers fail to apply justice practices appropriate to a given culture, they would have demonstrated transcultural justice incompetence. One of the implications of this concept is that managers should be trained to develop transcultural competence in applying justice principles. Because justice practices that are effective in one culture may be ineffective in another culture, managers should adopt a contingency approach when managing justice issues across cultures. There is no best way to manage justice issues across cultures. Managing justice across cultures depends on at least two variables: (a) the specific cultural syndromes of the country and (b) the fit between justice practices and these cultural syndromes.

To develop transcultural justice competence, managers may also use the cultural maps developed by Hofstede (1980, 1991), Schwartz (1994), Trompenaars (1993), Trompenaars and Hampden-Turner (1998), Fiske

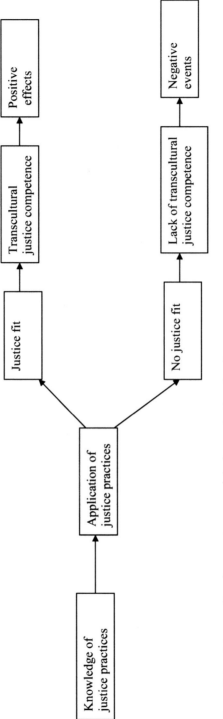

Figure 6.1. A transcultural competence model of organizational culture.

(1992) to determine the cultural distance between countries. Cultural distance measures the extent to which different cultures are similar or different (Shenkar, 2001). Such a measure may help managers adapt their justice practices to specific cultures. Particularly, it may help develop clusters of cultural justice behaviors. For instance, the Anglo cluster including Australia, Canada, New Zealand, the United Kingdom, and the United States may be different from the a Latin cluster comprising France, Italy, Portugal and Spain.

Using such clusters, managers may develop justice practices that may be appropriate for each cluster. However, within each cluster, variations may occur that may call for realignment to specific countries. Even within the same country, there are cultural variations that may require adaptation to specific social groups. Understanding employee reactions to justice is important because as Kim and Mauborgne (1997, p. 66) put it "Fair process profoundly influences attitudes and behaviors critical to high performance. It builds trust and unlocks ideas. With it, managers can achieve even the most painful and difficult goals while gaining the voluntary cooperation of the employees affected" (p. 66).

CONCLUSION

I have devoted this book to the study of cross-cultural factors that shape judgments of fairness as well as reactions to situations of fairness and unfairness. Despite the existence of cultural differences, some findings support the view that the cultural boundedness of Western-inspired managerial practices (at least when it comes to organizational justice) should not be overstated (Lam, Schaubroeck, & Aryee, 2002). Therefore, we must acknowledge that the purpose of conducting cross-cultural studies is not merely to demonstrate cultural variations in human behavior, but also to build better universal laws so that we can generalize from culture to culture (Kurosawa, 1992). Therefore, in this conclusion, I call for the development of a new subfield of organizational justice—comparative organizational justice.

I define comparative organizational justice as the study of employee perceptions of fairness between nations and societies. By studying comparative justice, scholars would not only be concerned about differences but also about similarities across cultures. However, comparative organizational justice is not limited to the study of the impact of culture on organizational justice. National culture represents only a part, albeit an important part, of the national-level context of work (Parboteeah & Cullen, 2003). Thus, comparative organizational justice goes beyond cross-cultural comparisons and addresses such issues as the impact of societal transformations and economic development on organizational justice. In the following sections, I discuss four topics that may be covered

A Cultural Perspective of Organizational Justice, 151–158

under the study of comparative organizational justice: (1) the nature of procedural justice, (2) the construct of cosmic justice, (3) the impact of social changes, and (4) the role of economic development.

THE NATURE OF PROCEDURAL JUSTICE ACROSS CULTURES

Berg and Mussen (1975) recognize that the meaning of justice varies not only among individuals but also among cultures, civilizations, and historical eras. For example, in the United States and other industrialized countries, procedures may be of a formal nature, written, documented, and communicated to employees. In other cultures, however, these procedures may be unwritten and often based on informal encounters. Thus, when employees in the United States assess the fairness of procedures in their organizations, they are referring to formal procedures. However, in other countries, when employees assess the fairness of organizational procedures, they are probably referring to formal as well as informal procedures. It is therefore important to consider the extent to which the nature of procedural justice may be different across cultures.

The distinction between formal and informal procedures has recently been acknowledged by Blader and Tyler (2003a). These authors refer to formal and informal sources of procedural justice. Formal sources refer to the formal and official rules and procedures, whereas informal sources refer to the experiences people have of their specific group authorities who manage their work lives. This distinction tends to lead to the distinction between procedural justice and interactional justice. Procedural justice refers to the fairness of formal procedures as they are spelled out in written documents and interactional justice refers to the fairness of social interactions during the enactment of those procedures. However, in this section, the distinction made deals with written, codified procedures versus unwritten, informal procedures. Lind, Tyler, and Huo's (1997) contention that procedural justice is defined much the same way across different cultural contexts may not always hold true.

One may also explore cultural differences in two areas; (a) shock in response to perceived injustice and (b) ways of dealing with the shock. In Eastern cultures, face saving is very important. Thus, exploring the impact of face saving on voice may lead to a better understanding of the voice effect in such cultures. James (1993) suggests that being accustomed to greater power distance may limit employee expectations about fairness and reactions to injustices. In high power distance cultures, for example, employees may not expect voice. Organizational justice scholars may also address the effect of culture on third party reactions to injustice. Third party reactions to injustice may be an important area of concern particularly in relation-centered cultures. To the extent that social identity issues may be salient in collectivist cultures where the in-group/out-group distinction is prevalent, injustice to an in-group member may be perceived as injustice to oneself and may therefore elicit strong emotional reactions. The extent to which this is so needs empirical investigations. Some cultures may also rely on supernatural beings to dispense justice.

EXPLORING THE CONSTRUCT OF COSMIC JUSTICE

In some cultures, people may rely on other agents of justice, such as God, spirits or ancestors to dispense justice. It is not uncommon that people in some cultures use these "justice agents" to explain their fortune or misfortune in organizations. Although this idea of cosmic justice has never been explored in organizational justice, it remains intuitively appealing. Cosmic justice may influence the sense of accountability when injustice occurs. People who believe that their misfortune is due to other supernatural forces may be less likely to blame the perpetrator of an injustice. Instead, they may conclude that the person's plight was preordained in some cosmic order. For instance, Muslims often think that the world is preordained and what happens to people on earth is already written in advance. Thus, when a person experiences a severe injustice, such as being laid off, the victim or observers may explain his or her fate by relying on divine predictions.

The construct of cosmic justice may find some support in Fiske's element of Communal Sharing. Fiske (1992) suggests two ways for people in Communal Sharing relationships to explain misfortune. First, people search for a transgression when they suffer a misfortune. People also treat a victim of misfortune as contaminating and contagious, as if the victim had committed some polluting violation that tainted the Communal Sharing relationship. This is illustrated by the story of Job in the Old Testament of the Christian Bible. Second, this may tend to entertain the possibility that any member of the group is suffering because of the transgressions of any other member. Applied to organizational justice, this attitude may help define injustice in terms of the consequence of a transgression rather than the act of another person that can easily be identified and confronted. When people hold such beliefs, an unfair treatment may well be seen as the direct consequence of a transgression. Thus, one suffers injustice because a type of relationship has been broken. In this regard, the immediate offender may not be perceived as the "real" actor of the injustice.

Because religious practices and beliefs define the ultimate purposes of human life, they may be important in assessing what is fair or unfair and how to react to unfairness. Thus, religious beliefs may influence justice judgments (Finkel, Crystal, & Watanabe, 2001). Comparing the United States and Japan, Finkel, Crystal, and Watanabe (2001) speculate that religious and philosophical differences between Japanese and American cultures—around God and nature, and human relationships to God and nature suggest that unfairness disparities may arise with regard to uncontrollable events. The religious underpinnings of Japanese culture derived from Buddhist and Confucian teachings that encourage acceptance of life's vicissitudes in contrary to the Judeo-Christian tradition, in which humankind's actions can directly evoke benevolence or wrath of God. These differences may influence how people react to misfortune in both cultures. These authors noted that Americans designated misfortune cases as unfair far more often than Japanese. Although the sense of unfairness was strong in both cultures, what was emphasized bore a local connotation.

SOCIAL CHANGES AND ORGANIZATIONAL JUSTICE

No culture is immune to change. As social changes may affect organizations, organizations in return may drive social changes. Organizations are important collective actors in the transition, maintenance, and change of cultural values within virtually all contemporary societies (Kabanoff, 1997). Social norms change overtime and moral standards change when we move across people and overtime (Cropanzano, Chrobot-Mason, Rupp, & Prehar, 2004). Change may influence justice expectations and preferences. He, Chen, and Zhang (2004) found that in China, employees of enterprises that experienced a greater degree of ownership reform expressed stronger preferences for differential allocation rules but weaker preferences for equality rules. As cultures change, so might the psychological dimensions that they affect. Younger participants may not identify with traditional cultural beliefs and values, and therefore may not exhibit the psychological tendencies shown by older participants (Brockner, 2003). Although cultures change and do not remain always static, few studies have investigated the impact of cultural change on organizational justice.

We know that ascribed status is often common in collectivist cultures. However, as these cultures become democratic and adopt free-market principles, people may acquire high status through professional skills and business acumen, thus embracing the concept of achieved status. People no longer have to rely on their birthright to acquire ascribed status. Giacobbe-Miller, Miller, Zhang, and Victorov (2003) conducted a comparative study including samples of American, Chinese, and Russian managers.

Their findings showed that U.S. managers allocated the most and Chinese managers allocated the least for productivity, whereas Chinese managers allocated significantly more to equality than U.S. managers. Exposure to Western business and employment practices tends to lead to a convergence of work related values and expectations across cultures (e.g., Ralston, Gustafson, Cheung, & Terpstra, 1993). Forces of technological and organizational rationality drive enterprises toward common operational systems at the macro and microlevels (Child, 1981).

In a previous study, Chen (1995) found that Chinese employees were economically oriented and preferred to invoke differential rules for the allocation of both material and socioemotional rewards, whereas their American counterparts were humanistically oriented and preferred performance rules for the allocation of material rewards but equality rules for socioemotional rewards. The author explained these findings by invoking changes occurring in the two cultures. Chen (1995) concluded that the Chinese's preferences were consistent with efforts to encourage individual responsibility and to link rewards to performance, whereas the Americans' preferences for equality went well with recent emphasis on team-based reorganization in American businesses. This conclusion is in line with the contention that social changes may influence justice judgments.

Meindl, Cheng, and Jun (1990) suggest that as nations advance and converge in terms of technological advances and economic development, their organizations and management practices may become similar. Such convergence may perhaps explain the similarities among cultures. Meindl, Cheng, and Jun (1990) conducted an empirical study comparing American and Chinese managers' allocation patterns. They found that the definitions of fairness and the preferences for highly differentiated and equity-based allocation schemes among Chinese managers were similar to those of their American counterparts. Specifically, both groups displayed allocations that reflected highly differentiated patterns consistent with the equity logic when productivity was emphasized and interdependence among recipients was low. However, Russian managers were significantly different from Chinese managers (in terms of collectivistic orientation) but they were not different from U.S. managers in their distribution for either equality or productivity. The authors concluded that distributive justice values convergence has occurred among the Russian managers. Thus, the convergence hypothesis may help shed light on the impact of societal change on organizational justice. As change spreads across the globe will employees tend to develop similar norms related to workplace fairness? Although few empirical studies have tested the hypothesis, it is important for organizational justice scholars to assess the extent to which social changes influence perceptions of organizational justice (Beugré, 2002).

ECONOMIC DEVELOPMENT AND ORGANIZATIONAL JUSTICE

Comparing economic systems is an effective way of studying the impact of culture on organizational justice because economic systems affect every aspect of life (e.g., Fiske, 2002). The level of economic development of a country may influence judgments of fairness. In wealthier countries, employees may expect higher salaries and benefits whereas in poorer countries where jobs are scarce, employees may be satisfied with the minimum. As the level of economic development rises, employees' expectations may rise. Thus, justice expectations may rise as a country becomes wealthy. A fundamental assumption in the organizational justice literature is that outcomes are judged unfair when they are lower than they should be compared to some standards (e.g., Adams, 1965; Deutsch, 1985; Folger & Cropanzano, 1998; Homans, 1961). What happens when these standards are relatively low? How can justice be explained in a culture of scarcity as compared to a culture of abundance?

As the world's wealthiest nation, the United States is considered as a culture of abundance, whereas most African countries are characterized as cultures of scarcity. Which allocation rules would prevail in the former compared to the latter? Perhaps, the equity rule may considered as fair in the former, whereas the need rule may be considered fair in the latter. The lack of basic opportunities in cultures of scarcity may lead people to tolerate injustices and hold low standards of fairness. Because job opportunities are scarce in such cultures, people may think that having a job is better than nothing at all and therefore tolerate workplace injustices. In such cultures of scarcity, people may live by diminished expectations. However, as some of these countries prosper, expectations may rise and preferences for allocation rules may change. Perhaps, economic progress may change cultural values and subsequently alter justice judgments.

Level of economic development may influence the degree of distributive fairness and the preference for allocation rules. In wealthy countries, employees may receive better compensation than in poor countries. In such countries, concerns for economic productivity would influence distribution rules in the workplace. Managers may use the equity rule to foster economic productivity. Thus, employees may tend to consider the equity rule as the fairest rule for outcome distribution. Economic development may also influence procedural justice insofar that as societies focus on economic productivity, the development and implementation of formal rules become essential ingredients for maintaining an acceptable level of economic productivity. Economic development also implies high levels of formal education. As employees become well educated, they will expect more not only in terms of economic compensation but also in their desire to influence decisions concerning their daily work activities. Thus, the preference for voice may be higher in developed countries than in less developed countries. Level of economic development may also influence interactional justice. Because job opportunities are scarce in poor countries, employees may be less likely to react overtly to unfair interpersonal treatment for fear of losing their jobs.

Economic development undoubtedly leads to the emergence of social disparities, creating groups of *haves* and *have nots*. It is possible that justice issues may be influenced by people's social status in a particular society. Kluegel, Mason, and Wegener (1995) found that in most countries, it was the disadvantaged that favored equality, while those at the top of the income ladder support equity principles typically based on merit. Those who hold higher social status (wealth, education, power) may have different views concerning the distribution of outcomes. Sabbagh (2003) found that in Israel, in most cases, differentiation is favored more strongly by advantaged respondents than by disadvantaged ones. Extrapolating these findings, one may speculate that as countries move toward free market economies, employees may tend to favor equity as the preferred rule of outcome distribution.

Although research on the link between economic development and organizational justice is nonexistent or scarce at best, previous studies comparing different cultures may help shed light on the relationship between the two concepts. In discussing the applicability of American management theories to China, Shenkar and Von Glinow (1994) suggested that equity theory (e.g., Adams, 1965) was applicable to China albeit with some adjustments. With the implementation of economic reforms in China, the authors argued, there was the existence of comparison others, thus rendering applicable equity theory. For instance, the existence of comparison others may create a sense of relative deprivation for some employees, what was called "the red eye disease" (Shenkar and Von Glinow, 1994).

As these findings illustrate, justice perceptions are dynamic and can change rapidly in a fast-moving economy (Leung & Kwong, 2003). This assumption is illustrated by the findings of two studies (e.g., Leung, Smith, Wang, and Sun, 1996; Leung, Wang, and Smith, 2001). Leung, Smith, Wang, and Sun (1996) conducted a survey on Chinese local employees working in international joint ventures. They found that these employees did not use the expatriates as comparison others and were satisfied with their pay even though it was much lower than that of expatriates. Five years later, Leung, Wang, and Smith (2001) replicated the survey on a similar sample. Surprisingly, they found that respondents not only used expatriates as comparison others but they were considering their pay as unfair. In an empirical study testing the influence of culture on preferences for allocation rules, Murphy-Berman, Berman, Singh,

Packauri, and Kumar (1984) and Berman, Murphy-Berman, and Singh (1985) found that Indians prefer the need norm compared to their American counterparts. Although Leung (1988) explained these findings by arguing that resources were scarce in India, such an explanation may not hold today, because of the offshoring boom in India that may increase the standard of living there. Perhaps, replicating these studies in today' economic context in India may yield different results.

Despite these promising areas of research, the subfield of comparative organizational justice cannot prosper without sound research methodologies. For instance, most cross-cultural studies have used instruments developed in one culture to study the same phenomenon in other countries. Such an approach presents several caveats. First, it is not evident that the instrument captures the same phenomenon in the country of application. As an example in point, using an instrument developed in the United States to study procedural justice may miss to identify the very nature of procedural justice in the Chinese society. As acknowledged by Morris and Leung (2000), justice theories developed and confirmed in the United States should not be automatically assumed to be valid in different cultures. Perhaps, one way to overcome this caveat is to develop instruments that capture the true reality of the concept in the country where the study is being conducted. This approach also raises another issue. How can we compare the phenomenon of study when different measures are used?

Although there is no easy answer to this question, scholars may at least express the view that the phenomenon exists in both cultures but is expressed differently. Second, errors in translation and back translation of research instruments may bias comparative studies. Although such errors are reduced in most studies, these approaches do not always yield the expected results. Despite careful translations, survey questions may be subject to misinterpretation and biases (Barden, Steensma, and Lyles, 2005). Third, most comparative studies used student samples. Although studies using student samples are methodologically sound, their results cannot always be generalized to nonstudent samples. With sound research methodologies, the subfield of comparative organizational justice may spur research that is not limited to cross-cultural analyzes but encompasses the effects of societal transformations sweeping our world on employee perceptions of fairness. It is my hope that this book will stimulate organizational justice scholars to focus their effort on comparative organizational justice. When this happens, the present book would have accomplished its objective.

ABOUT THE AUTHOR

Dr. Constant D. Beugré (PhD, Rensselaer Polytechnic Institute) is an associate professor of management at Delaware State University, School of Management where he teaches courses in organizational behavior, human resources management at the undergraduate level, and organizational leadership at the graduate level. Prior to joining Delaware State University, Dr. Beugré was an assistant professor of management and information systems at Kent State University, Tuscarawas Campus. Dr. Beugré has been a visiting fellow at Harvard University in 1996. His research interests include organizational justice and offshoring. Dr. Beugré has published three books including the present one and more than 30 referred journal articles.

REFERENCES

Adams, J. S. (1963). Toward an understanding of inequity. *Journal of Abnormal Social Psychology, 67,* 421-436.

Adams, S. J. (1965). Inequity in social exchange. In L. Berkowitz (Ed.), *Advances in social experimental psychology* (Vol. 2, pp. 267-299). New York: Academic Press.

Adler, N. J. (1983). Cross-cultural management research: The ostrich and the trend. *Academy of Management Review, 8,* 226-232.

Akasu, K., & Asao, K. (1993). Sociolinguistic factors influencing communication in Japan and the United States. In W. B. Gudykunst (Ed.), *Communication in Japan and the United States* (pp. 88-121). Albany: State University of New York Press.

Alexander, R. (2004). The role of whistleblowers in the fight against economic crime. *Journal of Financial Crime, 12*(2), 131-137.

Alexander, S., & Ruderman, M. (1987). The role of procedural and distributive justice in organizational justice. *Social Justice Research, 1,* 177-198.

Ambrose, M. L. (2002). Contemporary justice research: A new look at familiar questions. *Organizational Behavior and Human Decision Processes, 89,* 803-812.

Ambrose, M. L., & Arnaud, A. (2005). Are procedural justice and distributive justice conceptually distinct? In In J. Gerald & J. A. Colquitt (Eds.), *Handbook of organizational justice* (pp. 59-84). Mahwah, NJ: Erlbaum.

Ambrose, M. L., & Kulik, C. T. (2001). How do I know that's fair? A categorization approach of fairness judgments. In S. Gilliland, D. Steiner, & D. Skarlicki (Eds.), *Theoretical and cultural perspectives on organizational justice* (pp. 35-61). Greenwich, CT: Information Age Publishing.

Ambrose, M. L., Seabright, M. A., & Schminke, M. (2002). Sabotage in the workplace: The role of organizational injustice. *Organizational Behavior and Human Decision Processes, 89,* 947-965.

Babcok, L., Lowenstein, G., Issacharoff, S., & Camerer, C. (1995). Biased judgments of fairness in bargaining. *American Economic Review, 5*(5), 1337-1343.

Bandura, A. (1982). Self-efficacy mechanism in human agency. *American Psychologist, 37*, 122-147.

Bandura, A. (1986). *Social foundations of thought and action. A social cognitive theory.* Englewood Cliffs, NJ: Prentice-Hall.

Barclay, L., Skarlicki, D. P., & Pugh, S. D. (2005). Exploring the role of emotions in injustice perceptions and retaliation. *Journal of Applied Psychology, 90*, 629-643.

Barden, J. Q., Steensma, H. K., & Lyles, M. A. (2005). The influence of parent control structure on parent conflict in Vietnamese international joint ventures: An organizational justice-based contingency approach. *Journal of International Business Studies, 36*, 156-174.

Barling, J., & Phillips, M. (1993). Interactional, formal, and distributive justice in the workplace: An exploratory study. *Journal of Psychology, 127*, 649-656.

Baron, R. A., Neuman, J. H., & Geddes, D. (1999). Social and personal determinants of workplace aggression: Evidence for the impact of perceived injustice and the Type A behavior pattern. *Aggressive Behavior, 25*, 281-296.

Barrett-Howard, E., & Lamm, H. (1986). Procedural and distributive justice: Definitions and beliefs of West German university students. *Law & Society Review, 39*, 875-892.

Baumeister, R. F., & Leary, M. R. (1995). The need to belong: Desire for interpersonal attachments as a fundamental human motivation. *Psychological Bulletin, 117*, 497-529.

Bazerman, M. H. (1993). Fairness, social comparison, and irrationality. In J. K. Murnighan (Ed.), *Social psychology in organizations: Advances in theory and research* (pp. 184-203). Englewood Cliffs, NJ: Prentice Hall.

Berg, N. E., & Mussen, P. (1975). The origins and development of concepts of justice. *Journal of Social Sciences, 31*(3), 183-201.

Berger, C. R. (1979). Beyond initial understanding: Uncertainty, understanding, and the development of interpersonal relationships. In H. Giles & R. N. St. Clair (Eds.), *Language and social psychology* (pp. 122-144). Oxford: Blackwell.

Berger, C. R., & Bradac, J. J. (1982). *Language and social knowledge: Uncertainty in interpersonal relations.* London: Arnold.

Berger, C. R., & Calabrese, R. J. (1975). Some explorations in initial interaction and beyond: Toward a developmental theory of interpersonal communication. *Human Communication Theory, 1*, 99-112.

Berger, C. R., & Gundykunst, W. B. (1991). Uncertainty and communication. In B. Dervin & M. Voight (Eds.), *Progress in communication sciences* (pp. 20-45). Norwood, NJ: Ablex.

Berman, J. J., Murphy-Berman, V., & Singh, P. (1985). Cross-cultural similarities and differences in perceptions of fairness. *Journal of Cross-Cultural Psychology, 16*, 55-67.

Beugré, C. D. (1998a). *Managing fairness in organizations.* Englewoods, CT: Quorum Books.

Beugré, C. D. (1998b). *La motivation au travail des cadres africains* [Work motivation of African managers']. Paris: Les Editions L'Harmathan.

Beugré, C. D. (1998c). Understanding organizational insider-perpetrated workplace aggression: An integrated model. *Research in the Sociology of Organizations, 15,* 163-196.

Beugré, C. D. (2002). Understanding organizational justice and its impact on employees: An African perspective. *International Journal of Human Resource Management, 13*(7), 1-14.

Beugré, C. D. (2005a). Understanding injustice-related aggression in organizations: A cognitive model. *International Journal of Human Resources Management, 1*(7), 1120-1136.

Beugré, C. D. (2005b). Reacting aggressively to injustice at work: A cognitive stage model. *Journal of Business and Psychology, 20*(2), 291-301.

Beugré, C. D., & Baron, R. A. (2001). Perceptions of systemic justice: The effects of distributive, procedural, and interactional justice. *Journal of Applied Social Psychology, 31,* 324-339.

Bierbrauer, G. (1990). Toward an understanding of legal culture: Variations in individualism and collectivism between Kurds, Lebanese, and Germans. *Law and Society Review, 28,* 243-264.

Bies, R. J. (1987). The predicament of injustice: The management of moral outrage. In L. L. Cummings & B. M. Staw (Eds.), *Research in Organizational Behavior* (pp. 289-319). Greenwich, CT: JAI Press.

Bies, R. J. (2001). Interactional (in)justice: The scared and the profane. In J. Greenberg & R. Cropanzano (Eds.), *Advances in organizational justice* (pp. 89-118). Palo Alto, CA: Stanford University Press.

Bies, R. J. (2005). Are procedural justice and interactional justice conceptually distinct? In J. Gerald & J. A. Colquitt (Eds.), *Handbook of organizational justice* (pp. 85-112). Mahwah, NJ: Erlbaum.

Bies, R. J., & Greenberg, J. (2002). Justice, culture, and corporate image: The swoosh, the sweatshops, and the sway of public opinion. In M. J. Gannon & K. L. Newman (Eds.), *The Blackwell handbook of cross-cultural management* (pp. 320-334). Oxford, England. Blackwell.

Bies, R. J., & Moag, J. S. (1986). Interactional justice: Communication criteria of fairness. In R. J. Lewicki, B. H. Sheppard, & M. H. Bazerman (Eds.), *Research on negotiation in organizations* (Vol. 1, pp. 43-55). Greenwich, CT: JAI Press.

Bies, R. J., & Shapiro, D. L. (1987). Interactional fairness judgments: The influence of causal accounts. *Social Justice Research, 1,* 199-218.

Bies, R. J., & Shapiro, D. L. (1988). Voice and justification: Their influence on procedural fairness judgments. *Academy of Management Journal, 31,* 676-685.

Bies, R. J., Shapiro, D. L., & Cummings, L. L. (1988). Causal accounts and managing organizational conflict: It is not enough to say it's not my fault. *Communication Research, 15,* 381-399.

Bies, R. J., & Tripp, M. T. (1995). The use and abuse of power: Justice as social control. In R. Cropanzano & K. M. Kamar (Eds.), *Organizational politics, justice, and support* (pp. 131-145). Westport, CT: Quorum Books.

Bies, R. J., & Tripp, T. M. (1996). Beyond distrust: Getting even and the need for revenge. In R. M. Kramer & T. Tyler (Eds.), *Trust and organizations* (pp. 246-260). Thousand Oaks, CA: Sage.

Bies, R. J., & Tripp, T. M. (2001a). Hot flashes, open wounds: Injustice and the tyranny of its emotions. In S. W. Gilliland, D. D. Steiner, & D. P. Skalicki (Eds.), *Emerging perspectives on managing organizational justice* (pp. 203-221). Greenwich, CT: Information Age Publishing.

Bies, R. J., & Tripp, T. M. (2001b). A passion for justice: The rationality and morality of revenge. In R. Cropanzano (Ed.), *Justice in the workplace: From theory to practice* (Vol. 2, pp. 197-208). Mahwah, NJ: Erlbaum.

Black, J. S., & Gregersen, H. B. (1999). The right way to manage expats. *Harvard Business Review, 77*(2), 52-60.

Blader, S. L., Chang, C. C., & Tyler, T. R. (2001). Procedural justice and retaliation in organizations: Comparing cross-nationally the importance of fair group processes. *The International Journal of Conflict Management, 12*(4), 295-311.

Blader, S. L., & Tyler, T. R. (2003a). What constitutes fairness in work settings? A four- component model of procedural justice. *Human Resource Management Review, 13*, 107-126.

Blader, S. L., & Tyler, T. R. (2003b). A four-component model of procedural justice: Defining the meaning of a fair process. *Personality & Social Psychology Bulletin, 29*, 747-758.

Blader, S. L., & Tyler, T. R. (2005). How can theories of organizational justice explain the effects of fairness? In J. Gerald & J. A. Colquitt (Eds.), *Handbook of organizational justice* (pp. 229-354). Mahwah, NJ: Erlbaum.

Blau, P. M. (1964). *Exchange and power in social life*. New York: Wiley.

Blodgett, J. G., Hill, D. J., & Tax, S. S. (1997). The effects of distributive, procedural, and interactional justice on postcomplaint behavior. *Journal of Retailing, 73*, 185-210.

Bobocel, D. R., & Holmvall, C. M. (2001). Are interactional justice and procedural justice different? Framing the debate. In S. Gilliland, D. Steiner, & D. Skarlicki (Eds.), *Theoretical and cultural perspectives on organizational justice* (pp. 85-108). Greenwich, CT: Information Age Publishing.

Boeckman, R. J., & Tyler, T. R. (1997). Commensense justice and inclusion within the moral community: When do people receive procedural protections from others? *Psychology, Public Policy, and Law, 3*, 362-380.

Boer, E. M., Bakker, A. B., Syroit, J. E., & Schaufeli, W. B. (2002). Unfairness work as a predictor of absenteeism. *Journal of Organizational Behavior, 23*, 181-197.

Bond, M. H., Leung, K., & Schwartz, S. (1992). Explaining choices in procedural and distributive justice across cultures. *International Journal of Psychology, 27*(2),211-225.

Bond, M. H., Leung, K., & Wan, K. C. (1982). How does cultural collectivism operate? The impact of task and maintenance contribution on reward distribution. *Journal of Cross-Cultural Psychology, 13*,186-200.

Bond, M. H., Wan, K. C., Leung, K., & Giacalone, R. (1985). How are responses to verbal insult to cultural collectivism and power distance. *Journal of Cross-Cultural Psychology, 16*, 111-127.

Brockner, J. (2002). Making sense of procedural fairness: How high procedural fairness can reduce or heighten the influence of outcome favorability, *Academy of Management Review, 27*, 58-76.

Brockner, J. (2003). Unpacking country effects: On the need to operationalize the psychological determinants of cross-national differences. *Research in Organizational Behavior, 25,* 333-367.

Brockner, J. (2006, March). Why it is so hard to be fair? *Harvard Business Review, 84*(3), 122-129.

Brockner, J., Ackerman, G., & Fairchild, G. (2001). When do elements of procedural fairness make a difference? A classification of moderating differences. In J. Greenberg & R. Cropanzano (Eds.), *Advances in organizational justice* (pp. 179-212). Stanford, CA: Stanford University Press.

Brockner, J., Ackerman, G., Greenberg, J., Gelfand, M. J., Francesco, A. M., Chen, Z. X., et al. (2001). Culture and procedural justice: The influence of power distance on reactions to voice. *Journal of Experimental Social Psychology, 37,* 300-315.

Brockner, J., Chen, Y. R., Mannix, E. A., Leung, K., & Skarlicki, D. P. (2000). Culture and procedural fairness: When the effects of what you do depend on how you do it? *Administrative Science Quarterly, 45,* 138-159.

Brockner, J., Tyler, R. T., & Cooper-Schneider, R. (1992). The influence of prior commitment to an institution on reactions to perceived unfairness: The higher they are, the harder they fall. *Administrative Science Quarterly, 37,* 241-261.

Brockner, J., & Wiesenfeld, B. M. (1996). An integrated framework for explaining reactions to decisions: Interactive effects of outcomes and procedures. *Psychological Bulletin, 120,* 189-208.

Campbell, D. T. (1964). Distinguishing differences of perception from failures of communication in cross-cultural studies. In F. S. C. Northrop & H. H. Livington (Eds.), *Cross-cultural understanding of epistemology in anthropology* (pp. 308-336). New York: Harper & Row.

Chao, G. T., & Moon, H. (2005). The cultural mosaic: A metatheory for understanding the complexity of culture. *Journal of Applied Psychology, 90,* 1128-1140.

Chattopadhyay, P., Tluchowska, M., & George, E. (2004). Identifying the ingroup: A closer look at the influence of demographic dissimilarity on employee social identity. *Academy of Management Review, 29,* 180-202.

Chen, C. C. (1995). New trends in rewards allocation preferences: A Sino U.S. comparison. *Academy of Management Journal, 38,* 408-428.

Chen, C. C., Chen, Y. R., & Xin, K. (2004). Guanxi practices and trust in management: A procedural justice perspective. *Organization Science, 15,* 200-209.

Chen, C. C., Choi, J., & Chi, S. C. (2002). Making justice sense of local-expatriate compensation disparity: Mitigation by local referents, ideological explanations, and interpersonal sensitivity in China-foreign joint ventures. *Academy of Management Journal, 45,* 807-817.

Chen, C. C., Meindl, J., & Hui, H. (1998). Deciding on equity or parity: A test of situational, cultural, and individual factors. *Journal of Organizational Behavior, 19,* 115-129.

Chen, C. C., Meindl, J., & Hunt, R. G. (1997). Testing the effects of vertical and horizontal collectivism: A study of reward allocation preferences in China. *Journal of Cross-Cultural Psychology, 28,* 44-70.

Chi, S. C., & Lo, H. H. (2003). Taiwanese employees' perceptions of co-workers' punitive events. *The Journal of Social Psychology, 143*(2), 27-42.

Child, J. (1981). Culture, contingency, and capitalism in the cross-national study of organizations. In L. L. Cummings & B. M. Staw (Eds.), *Research in Organizational Behavior* (Vol. 3, pp. 303-356). Greenwich, CT: JAI Press.

Cobb, A. T., Wooten, K. C., & Folger, R. (1995). Justice in the making: Toward understanding the theory and practice in organizational change and development. In W. A. Pasmore & R. W. Woodman (Eds.), *Research in Organizational Change and Development* (Vol. 8, pp. 243-295). New York: JAI Press.

Cohen, R. L. (1982). Perceiving justice: An attributional perspective. In J. Greenberg & R. L. Cohen (Eds.), *Equity and justice in social behavior* (pp. 119-160). New York: Academic Press.

Cohen-Charash, Y., & Spector, P. E. (2001). The role of justice in organizations: A meta-analysis. *Organizational Behavior and Human Decision Processes, 89,* 1-44.

Colella, A. (2001). Coworker distributive fairness judgments of the workplace accommodation of employees with disabilities. *Academy of Management Review, 26,* 100-116.

Colquitt, J. A. (2001). On the dimensionality of organizational justice: A construct validation of a measure. *Journal of Applied Psychology, 86,* 386-400.

Colquitt, J. A., Conlon, D. E., Wesson, M. J., Porter, C. O. L. H., & Ng., K. Y. (2001). Justice at the millennium: A meta-analytic review of 25 years of organizational justice research. *Journal of Applied Psychology, 86,* 425-445.

Colquitt, J., & Greenberg, J. (2003). Organizational justice: A fair assessment of the state of the literature. In J. Greenberg (Ed.), *Organizational behavior: The state of the science* (pp. 165-210). Mahwah, NJ: Erlbaum.

Colquitt, J., & Greenberg, J. (2005, Eds.). *Handbook of organizational justice.* Mahwah, NJ: Erlbaum.

Colquitt, J. A., & Greenberg, J. (2001). Doing justice to organizational justice. In S. W. Gilliland, D. D. Steiner, & D. Skarlicki (Eds.), *Theoretical and cultural perspectives on organizational justice* (pp. 217-242). Greenwich, CT: Information Age Publishing.

Colquitt, J. A., Noe, R. A., & Jackson, C. L. (2002). Justice in teams: Antecedents and consequences of procedural justice climate. *Personnel Psychology, 55,* 83-109.

Colquitt, J. A., & Shaw, J. C. (2005). How should organizational justice be measured? In J. Gerald & J. A. Colquitt (Eds.), *Handbook of organizational justice* (pp. 113-152). Mahwah, NJ: Erlbaum.

Conlon, D. B., Porter, C. O. L. H., & McLean-Parks, J. (2004). The fairness of decision rules. *Journal of Management, 30,* 329-349.

Conner, D. S. (2003). Socially appraising justice: A cross-cultural perspective. *Social Justice Research, 16,* 29-39.

Cook, S. W. (1990). Toward a psychology of improving justice: Research on extending the equality principle to victims of injustice. *Journal of Social Issues, 46,* 147-162.

Cropanzano, R., & Ambrose, M. L. (2001). Procedural and distributive justice are more similar than you think: A monistic perspective and a research agenda.

In J. Greenberg & R. Cropanzano (Eds.), *Advances in organizational justice* (pp. 119-151). Stanford, CA: Stanford University Press.

Cropanzano, R., & Byrne, Z. S. (2001). When it is time to stop writing policies: An inquiry into procedural injustice. *Human Resource Management Review, 11,* 31-54.

Cropanzano, R., Byrne, Z. S., Bobocel, D. R., & Rupp, D. R. (2001). Moral virtues, fairness heuristics, social entities, and other denizens of organizational justice. *Journal of Vocational Behavior, 58,* 164-209.

Cropanzano, R., Chrobot-Mason, D., Rupp, D. E., & Prehar, C. A. (2004). Accountability for injustice. *Human Resource Management Review, 14,* 107-133.

Cropanzano, R., & Folger, R. (1989). Referent cognitions and task decision autonomy: Beyond equity theory. *Journal of Applied Psychology, 74,* 293-299.

Cropanzano, R., Goldman, B. M., & Folger, R. (2005). Self-interest: Defining and understanding a human motive. *Journal of Organizational Behavior, 26,* 985-991.

Cropanzano, R., & Greenberg, J. (1997). Progress in organizational justice: Tunneling through the maze. In C. L. Cooper & I. T. Robertson (Eds.), *International review of industrial and organizational psychology* (pp. 317-372). New York: Wiley.

Cropanzano, R., Prehar, C. A., & Chen, P. Y. (2002). Using social exchange theory to distinguish procedural justice from interactional justice. *Group and Organization Management, 27,* 324-351.

Cropanzano, R., & Rupp, D. E. (2002). Some reflections on the morality of organizational justice. In S. W. Gilliland, D. D. Steiner, & D. P. Skarlicki (Eds.), *Emerging perspectives on managing organizational justice* (pp. 225-278). Greenwich, CT: Information Age Publishing.

Cropanzano, R. S., Rupp, D. E., Mohler, C. J., & Schminke, M. (2001). Three roads to organizational justice . In G. Ferris (Ed.), *Research in personnel and human resource management* (pp. 1-113). Oxford, England: Elsevier Science.

Cropanzano, R., & Schminke, M. (2001). Using social justice to build effective work groups. In M. E. Turner (Ed.), *Groups at work: Theory and research* (pp. 143-172). Mahwah, NJ: Erlbaum.

Crosby, F. (1976). A model of egoistic relative deprivation. *Psychological Review, 23,* 85-113.

Cullen, J. B., & Parboteeah, K. P. (2005). *Multinational management: A strategic approach* (3rd ed.). Cincinnati, OH: Thomson/South-Western.

Cushner, K, & Brislin, R. (1996). *Intercultural interactions: A practical guide.* Thousand Oaks, CA: Sage.

Daly, J. P., & Geyer, P. D. (1994). The role of fairness in implementing large-scale change: Employee evaluations of process and outcomes in seven facility relocations. *Journal of Organizational Behavior, 15,* 623-638.

Darley, J. M., & Pittman, T. S. (2003). The psychology of compensatory and retributive justice. *Personality and Social Psychology Review, 7,* 324-336.

Davidson, M., & Friedman, R. A. (1998). When excuses don't work: The persistent injustice effect among black managers. *Administrative Science Quarterly, 43,* 154-183.

Deci, E. L. (1975). *Intrinsic motivation.* New York: Plenum Press.

Deutsch, M. (1975). Equity, equality, and need: What determines which value will be used as the basis of distributive justice? *Journal of Social Issues, 31,* 137-149.

Deutsch, M. (1985). *Distributive justice: A social-psychological perspective.* New Haven, CT: Yale University Press.

DeVos, G. A. (1990). Self in society: A multilevel, psychocultural analysis. In G. A. DeVos & M. Suarez-Orozco (Eds.), *Status inequality: The self in culture* (pp. 17-74). Newbury Park, CA: Sage.

Erez, M. (2000). Make management practice fit the national culture. In E. A. Locke, (Ed.), *Blackwell handbook of principles of organizational behavior* (pp. 418-434). Oxford, England: Blackwell.

Erdogan, B., & Liden, R. C. (2006). Collectivism as a moderator of responses to organizational justice: Implications for leader-member exchange and ingratiation. *Journal of Organizational Behavior, 27,* 1-17.

Festinger, L. (1954). A theory of social comparison processes. *Human Relations, 7,* 11-40.

Fields, D., Pang, M., & Chiu, C. (2000). Distributive and procedural justice as predictors of employee outcomes in Hong Kong. *Journal of Organizational Behavior, 21,* 547-562.

Finkel, N. J. (2000). But it's not fair: Commonsense notions of unfairness. *Psychology, Public Policy, & Law, 6,* 898-952.

Finkel, N. J., Crystal, D. S., & Watanabe, H. (2001). Commonsense notions of unfairness in Japan and the United States. *Psychology, Public Policy, and Law, 7*(2), 345-380.

Fiske, A. P. (1991). *Structures of social life: The four elementary forms of human relations.* New York: Free Press.

Fiske, A. P. (1992). The four elementary forms of sociality: Framework for a unified theory of social relations. *Psychological Review, 99,* 689-723.

Fiske, A. P. (2002). Using individualism and collectivism to compare cultures: A critique of the validity and measurement of the constructs: Comment on Oyserman et al. (2002). *Psychological Bulletin, 128,* 78-88.

Foa, U. G., & Foa, E. B. (1974). *Societal structures of the mind.* Springfield, IL: Thomas.

Folger, R. (1977). Distributive and procedural justice: Combined impact of voice and improvement on experienced inequity. *Journal of Personality and Social Psychology, 35,* 108-119.

Folger, R. (1986). Rethinking equity theory: A referent cognitions model. In H. W. Bieerhoff, R. L. Cohen, & J. Greenberg (Eds.), *Justice in social relations* (pp. 145-162). New York: Plenum.

Folger, R. (1987). Distributive and procedural justice in the workplace. *Social Justice Research, 1*(2), 143-159.

Folger, R. (1993). Reactions to mistreatment at work. In J. K. Murnighan (Ed.), *Social psychology in organizations: Advances in theory and research* (pp. 161-183). Englewood Cliffs, NJ: Prentice Hall.

Folger, R. (1998). Fairness as a moral virtue. In M. Schminke (Ed.), *Managerial ethics: Moral management of people and process* (pp. 13-34). Mahwah, NJ: Erlbaum.

Folger, R. (2001). Fairness as deonance. In S. Gilliland, D. D. Steiner, & D. Skalicki (Eds.), *Theoretical and cultural perspectives on organizational justice* (pp. 3-33). Greenwich, CT: Information Age Publishing.

Folger, R., & Bies, R. J. (1989). Managing responsibilities and procedural justice. *Employee Responsibilities and Rights Journal, 2*(2), 79-90.

Folger, R., & Cropanzano, R. (1998). *Organizational justice and human resource management.* Beverly Hills, CA: Sage.

Folger, R., & Cropanzano, R. (2001). Fairness theory: Justice as accountability. In J. Greenberg R. Cropanzano (Eds.), *Advances in organizational justice* (pp. 1-55). Stanford, CA: Stanford University Press.

Folger, R., Cropanzano, R., & Goldman, B. (2005). What is the relationship between justice and morality? In J. Gerald & J. A. Colquitt (Eds.), *Handbook of organizational justice* (pp. 215-245). Mahwah, NJ: Erlbaum.

Folger, R., & Greenberg, J. (1985). Procedural justice: An interpretative analysis of personnel systems. In K. Rowland & G. Ferris (Eds.), *Research in personnel and human resources management* (Vol. 3, pp. 141-183). Greenwich, CT: JAI Press.

Folger, R., & Konovsky, M A. (1989). Effects of procedural and distributive justice on reactions to pay raise decisions. *Academy of Management Journal, 32,* 115-130.

Folger, R., & Rosenfield, D., Grove, J., & Corkran, L. (1979). Effects of voice and peer opinions on responses to inequity. *Journal of Personality and Social Psychology, 37,* 2253-2261.

Folger, R., & Skarlicki, D. P. (1999). Unfairness and resistance to change: Hardship as mistreatment. *Journal of Organizational Change Management, 12*(1), 35-50.

Friedman, R. A., & Robinson, R. J. (1993). Justice for all? Union versus management responses to unjust acts and social accounts. *International Journal of Conflict Management, 4,* 99-117.

Furby, L. (1986). Psychology and justice. In R. L. Cohen (Ed.), *Justice: Views from the social sciences* (pp. 153-203). New York: Plenum.

Gelfand, M. J., & Realo, A. (1999). Individualism-collectivism and accountability in intergrorp negotiations. *Journal of Applied Psychology, 84,* 721-736.

Gelfand, M. J., Lim, B. C., & Raver, J. L. (2004). Culture and accountability in organizations: variations in forms of social control across cultures. *Human Resource Management Review, 14,* 135-160.

Ghoshal, S., & Bartlett, C. A. (1990). The multinational corporation as an interorganizational network. *Academy of Management Review, 15,* 603-625.

Giacobbe-Miller, J. K., Miller, D. J., & Zhang, W. (1997). Equity, equality and need as determinants of pay allocations: A comparative study of Chinese and U.S. managers. *Employee Relations, 19,* 309-320.

Giacobbe-Miller, J. K., Miller, D. J., Zhang, W., & Victorov, V. I. (2003). Country and organizational-level adaptation to foreign workplace ideologies: A comparative study of distributive justice values in China, Russia and the United States. *Journal of International Business Studies, 34,* 389-406.

Gillepsie, J. Z., & Greenberg, J. (2005). Are the goals of organizational justice self-interested? In In J. Gerald & J. A. Colquitt (Eds.), *Handbook of organizational justice* (pp. 179-213). Mahwah, NJ: Erlbaum.

Gilliland, S. W., Groth, M., Baker, IV, R. C., Dew, A. F., Polly, L. M., & Langdon, J. C. (2001). Improving applicants' reactions to rejection letters: An application of fairness theory. *Personnel Psychology, 54,* 669-703.

Goldman, B. M., & Thatcher, S. M. B. (2002). A social information processing view of organizational justice. In S. W. Gilliland, D. D. Steiner, & D. P. Skalicki (Eds.), *Emerging perspectives on managing organizational justice* (pp. 103-130). Greenwich, CT: Information Age Publishing.

Gouveia, V. V., Clemente, M., & Espinosa, P. (2003). The horizontal and vertical attributes of individualism and collectivism in a Spanish population. *Journal of Social Psychology, 143*(1), 43-63.

Granovetter, M. (1985). Economic action and social structure: The problem of embeddness. *American Journal of Sociology, 82,* 929-964.

Greenberg, J. (1983). Overcoming egocentric bias in perceived fairness through self-awareness. *Social Psychology Quarterly, 46,* 55-61.

Greenberg, J. (1987a). A taxonomy of organizational justice theories. *Academy of Management Review, 12,* 9-22.

Greenberg, J. (1987b). Reactions to procedural injustices in payment distributions: Do the means justify the ends? *Journal of Applied Psychology, 72,* 55-61.

Greenberg, J. (1990a). Looking fair versus being fair: Managing impressions of organizational justice. *Research in Organizational Behavior, 12,* 111-157.

Greenberg, J. (1990b). Organizational justice: Yesterday, today, and tomorrow. *Journal of Management, 16,* 399-432.

Greenberg, J. (1990c). Employee theft as a reaction to underpayment inequity: The hidden costs of pay cuts. *Journal of Applied Psychology, 75,* 561-568.

Greenberg, J. (1993a). The social side of fairness: Interpersonal and informational classes of organizational justice. In R. Cropanzano (Ed.), *Justice in the workplace* (pp. 79-103). Mahwah, NJ: Erlbaum.

Greenberg, J. (1993b). Stealing in the name of justice: Informational and interpersonal moderators of theft reactions to underpayment inequity. *Organizational Behavior and Human Decision Processes, 54,* 81-103.

Greenberg, J. (1994). Using socially fair treatment to promote acceptance of a work site smoking ban. *Journal of Applied Psychology, 79,* 288-297.

Greenberg, J. (1996). The quest for justice on the job: Essays and experiments. Thousand Oaks, CA: Sage.

Greenberg, J. (2001a). Studying organizational justice cross-culturally: Fundamental challenges. *International Journal of Conflict Management, 12,* 365-375.

Greenberg, J. (2001b). The seven loose canons of organizational justice. In J. Greenberg & R. Cropanzano (Eds.), *Advances in organizational justice* (pp. 245-271). Stanford, CA: Stanford University Press.

Greenberg, J. (2002). Who stole the money and when? Individual and situational determinants of employee theft. *Organizational Behavior and Human Decision Processes, 89,* 985-1003.

Greenberg, J. (2006). Losing sleep over organizational injustice: Attenuating insomniac reactions to underpayment inequity with supervisory training in interactional justice. *Journal of Applied Psychology, 91,* 58-69.

Greenberg, J., & Alge, B. J. (1998). Aggressive reactions to workplace injustice. in R. W. Griffin, A. O'Leary-Kelly, & J. Collins (Eds.), *Dysfunctional behavior in organizations: Violent behaviors in organizations* (Vol. 1, pp. 119-145). Greenwich, CT: JAI Press.

Greenberg, J., & Lind, E. A. (2000). The pursuit of organizational justice: From conceptualization to implication to application. In C. L. Cooper & E. A. Locke (Eds.), *Industrial/organizational psychology: What we know about theory and practice* (pp. 72-105). Oxford, England: Blackwell.

Greenberg, J., Solomon, S., & Pyszczynski, T. (1997). Terror management theory of self-esteem in cultural worldviews: Empirical assessments and conceptual refinements. In M. Zanna (Ed.), *Advances in experimental social psychology* (Vol. 29, pp. 61-139). New York: Academic Press.

Greenberg, J., Solomon, S., Rosenblatt, A., & Pyszczynski, T. (1990). Terror management theory of self-esteem and cultural views: Empirical assessments and conceptual refinements. In M. Zanna (Ed.), *Advances in experimental social psychology* (Vol. 29, pp. 61-139). New York: Academic Press.

Grover, S. T. (1991). Predicting the perceived fairness of parental leave policies. *Journal of Applied Psychology, 76,* 247-255.

Gundykunst, W. B., & Ting-Toomey, S. (1988). Culture and affective communication. *American Behavioral Scientist, 31,* 348-400.

Hall, R. H., & Xu, W. (1990). Run silent, run deep: Cultural influences in the Far East. *Organization Studies, 11,* 569-576.

Hamilton, V. L., & Hagiwara, S. (1992). Roles, responsibility, and accounts across cultures. *International Journal of Psychology, 27*(2), 157-179.

Hamilton, V. L., & Saunders, J. (1988). Punishment and the individual in the United States and Japan. *Law and Society Review, 22,* 301-328.

Hamilton, V. L., & Saunders, J. (1992). *Every day justice: Responsibility and the individual in Japan and the United States.* New Haven, CT: Yale University Press.

Hampden-Turner, C., & Trompenaars, A. (1993). *The seven cultures of capitalism: Value systems for creating wealth in the United States, Japan, Germany, France, Britain, Sweden, and the Netherlands.* New York: Currency/Doubleday.

He, W., Chen, C. C., & Zhang, L. (2004). Reward-allocation preferences of Chinese employees in the new millennium: The effects of ownership, reform, collectivism, and goal priority. *Organization Science, 15,* 221-231.

Hegtvedt, K. A., Clay-Warner, J., & Johnson, C. (2003). The social context of responses to injustice: Considering the indirect and direct effects of group-level factors. *Social Justice Research, 16*(4), 343-366.

Hegtvedt, K. A., & Cook, K. S. (2000). Distributive justice: Recent theoretical developments and applications. In J. Sanders & V. L. Hamilton (Eds.), *Handbook of justice research in law* (pp. 93-132). New York: Kluwer Academic.

Hertel, G., Aarts, H., & Zeelenberg, M. (2002). What do you think is fair? Effects of ingroup norms and outcome control on fairness judgments. *European Journal of Social Psychology, 33,* 327-341.

Hofstede, G. R. (1980). *Culture's consequences: International Differences in work relations.* Newbury Park, CA: Sage.

Hosftede, R. G. (1991). *Cultures and organizations: Software of the mind.* London: McGraw-Hill.

Hofstede, G. R., & Bond, M. H. (1984). Hofstede's culture dimensions: An independent validation using Rokeach's value survey. *Journal of Cross-Cultural Psychology, 15,* 417-433.

Hogg, M. A., & Terry, D. J. (2000). Social identity and self-categorization processes in organizational contexts. *Academy of Management Review, 25,* 121-140.

Homans, G. C. (1961). *Social behavior: Its elementary forms.* New York: Harcourt, Brace & World.

Hui, C., Lee, C., & Rousseau, D. M. (2004). Employment of relationship in China : Do workers relate to the organization or to people? *Organization Science, 15,* 232-240.

Hundley, G., & Kim, J. (1997). National culture and the factor affecting perceptions of pay fairness in Korea and the United States. *International Journal of Organizational Analysis, 5,* 325-341.

Inness, M., Barling, J., & Turner, N. (2005). Understanding supervisor-targeted aggression: A within-person, between-jobs design. *Journal of Applied Psychology, 90,* 731-739

Itoi, R., Obhuci, K. I., & Fukuno, M. (1996). A cross-cultural study of preference of accounts: Relationship closeness, harm severity, and motives of account making. *Journal of Applied Social Psychology, 26,* 913-934.

James, K. (1993). The social context of organizational justice: Cultural, intergroup and structural effects on justice behaviors and perceptions. In R. Cropanzano (Ed.), *Justice in the workplace: Approaching fairness in human resource management* (pp. 21-50). Hillsdale, NJ: Erlbaum.

Jawahar, I. M. (2002). A model of organizational justice and workplace aggression. *Journal of Management, 28,* 811-834.

Johnston, W. B. (1991). Global workforce 2000: The new world labor market. *Harvard Business Review, 69*(2),115-127.

Kabanoff, B. (1991). Equity, equality, power and conflict. *Academy of Management Review, 16,* 416-441.

Kabanoff, B. (1997). Organizational justice across cultures: Integrating organization-level and culture-level perspectives. In P. C. Early & M. Erez (Eds.), *New perspectives in industrial/organizational psychology* (pp. 676-712). San Francisco: The Lexicon Press.

Kahneman, D., Knestch, J. L., & Thaler, R. H. (1986). Fairness and the assumptions of economics. *Journal of Business, 59,* 285-300.

Kahneman, D., & Tversky, A. (1979). Prospect theory: An analysis of decision under uncertainty. *Econometrica, 47,* 263-291.

Kanter, R. (1991). Globalism-localism: A new human resources agenda. *Harvard Business Review, 69*(2), 9-10.

Kashima, Y., Kashima, E. S., Kim, U., & Gelfand, M. J. (2006). Describing the social world: How is a person, a group, and a relationship described in the East and the West? *Journal of Experimental Social Psychology, 42,* 388-396.

Kashima, Y, Siegal, M., Tanaka, K., & Isaka, H. (1988). Universalism in lay conceptions of distributive justice: A cross-cultural examination. *International Journal of Psychology, 23,* 51-64.

Kidder, L. H., & Miller, S. (1991). What is fair in Japan? In Vermunt R., & Steensma, H. (Eds.), *Social and psychological consequences of justice and injustice* (Vol. 2, pp. 139-154). New York: Plenum.

Kim, W. C., & Mauborgne, R. A. (1988). Becoming an effective global competitor. *Journal of Business Strategy, 9(1)*, 33-47.

Kim, W. C., & Mauborgne, R. A. (1991). Implementing global strategies: The role of procedural justice. *Strategic Management Journal, 12*, 125-143.

Kim, W. C., & Mauborgne, R. A. (1993a). Procedural justice, attitudes, and subsidiary top management compliance with multinationals' corporate strategic decisions. *Academy of Management Journal, 36*, 502-526.

Kim, W. C., & Mauborgne, R. A. (1993b). Effectively conceiving and executing multinationals' worldwide strategies. *Journal of International Business Studies, 24*(3), 419-448.

Kim, W. C., & Mauborgne, R. A. (1993c). Procedural justice theory and the multinational corporation. In S. Ghoshal & D. E. Westney (Eds), *Organizational theory and the multinational corporation* (pp. 237-255). London: McMillan.

Kim, W. C., & Mauborgne, R. A. (1993d). Making global strategies work. *Sloan Management Review, 34*(3), 11-27.

Kim, W. C., & Mauborgne, R. A. (1995). A procedural justice model of strategic decision making: Strategy content implications in the multinational. *Organization Science, 6*, 44-61.

Kim, W. C., & Mauborgne, R. A. (1996). Procedural justice and managers' in-role and extra-role behavior: The case of the multinational. *Management Science, 42*, 499-515.

Kim, W. C., & Mauborne, R. A. (1997). Fair process: Managing in the knowledge economy. *Harvard Business Review, 75*(4), 65-75.

Kim, K. I., Park, H. J., & Suzuki, N. (1990). Reward allocations in the United States, Japan, and Korea: A comparison of individualistic and collectivistic cultures. *Academy of Management Journal, 33*, 188-198.

Kluckhohn, C. (1951). Values and value-orientations in the theory of action: An exploration in definition and classification. In T. Parsons & E. Shils (Eds.), *Toward a general theory of action* (pp. 388-433). Cambridge, MA: Harvard University Press.

Kluegel, J. R., Mason, D. S., & Wegener, B. (Eds.). (1995). *Social justice and political change: Public opinion in capitalist and post-communist states.* New York: Aldine.

Konopaske, R., & Werner, S. (2002). Equity in non-North American contexts: Adapting equity theory to the new global business environment. *Human Resource Management Review, 12*, 405-418.

Kray, L. J., & Lind, E. A. (2002). The injustice of others: Social reports and the integration of others' experiences in organizational justice judgments. *Organizational Behavior and Human Decision Processes, 89*, 906-925.

Kurosawa, K. (1992). Responsibility and justice: A view across cultures. *International Journal of Psychology, 27*(2), 243-26.

Lam, S. S., Schaubroeck, J., & Aryee, S. (2002). Relationship between organizational justice and employee work outcomes: A cross-national study. *Journal of Organizational Behavior, 23*, 1-18.

Lamertz, K. (2002). The social construction of fairness: Social influence and sense making in organizations. *Journal of Organizational Behavior, 23*, 19-37.

Leadership at Halliburton. (2005). *Fortune, 151*(10), 22.

Lee, C., Pillutla, M., & Law, K. S. (2000). Power distance, gender, and organizational justice. *Journal of Management, 26*, 685-704.

Lerner, M. J. (1981). The justice motive in human relations. Some thoughts of what we know and need to know about justice. In M. J. Lerner & S. C. Lerner (Eds.), *The justice motive in social behavior* (pp. 11-35). New York: Plenum Press.

Lerner, M. J. (1982). Justice motive in human relations and the economic model of man. In V. Derlega & Grzelak (Eds.), *Cooperation and helping behavior* (pp. 249-277). New York Academic Press.

Leung, K. (1987). Some determinants of reactions to procedural models for conflict resolution: A cross-national study. *Journal of Personality and Social Psychology, 53*, 898-908.

Leung, K. (1988). Theoretical advances in justice behavior: Some cross-cultural input. In M. H. Bond (Ed.), *The cross-cultural challenge to social psychology* (pp. 218-229). Newbury Park, CA: Sage.

Leung, K. (1997). Negotiation and reward allocations across cultures. In P. C. Early & M. Erez (Eds.), *New perspectives on industrial/organizational psychology* (pp. 640-675). San Francisco: Jossey-Bass.

Leung, K. (2005). How generalizable are justice effects across cultures? In J. Gerald & J. A. Colquitt (Eds.), *Handbook of organizational justice* (pp. 555-586). Mahwah, NJ: Erlbaum.

Leung, K., & Bond, M. H. (1982). How Chinese and Americans reward task-related contributions: A preliminary study. *Psychologia, 25*, 32-39.

Leung, K., & Bond, M. H. (1984). The impact of cultural collectivism on reward allocation. *Journal of Personality and Social Psychology, 4*, 793-804.

Leung, K., & Iwawaka, S. (1988). Cultural collectivism and distributive behavior. *Journal of Cross-Cultural Psychology, 19*, 35-49.

Leung, K., & Kwong, J. Y. Y. (2003). Human resource management practices in international joint ventures in mainland China: A justice analysis. *Human Resource Management Review, 13*, 85-105.

Leung, K., & Lind, E. A. (1986). Procedural justice and culture: Effects of culture, gender, and investigator status on procedural preferences. *Journal of Personality and Social Psychology, 6*, 1134-1140.

Leung, K., & Morris, M. W. (2001). Justice through the lens of culture and ethnicity. In J. Sanders & V. L. Hamilton (Eds.), *Handbook of justice research in law* (pp. 343-378). New York: Kluwer Academic/Plenum.

Leung, K., & Park, H. J. (1986). Effects of interactional goal on choice of allocation rule: A cross-national study. *Organizational Behavior and Human Decision Processes, 37*, 111-120.

Leung, K., K., Smith, P. B., Wang, Z. M., & Sun, H. F. (1996). Job satisfaction in joint venture hotels in China: An organizational justice analysis. *Journal of International Business Studies, 27*, 947-962.

Leung, K., & Stephan, W. G. (1998). Perceptions of injustice in intercultural relations. *Applied and Preventive Psychology, 7*, 193-205.

Leung, K., & Tong, K. K. (2004). Justice across cultures: A three-stage model for intercultural negotiation. In M. Gelfand & J. Brett (Eds.), *The handbook of negotiation and culture* (pp. 313-333). Stanford, CA: Stanford UniversityPress.

Leung, K., Wang, Z. M., & Smith, P. B. (2001). Job attitudes and organizational justice in joint venture hotels in China: The role of expatriate managers. *International Journal of Human Resource Management, 12,* 926-945.

Leventhal, G. S. (1976). The distinction of rewards and resources in groups and organizations. In L. Berkowitz, & E. Walster (Eds.), *Advances in experimental social psychology* (Vol. 9, pp. 91-131). New York: Academic Press.

Leventhal, G. S., Karuza, J., & Fry, W. R. (1980). Beyond fairness: A theory of allocation preferences. In G. Mikula (Ed.), *Justice and social interaction* (pp. 167-218). New York: Springer-Verlag.

Lewin-Epstein, N., Kaplan, A., & Levanon, A. (2003). Distributive justice and attitudes toward the welfare state. *Social Justice Research, 16*(1), 1-27.

Lind, E. A. (2001). Fairness heuristic theory: Justice judgments as pivotal cognitions in organizational relations. In J. Greenberg & R. Cropanzano (Eds.), *Advances in organizational justice* (pp. 56-88). Stanford, CA: Stanford University Press.

Lind, E. A., & Early, C. P. (1992). Procedural justice and culture. *InternationaJournal of Psychology, 27*(2), 227-242.

Lind, E. A., Kray, L. J., & Thompson, L. (1998). The social construction of injustice: Fairness judgments in response to own and others' unfair treatment by authorities.*Organizational Behavior and Human Decision Processes, 75,* 1-22.

Lind, E. A., Kray, L. J., & Thompson, L. (2001). The social construction of injustice: Fairness judgments in response to own and others' unfair treatment by authorities. *Organizational Behavior and Human Decision Processes, 75,* 1-22.

Lind, E. A., Kulik, C. T., & Ambrose, M. L. (1993). Individual and corporate dispute resolution: Using procedural fairness as a decision heuristic. *Administrative Science Quarterly, 38,* 224-251.

Lind, E. A., & Tyler, T. R. (1988). *The social psychology of procedural justice.* New York: Plenum Press.

Lind, E. A., & Tyler, T. R., Huo, Y. J. (1997). Procedural context and culture: variation in the antecedents of procedural justice judgments. *Journal of Personality and Social Psychology, 73,* 767-780.

Lind, E. A., & Van den Bos, K. (2002). When fairness works: Toward a general theory of uncertainty management. In B. M. Staw & R. M. Kramer (Eds.), *Research in Organizational Behavior* (Vol. 24, pp. 181-223). Greenwich, CT: JAI Press.

Lindell, M. K., & Brandt, C. J. (2000). Climate quality and consensus as mediators of the relationship between organizational antecedents and outcomes. *Journal of Applied Psychology, 85,* 331-348.

Luo, Y. (2005). How important are shared perceptions of procedural justice in cooperative alliances? *Academy of Management Journal, 48,* 695-709.

Lutz, C. (1988). *Unnatural emotions: Everyday sentiments on a Micronesian atoll and their challenge to Western theory.* Chicago: University of Chicago Press.

Marin, G. (1985). The preference for equity when judging the attractiveness and fairness of an allocator: The role of familiarity and culture. *Journal of Social Psychology, 125*, 543-549.

Markus, H. R., & Kitayama, S. (1991). Culture and the self: Implications for cognition, emotion, and motivation. *Psychological Bulletin, 98*(2), 224-253.

Martin, J. (1981). Relative deprivation: A theory of distributive injustice for an era of shrinking resources. *Research in Organizational Behavior, 3*, 53-107

Martin, J., Brickman, P., & Murray, A. (1984). Moral outrage and pragmatism: Explanations for collective action. *Journal of Personality and Social Psychology, 20*, 484-496.

Martin, J., & Harder, J. W. (1987). Bread and roses: Justice and the distribution of financial and socioemotional rewards. *Social Justice Research, 7*, 241-264.

McClelland, D. C. (1961). *The achieving society.* Princeton, NJ: Van-Nostrand.

McFarlin, D. B., & Sweeney, P. D. (2001). Cross-cultural applications of organizational justice. In R. Cropanzano (Ed.), *Justice in the workplace: From theory to practice* (Vol. 2, pp. 67-95). Mahwah, NJ: Erlbaum.

McFarlin, D. B., & Sweeney, P. D. (2006). *International management* (3rd ed.). New York: Houghton Mifflin.

Masterson, S. S., Lewis, K., Goldman, B. M., & Taylor, M. S. (2000). Integrating justice and social exchange. The differing effects of fair procedures and treatment of work relationships. *Academy of Management Journal, 43*, 738-748.

Meara, N. M. (2001). Just and virtuous leaders and organizations. *Journal of Vocational Behavior, 58*, 227-234.

Meindl, J. R., Cheng, Y. K., & Jun, L. (1990). Distributive justice in the workplace: Preliminary data on managerial preferences in the PRC. *Research in Personnel and Human Resources Management,* (Supplement 2), 221-236.

Menon, T., Morris, M. W., Chiu, C., & Hong, Y. (1999). Culture and construal of agency: Attribution to individual versus group dispositions. *Journal of Personalityand Social Psychology, 76*, 701-717.

Mesquita, B. (2001). Emotions in collectivist and individualist contexts. *Journal of Personality and Social Psychology, 80*, 68-74.

Messé, L. A., Hymes, R. W., & MacCoun, R. J. (1986). Group categorization and distributive justice decisions. In H. Bierhoff, R. L. Cohen, & Greenberg, J. (Eds.), *Justice in social relations* (pp. 227-248). New York: Plenum.

Messick, D. M., & Sentis, K. (1979). Fairness and preference. *Journal of Experimental Social Psychology, 15*, 418-434.

Messick, D. M., Bloom, S., Boldizar, J. P., & Samuelson, C. D. (1985). Why we are fairer than others. *Journal of Experimental Social Psychology, 21*, 480-500.

Mikula, G. (1986). The experience of injustice: Toward a better understanding of its phenomenology. In H. W. Bierhoff, R. I, Cohen, & J. Greenberg (Eds.), *Justice in social relations* (pp. 103-123). New York: Plenum.

Mikula, G. (1987). Exploring the experience of injustice. In G. R. Semin & B. Krahé (Eds.), *Issues in contemporary German social psychology* (pp. 74-96). London: Sage.

Miles, J. A., & Greenberg, J. (1993). Cross-national differences in preferences for distributive justice norms: The challenge of establishing fair resource allocations for the European Community. In J. Shaw, P. Kirkbride, K. Rowland, &

G. Ferris (Eds.), *Research in Personnel and Human Resources Management*, (Supplement 3), 133-156. Grenwich, CT: JAI Press.

Miller, D. T. (1999). The norm of self-interest. *American Psychologist, 54,* 1-8.

Montada, L. (1998). Justice: Just a rational choice? *Social Justice Research, 12,* 81-101.

Moorman, R. H. (1991). Relationship between organizational justice and organizational citizenship behaviors: Do fairness perceptions influence employee citizenship? *Journal of Applied Psychology, 76,* 845-855.

Mossholder, K. W., Bennett, N., & Martin, C. L. (1998). A multilevel analysis of procedural justice context. *Journal of Organizational Behavior, 19,* 131-141.

Morris, M. W., & Leung, K. (2000). Justice for all? Progress in research on cultural variation in the psychology of distributive and procedural justice. *Applied Psychology: An International Review, 49,* 100-132.

Morris, M. W., Leung, K., Ames, D., & Lickel, B. (1999). Views from inside and outside: Integrating emic and etic insights about culture and justice judgment. *Academy of Management Review, 24,* 781-796.

Morris, M. W., & Peng, K. (1994). Culture and cause: American and Chinese attributions for social and physical events. *Journal of Personality and Social Psychology, 67,* 949-971.

Mullin, B. A., & Hoog, M. A. (1999). Motivations for group membership: The role of subjective importance and uncertainty reduction. *Basic and Applied Social Psychology, 21*(2) 91-102.

Murphy-Berman, V., & Berman, J. J. (2002). Cross-cultural differences in perceptions of distributive justice: A comparison of Hong Kong and Indonesia. *Journal of Cross-Cultural Psychology, 33,* 157-170.

Murphy-Berman, V., Berman, J. J., Singh, P., Packauri, A., & Kumar, P. (1984). Factors affecting allocation to needy and meritorious recipients: A cross-cultural comparison. *Journal of Personality and Social Psychology, 46,* 1267-1272.

Naumann, S. E., & Bennett, N. (2000). A case for procedural justice climate: Development and test of a multilevel model. *Academy of Management Journal, 43,* 881-889.

Novelli, L., Kirkman, B. L., & Shapiro, D. L. (1995). Effective implementation of organizational change: An organizational justice perspective. In C. L. Cooper & D. M. Rousseau (Eds.), *Trends in organizational behavior* (Vol. 2, pp. 15-36). New York: Wiley.

Obhuci, K. I., & Takahashi, Y. (1994). Cultural styles of conflict management in Japanese and Americans: Passivity, covertness, and effectiveness of strategies. *Journal of Applied Social Psychology, 24,* 1345-1366.

Opotow, S. (1990). Moral exclusion and injustice: An introduction. *Journal of Social Issues, 46*(1), 1-20.

Paese, P. W., & Yonker, R. D. (2001). Toward a better understanding of egocentric fairness judgments in negotiation. *The International Journal of Conflict Management, 12*(2), 114-131.

Parboteeah, K. P., & Cullen, J. B. (2003). Social institutions and work centrality: Explorations beyond national culture. *Organization Science, 14,* 137-148.

Pearce, J. L., Branyiczki, L., & Bakacsi, G. (1994). Person-based reward systems: A theory of organizational reward practices in reform-communist organizations. *Journal of Organizational Behavior, 15,* 261-282.

Pfeffer, J. R., & Salancik, G. R. (1978). *The external control of organizations: A resource dependency perspective.* New York: Harper & Row.

Pillai, R., Williams, E. S., & Tan, J. J. (2001). Are the scales tipped in favor of procedural or distributive justice? An investigation of the U.S., India, Germany, and Hong Kong (China). *The International Journal of Conflict Management, 12,* 312-332.

Pinder, C. C., & Harlos, K. P. (2001). Employee silence: Quiescence and acquiescence as responses to perceived injustice. *Research in Personnel and Human Resources Management, 20,* 331-369.

Price, K. H., Hall, T. W., Van den Bos, K., Hunton, J. E., Lovett, S., & Tippett, M. J. (2001). Features of the value function for voice and their consistency across participants from four countries: Great Britain, Mexico, the Netherlands, and the United States. *Organizational Behavior and Human Decision Processes, 84,* 95-121.

Rahim, M. A., Magner, N. R., & Shapiro, D. L. (2000). Do justice perceptions influence styles of handling conflict with supervisor? What justice perceptions, precisely? *International Journal of Conflict Management, 11,* 5-26.

Ralston, D. A., Gustafson, D. J., & Cheung, F. M. , & Terpstra, R. H. (1993). Differences in managerial values: A study of US, Hong Kong, and PRC managers. *Journal of International Business Studies, 24,* 249-275.

Ralston, D. A., Holt, D. H., Terpstra, R. H., & Kai-Cheng, Y. (1997). The impact of national culture and economic ideology on managerial values: A study of the United States, Russia, Japan, and China. *Journal of International Business Studies* (First Quarter), 28, 177-207.

Rawls, J. (1971). *A theory of justice.* Cambridge, MA: Harvard University Press.

Roberson, Q. M., & Colquitt, J. A. (2005). Shared and configural justice: A social network model of justice in teams. *Academy of Management Review, 30,* 595-607.

Rodriguez, C. (2001). *International management: A cultural approach* (2nd ed.). Cincinnati, OH: Southwestern College.

Rokeach, M. (1973). *The nature of human values.* New York: Free Press.

Ross, L. (1977). The intuitive psychologist and his shortcomings: Distortions in the attribution process. In L. Berkowitz (Ed.), *Advances in experimental social psychology* (Vol. 10, pp. 174-221). New York: Academic Press.

Rotter, J. B. (1966). Generalized expectations for internal versus external control of reinforcement. *Psychological Monograph, 109,* 1-28.

Rozin, P., Lowery, L., Imada, S., Haidt, J. (1999). The CAD triad hypothesis: A mapping between three moral emotions (contempt, anger, disgust) and three moral codes (community, autonomy, divinity). *Journal of Personality and Social Psychology, 76,* 574-586.

Runciman, W. G. (1966). *Relative deprivation and social justice: A study of attitudes to social inequality in twentieth century England.* Berkeley, CA: University of California Press.

Rupp, D. E., & Cropanzano, R. (2002). The mediating effects of social exchange relationships in predicting workplace outcomes from multifoci organizational justice. *Organizational Behavior and Human Decision Processes, 89,* 925-946.

Rutte, C. G., & Messick, D. M. (1995). An integrated model of perceived unfairness in organizations. *Social Justice Research, 3,* 239-261.

Sabbagh, C. (2003). Evaluating society's spheres of justice: The Israeli case. *Social Psychology Quarterly, 66*(3), 254-271.

Scheer, L. K., Kumar, N., & Steenkamp, J. B. E. M. (2003). Reactions to perceived inequity in US and Dutch interorganizational relationships. *Academy of Management Journal, 46,* 303-316.

Schlenker, B. R., Britt, T. W., Pennington, J., Murphy, R., & Doherty, K. (1994). The triangle of responsibility. *Psychological Review, 10,* 632-652.

Schneider, B. (1987). The people make the place. *Personnel Psychology, 40,* 437-453.

Schwartz, S. H. (1990). Individualism-collectivism: Critique and proposed refinements. *Journal of Cross-Cultural Psychology, 21,* 139-157.

Schwartz, S. H. (1992). Universals in the content and structure of values: Theoretical advances and empirical tests in 20 countries. In M. Zanna (Ed.), *Advances in experimental social psychology* (Vol. 25, pp. 1-65). Orlando, FL: Academic Press.

Schwartz, S. H. (1994). Beyond individualism/collectivism: New cultural dimensions of values. In U. Kim, H. C. Triandis, C. Kagitcibasi, S. C. Choi, & G. Yoon (Eds.), *Individualism and collectivism: Theory, method, and applications* (pp. 85-119). Thousand Oaks, CA: Sage.

Schwartz, S. H., & Bilsky, W. (1987). Toward a psychological structure of human values. *Journal of Personality and Social Psychology, 53,* 550-562.

Schwartz, S. H., & Bilsky, W. (1990). Toward a theory of the universal content and structure of values: Extensions and cross-cultural replications. *Journal of Personality and Social Psychology, 58,* 878-891.

Shane, S. A. (1992). Why do some societies invent more than others? *Journal of Business Venturing, 7,* 29-46.

Shapiro, D. L. (2001). The death of justice theory is likely if theorists neglect the wheels already invented and the voices of the injustice victims. *Journal of Vocational Behavior, 58,* 235-242.

Shapiro, D. L., & Kirkman, B. L. (1999). Employees' reactions to the change to work teams: The influence of anticipatory injustice. *Journal of Organizational Change Management, 12,* 51-66.

Shapiro, D. L., & Kirkman, B. L. (2001). Anticipatory injustice: The consequences of expecting injustice in the workplace. In J. Greenberg & R. Cropanzano (Eds.), *Advances in organizational justice* (pp. 152-178). Stanford, CA: Stanford University Press.

Shaver, K. G. (1985). *The attribution of blame: Causality, responsibility, and blameworthiness.* New York: Springer-Verlag.

Shenkar, O. (1990). International joint ventures' problems in China: Risks and remedies. *Long Range Planning, 23,* 82-90.

Shenkar, O. (2001). Cultural distance revisited: Towards a more rigorous conceptualization and measurement of cultural differences. *Journal of International Business Studies, 32,* 519-535.

Shenkar, O., & Von Glinow, M. A. (1994). Paradoxes of organizational theory and research: using the case of China to illustrate national contingency. *Management Science, 40*(1), 56-71.

Sheppard, B. H., Lewicki, R. J., & Minton, J. W. (1992). *Organizational justice: The search of fairness in the workplace.* New York: Lexington Books.

Skarlicki, D. P. (2001). Cross-cultural perspectives of organizational justice. *The International Journal of Conflict Management, 12*(4), 292-294.

Skarlicki, D. P., & Folger, R. (1997). Retaliation in the workplace: The role of distributive, procedural, and interactional justice. *Journal of Applied Psychology, 82,* 434-443.

Skitka, L. J., & Tetlock, P. (1992). Allocating scarce resources: A contingency model of distributive justice. *Journal of Experimental and Social Psychology, 28,* 491-522.

Smithson, M., & Foddy, M. (1999). Theories and strategies for the study of social dilemmas. In M. Foddy, M. Smithson, S. Schneider, & M. Hogg (Eds.), *Resolving social dilemmas* (pp. 1-14). Philadelphia: Psychology Press.

Sober, E., & Wilson, D. S. (1998). *Unto others: The evolution and psychology of unselfish behavior.* Cambridge, MA: Harvard University Press.

Steiner, D. D. (2001). Cultural influences on perceptions of distributive and procedural justice In S. Gilliland, D. Steiner, & D. Skarlicki (Eds.), *Theoretical and cultural perspectives on organizational justice* (pp. 35-62). Greenwich, CT: Information Age Publishing.

Steiner, D. D., & Gilliland, S. W. (1996). Fairness reactions to personnel selection techniques in France and the United States. *Journal of Applied Psychology, 81,* 134-141.

Stone, D. L., & Stone-Romero, E. F. (2001). The religious underpinnings of social justice conceptions. In S. W. Gilliland, D. D. Steiner, D. P. Skalicki (Eds.), *Emerging perspectives on managing organizational justice* (pp. 35-75). Greenwich, CT: Information Age Publishing.

Sugawara, I., & Huo, Y. J. (1994). Disputes in Japan: A cross-cultural test of the procedural justice model. *Social Justice Research, 7*(2), 129-144.

Sully, de Luque, M., & Sommer, S. (2000). The impact of culture on feedback-seeking behavior: An integrated model and propositions. *Academy of Management Review, 25,* 829-949.

Sweeney, P. D., & McFarlin, D. B. (1993). Workers' evaluations of the ends and the means: An examination of four models of distributive and procedural justice. *Organizational Behavior and Human Decision Processes, 55,* 23-40.

Sweeney, P. D., & McFarlin, D. B. (1997). Process and outcome: Gender differences in the assessment of justice. *Journal of Organizational Behavior, 18,* 83-98.

Taggart, J. H. (1997). Autonomy and procedural justice: A framework for evaluating subsidiary strategy. *Journal of International Business Studies, 28,* 51-76.

Tajfel, H. (1978). Social categorization, social identity and social comparison. In H. Tajfel (Ed.), *Differentiation between groups: Studies in the social psychology of intergroup relations* (pp. 61-76). New York: Academic Press.

Tajfel, H. (1982). Social identity and intergroup relations. Cambridge, England: Cambridge University Press.

Tajfel, H., & Turner, J. (1979). An integrative theory of intergroup conflict. In Austin, W. G. & Worchel, S. (Eds.), *The social psychology of intergroup relations* (pp. 33-47). Monterey, CA: Brooks/Cole.

Takaku, S. (2000). Culture and status as influences on account giving: A comparison between the United States and Japan. *Journal of Applied Social Psychology, 30*(2), 371-388.

Tanaka, K. (1999). Judgments of fairness by just world believers. *The Journal of Social Psychology, 139*(5), 631-638.

Tangirala, S., & Alge, B. J. (2006). Reactions to unfair events in computer-mediated groups: A test of uncertainty management theory. *Organizational Behavior and Human Decision Processes, 100,* 1-20.

Tannenbaum, A. S. (1980). Organizational psychology. In H. C. Triandis & R. W. Brislin (Eds.), *Handbook of cross-cultural psychology* (Vol. 5, pp. 281-334). Boston: Allyn & Bacon.

Tata, J. (2005). The influence of national culture on the perceived fairness of grading procedures: A comparison of the United States and China. *The Journal of Psychology, 239*(5), 401-412.

Tepper, B. J. (2001). Health consequences of organizational injustices: Tests of main andinteractive effects. *Organizational Behavior and Human Decision Processes, 29,* 1-19.

Tetlock, P. E. (1992). The impact of accountability on judgment and choice: Toward a social contingency model. *Advances in Experimental Social Psychology, 25,* 331-376.

The truth about Halliburton. (2005, April 18). *Fortune, 151*(7), 74-88.

Thibaut, J. W., & Kelly, H. H. (1959). *The social psychology of groups.* Hillsdale, NJ: Erlbaum.

Thibaut, J. W., & Walker, L. (1975). *Procedural Justice: A psychological analysis.* Hillsdale, NJ: Erlbaum.

Tornblum, K., Jonsson, D., & Foa, U. (1985). Nationality, resource class, and preferences among three allocation rules: Sweden vs. US. *International Journal of Intercultural Relations, 9,* 51-77.

Toy, S. (1995). Will les affaires lead to reform in la France? *Business Week, 3413,* 14-15.

Triandis, H. C. (1989). The self and social behavior in differing cultural contexts. *Psychological Review, 96,* 506-520.

Triandis, H. C. (1994). *Culture and social behavior.* New York: McGraw-Hill.

Triandis, H. C. (1995). *Individualism and collectivism.* Boulder, CO: Westview Press.

Triandis, H. C. (1996). The psychological measurement of cultural syndromes. *American Psychologist, 51,* 407-415.

Triandis, H. C. (2002). Generic individualism and collectivism. In M. J. Gannon & K. L. Newman (Eds.), *The Blackwell handbook of cross-cultural management* (pp. 16-45). Oxford, England: Blackwell.

Triandis, H. C., & Bhawur, D. P. S. (1997). Culture theory and the meaning of relatedness. In P. C. Early & M. Erez (Eds.), *New perspectives on international industrial/organizational psychology.* San Francisco: New Lexington Press.

Tripp, T. M., Bies, R. J., & Aquino, K. (2002). Poetic justice or petty jealousy? The aesthetics of revenge. *Organizational Behavior and Human Decision Processes, 89,* 966-984.

Trompenaars, F. (1993). *Riding the waves of culture* (1st ed.). New York: McGraw-Hill.

Trompenaars, F., & Hampden-Turner, C. (1998). *Riding the waves of culture: Understanding cultural diversity in global business* (2nd ed.). New York: McGraw-Hill.

Turillo C. J., Folger, R., Lavelle, J. J., Umphress, E. E., & Gee, J. O. (2002). Is virtue its own reward? Self-sacrificial decisions for the sake of fairness. *Organizational Behavior and Human Decision Processes, 89,* 839–865.

Turner, J. C. (1985). Social categorization and the self-concept: A social cognitive theory of group behavior. In E. J. Lawler (Ed.), *Advances in group processes: Theory and research* (Vol. 2, pp. 77-122). Greenwich, CT: JAI Press.

Tyler, T. R. (1987). Conditions leading to value-expressive effects in judgments of procedural justice: A test of four models. *Journal of Personality and Social Psychology, 52,* 333-344.

Tyler, T. R. (1989). The psychology of procedural justice: A test of the group-value model. *Journal of Personality and Social Psychology, 57,* 830-838.

Tyler, T. R. (1994). Psychological models on the justice motive: Antecedents of distributive and procedural justice. *Journal of Personality and Social Psychology, 67*(5) 850-863.

Tyler, T. R., & Blader, S. L. (2000). *Cooperation in groups: Procedural justice, social identity, and behavioral engagement.* Philadelphia: Psychology Press.

Tyler, T. R., & Blader, S. L. (2001). Identity and cooperative behavior in groups. *Group Processes & Intergroup Relations, 4,* 207-226.

Tyler, T. R., & Blader, S. L. (2002). Autonomous vs. comparative status: Must we bebetter than others to feel good about ourselves? *Organizational Behavior and Human Decision Processes, 89,* 813-838.

Tyler, T. R., & Blader, S. L. (2003a). Social identity and fairness judgments. In S. Gilliland, D. Steiner, & D. Skarlicki (Eds.), *Social issues in management* (Vol. 3, pp. 67-96). Greenwich, CT: Information Age Publishing.

Tyler, T. R., & Blader, S. L. (2003b). The group engagement model: Procedural justice, social identity, and cooperative behavior. *Personality and Social Psychology Review, 7,* 349-361.

Tyler, T., & Boeckman, R. J. (1997). Three strikes and you are out, but why? *Law and Society Review, 3,* 327-265.

Tyler, T., Boeckman, R. J., Smith, J. J., & Huo, Y. J. (1997). *Social justice in a diverse society.* Boulder, CO: Westview Press.

Tyler, T. R., & Caine, A. (1981). The influence of outcomes and procedures on satisfaction with former leaders. *Journal of Personality and Social Psychology, 41,* 642-655.

Tyler, T. R., & Folger, R. (1980). Distributive and procedural aspects of satisfaction with citizens' police encounters. *Basic and Applied Social Psychology, 1,* 281-292.

Tyler, T. R., & Lind, E. A. (1992). A relational model of authority in groups: *Advances in Experimental Social Psychology, 15,* 115-191.

Umphress, E., Labianca, G., Scholten, L., Kass, E., & Brass, D. (2000). The social construction of organizational justice perceptions: A social networks approach. *Proceedings of the Academy of Management, Toronto, Canada.*

Van den Bos, K. (1999). What are we talking about when we talk about no-voice procedures? On the psychology of the fair outcome effect. *Journal of Experimental Social Psychology, 35,* 560-577.

Van den Bos, K. (2001a). Fairness heuristic theory: Assessing the information to which people are reacting has a pivotal role in understanding organizational justice. In S. Gilliland, D. Steiner, & D. Skarlicki (Eds.), *Theoretical and cultural perspectives on organizational justice* (pp. 63-84). Greenwich, CT: Information Age Publishing.

Van den Bos, K. (2001b). Uncertainty management: The influence of uncertainty salience on reactions to perceived procedural fairness. *Journal of Personality and Social Psychology, 80,* 931-941.

Van den Bos, K. (2002). Uncertainty management by means of fairness judgments. In M. P. Zanna (Ed.), *Advances in experimental social psychology* (Vol. 34, pp. 1-60). San Diego, CA: Academic Press.

Van den Bos, K. (2005). What is responsible for the fair process effect? In J. Gerald & J. A. Colquitt (Eds.), *Handbook of organizational justice* (pp. 273-300). Mahwah, NJ: Erlbaum.

Van den Bos, K., & Lind, E. A. (2002). Uncertainty management by means of fairness judgments. In M. P. Zanna (Ed.), *Advances in experimental social psychology* (Vol. 34, pp. 1-60). San Diego, CA: Academic Press.

Van den Bos, K. Lind, E. A., & Wilke, H. A. M., (2001). The psychology of procedural and distributive justice viewed from the perspective of fairness heuristic theory. In R. Cropanzano (Ed.), *Justice in the workplace: From theory to practice* (Vol. 2, pp. 49-66). Mahwah, NJ: Erlbaum.

Van den Bos, K., Lind, E. A., Vermunt, R., & Wilke, H. A. M. (1997). How do I judge my outcome when I do not know the outcome of others? The psychology of the fair process effect. *Journal of Personality and Social Psychology, 72,* 1034-1046.

Van den Bos, K., & Miedema, J. (2000). Toward understanding why fairness matters: The influence of mortality salience on reactions to procedural fairness. *Journal of Personality and Social Psychology, 79,* 355-366.

Van den Bos, K., & Spruijt, N. (2002). Appropriateness of decisions as a moderator of the psychology of voice. *European Journal of Social Psychology, 32,* 57-72.

Van den Bos, K. Vermunt, R., & Wilke, H. A. M. (1997). Procedural and distributive justice: What is fair depends more on what comes first than on what comes next. *Journal of Personality and Social Psychology, 72,* 95-104.

Van den Bos, K. Wilke, H. A. M., & Lind, E. A. (1998). When do we need procedural fairness? The role of trust in authority. *Journal of Personality and Social Psychology, 74,* 1449-1458.

Van den Bos, K. Wilke, H. A. M., & Lind, E. A. (2001). The psychology of procedural and distributive justice viewed from the perspective of fairness heuristic theory. In R. Cropanzano (Ed.), *Justice in the workplace: From theory to practice* (Vol. 2, pp. 49-66). Mahwah, NJ: Erlbaum.

Van den Bos, K. Wilke, H. A. M., Lind, E. A., & Vermunt, R. (1998). Evaluating outcomes by means of the fair process effect: Evidence of different processes in fairness and satisfaction judgments. *Journal of Personality and Social Psychology, 74,* 1493-1503.

Wagner, III, J. A. (1995). Studies of individualism-collectivism: Effects on cooperation in groups. *Academy of Management Journal, 38,* 152-172.

Walster, E. G. W., Walster, G. W., & Berscheid, E. (1976). New directions in equity research. In L. Berkowitz (Ed.), *Advances in experimental social psychology* (Vol. 9, pp. 1-43). New York: Academic Press.

Walster, E., Walster, G. W., & Berscheid, E. (1978). *Equity: Theory and research.* Boston: Allyn and Bacon.

Weick, K. E. (1966). The concept of equity in the perception of pay. *Administrative Science Quarterly, 11,* 414-439.

Zuckerman, M. (1979). Attributions of success and failure revisited: The motivational bias is alive and well in attribution theory. *Journal of Personality, 47,* 245-287.

AUTHOR INDEX

SUBJECT INDEX

Printed in the United States
83111LV00003B/56/A